THE GOSPEL BEFORE MARK

THE GOSPEL BEFORE MARK

By

PIERSON PARKER

THE UNIVERSITY OF CHICAGO PRESS

CHICAGO · ILLINOIS

THE UNIVERSITY OF CHICAGO PRESS, CHICAGO 37
Cambridge University Press, London, N.W. 1, England
The University of Toronto Press, Toronto 5, Canada

To

CHESTER CHARLTON McCOWN

TABLE OF CONTENTS

I

INTRODUCTION

THE Christian Church has been split many times. Yet no schism, not even the Protestant Reformation, was more decisive or more tragic than a controversy which shook the Church at its beginning. This was the so-called "Judaizing controversy."

The first Christians were Jews, living in Palestine. There were thousands of them, says the Book of Acts, and they came from every class. Some were "unlearned and ignorant men." Others were educated, and many of them were Pharisees. At first these converts did not call themselves "Christians"—that name came later—but "Nazoreans," perhaps after Jesus of Nazareth. They called their new-found faith "The Way." For all their enthusiasm for The Way, these Jewish Christians considered themselves good Jews—better Jews, indeed, than their unconverted brethren, for they had found the Messiah. That was the great feature which distinguished them from other Jews. They *knew* that Jesus was the Messiah, for he had proved it by rising from the dead. Another difference was that they believed themselves especially endowed by the Holy Spirit of God.

They, or at least their leaders, had known Jesus personally. They knew that he had been a Jew and that he had never once stepped outside the Jewish faith. He had been faithful to the Torah, the Law of Moses, and had said, "One jot or tittle shall not pass from the Torah till all things be accomplished. . . . Whosoever breaks one of the least of these commandments shall be called least in the Kingdom of Heaven; but whosoever does and teaches them shall be called great in the Kingdom of Heaven." He had come, he said, to fulfil the Scriptures, that great literary and religious heritage of Israel. He had come as Messiah or Christ,[1] and, next to the sacred name of God, this was the

1. "Messiah" is a Hebrew term, "Christ" a Greek one. Both mean "Anointed One," i.e., the One anointed and designated of God to fulfil his purpose.

holiest in Israel's language. It could not have occurred to these Jewish Christians that one could accept Messiah without accepting the Israel for whom Messiah came. That is, it could not have occurred to them that one could follow Jesus Christ without first being a circumcised Jew. It could not have occurred to them until it happened.

It did happen. Paul seems to have been chiefly responsible at first. Christianity, he saw, was much too great for the narrow particularism of the Jews' religion. Great and holy as the Mosaic Law was, it could not by itself save a man. It could define sin, thus making sin's reality more stark and horrible, but it could neither force a man to be good nor gain for him the forgiveness of God. Jesus Christ, through his atonement, did insure that forgiveness. Therefore in Christ the Law was not denied but transcended and superseded. Therefore the Gentile could come directly to the divine salvation without traversing the intermediary steps of Law, ceremonial, and circumcision.

Many Christian leaders took Paul's side—Mark, Barnabas, Silas, and, eventually, Peter himself. Many, however, did not. The issue was joined. The ensuing convulsion split the Church, and, within a generation after Jesus' death, the two branches of Christendom started on their separate ways. The Jewish branch continued for several centuries among small communities living, in the main, east of the Jordan River. After the first century this branch never regained the vitality it once had had, and in time it disappeared. Thus the decision of history was given on the gentile side of the controversy. The decision was right. Yet we ought not glibly to call it right without first seeing how much the Jewish Christians had on their side.

While the Judaizing controversy was going on, many New Testament books were being written. Some were written explicitly to meet it. In Galatians, for example, Paul defends his case against persons who had gone among his Galatian converts, persuading them that he was wrong. Part of the Corinthian correspondence likewise shows his extreme anxiety about the problem. Even when the controversy was not to the fore, Paul had frequently to defend his right to speak against other leaders who denied that right. Part of the controversy is described in the Book of Acts. Some scholars think that it is reflected also in Revelation and in the Epistle to the Hebrews.

What has not been fully recognized, up to now, is that this same controversy affected the Gospels too. Specifically, it affected the composition of Matthew and Mark, less directly of Luke.[2] That this was indeed the case is indicated by a mass of evidence which it is the purpose of this book to set forth.

The Gospel of Matthew contains three principal types of material. About half of it consists of passages that are found also in the Gospel of Mark. Matthew is much longer than Mark, and actually about 90 per cent of Mark reappears in Matthew, though often in a more condensed and polished form. This duplication has led the Church generally to prefer Matthew to Mark. (In the Book of Common Prayer, for example, the Communion Gospels are taken from Matthew thirty-eight times, from Mark only six. Even on St. Mark's Day his Gospel is not used.) Most non-Roman scholars have concluded that the author of Matthew used Mark as his basic source.[3] Roman Catholic scholars are forbidden to admit this, and they prefer to say that Mark copied and abridged from Matthew.

About one-fourth of Matthew, while having no parallel in Mark, is paralleled in Luke. This consists mostly of teachings of Jesus, though there are a few narratives. Apparently the authors of Matthew and Luke used a common source, a book of Jesus' teachings, which has disappeared except as we can recover it from these two Gospels. This source is labeled "Q" (from German *Quelle*, "source").[4] Q seems to be pro-Gentile in tone. It is chiefly concerned with our Lord's ethical teachings and contains many sayings about being worthy, bearing good fruit, and the like.

Then about one-fourth of Matthew (slightly more than the Q

2. And apparently not at all of John. The present study will deal very little with the Gospel of John.

3. The evidence on which this conclusion has been based is summarized below, chap. xv, Sec. A.

4. Some scholars use "Q" for the actual passages common to Matthew and Luke and "S" for the book from which they were supposedly taken. It seems simpler, however, to use "Q" in both senses. No ambiguity will result.

material) has no parallel in any other Gospel. This material is conveniently designated "M." Like Q, M is mostly teachings of Jesus. Unlike Q, however, M deals largely with matters of special interest to *Jewish* Christians. Furthermore, when separated out from the rest of the Gospel,[5] M presents a most disjointed appearance. It is full of broken sentences and half-told incidents and sayings. Thus M is very homogeneous in content but very disconnected in form. This presents a difficult problem. Where did the author of Matthew get this material? And why did he use it? To these questions three chief answers have been proposed.

One suggestion is that M, like Q, represents a book and that this book disappeared after the author of Matthew used it. This was the theory of Canon B. H. Streeter.[6] One objection to it is the amorphous, atomistic character of M itself: As a book, or even as selections from a book, M is most unconvincing. Another objection is that we are required to postulate so many hypothetical sources; for, besides Q and M, Streeter thought that there was a book "L," used by Luke only, and an earlier edition of Luke (Streeter called it "Proto-Luke"), both of which have disappeared. The evidence for L and Proto-Luke as actual books is considerably stronger than that for M.

Another frequent suggestion is that M is simply the editorial additions which the compiler of Matthew made to his material. Certainly the form (or, rather, the formlessness) of M would fit that theory. On the other hand, Matthew was apparently composed in Greek, for Gentiles, and a full generation after the Jewish and gentile churches had separated. It is not easy to see why the author should have added all this Jewish material at such a time. If this is not a fatal objection to the theory, it does suggest that we look for a fuller and more satisfactory explanation.

A third possibility, often put forward, is that M and Q are from the same document. Then M would be merely parts of the common Sayings Source that were not used by Luke. Now M

5. As in chap. ii, below.
6. *The Four Gospels* (2d ed.; London: Macmillan & Co., 1930), pp. 227 ff.

and Q are of about the same length, and both deal mainly with teachings of Jesus. In all other respects, however—vocabulary, style, arrangement, and choice of material—they differ. Indeed, so great is this difference that, as we hope to show, M and Q simply cannot have had the same origin.

These theories, and the objections to them, have been sketched briefly here and will be more fully elaborated in later pages. Now, however, it is worth while to state what the following study is intended to prove. The thesis is this:

There was an early Jewish Christian Gospel written several years before our Gospel of Mark. Perhaps this Jewish Christian Gospel was written originally in Aramaic, the language of Palestine. In any case it contained much that was of interest chiefly to Christian Jews in Palestine. Also it recorded sayings of Jesus which, taken out of context, could be and doubtless were used by Jewish Christians against their gentile opponents. It came into the hands of John Mark, a protagonist for the gentile side of the controversy, at a time when that controversy was at white heat. Mark excised from the Gospel what seemed to be anti-gentile portions, and he somewhat revised the remainder—all in the interest of the gentile Christian Church. Years later the compiler of Matthew also made use of the Jewish Christian Gospel. By his time, however, the controversy had subsided, so that excision and pro-gentile transformation seemed less urgent. What the compiler of Matthew did do was to combine his Jewish Christian source with the pro-gentile Q. Thus canonical Matthew is drawn not from our present Gospel of Mark but from Mark's immediate ancestor. Luke, however, used canonical Mark and did not use its Jewish Christian progenitor.

Thus M never did exist by itself in any form. M is simply those parts of the Jewish Christian Gospel which Mark left out.

Hereafter we shall designate the Jewish Christian Gospel as "K" (from Greek *progonos koinos*, "common ancestor"), since it was the common ancestor of Matthew and Mark and less directly of Luke. In diagram, and ignoring for the present Luke's special materials, the formation of the first three canonical Gospels was like this:

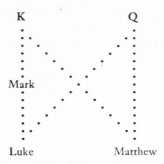

To New Testament scholars this will certainly appear, at first, as a strange explanation of the relationships between our first three Gospels. It is not lightly made. The evidence for it is of four kinds:

1. *Evidence from vocabulary and style.*—There is a consistent and distinct set of expressions which runs all through Mark, M, and Matthew's parallels to Mark. It is very different from the language of Q, and Q has its own distinctive manner of expression. The K style is too positive, too all-pervading, to be explained as the work of a later editor. It points to a prior unity of M and the Markan material.

2. *Evidence from structure.*—The structural defects of M are most simply acounted for if M is the parings that were left over from Mark's revision. Certain features in the arrangement of Mark itself, and equally important structural features in Matthew, point unmistakably to the same conclusion.

3. *Evidence from content.*—This explanation of the content of M, Mark, and Matthew fits the known facts about the Jewish and gentile churches in the first century. As we shall try to show, it fits the facts better than have most previous theories.

4. *Bearing on the Synoptic Problem as a whole.*—By "Synoptic Problem" is meant the problem of the relationships between all three Gospels, Matthew, Mark, and Luke. It is believed that the identification of the K source simplifies the solution to this problem enormously.

The evidence will be presented in the order indicated. First, however, it will be convenient for the reader to have before him the text of Matthew's special materials, the so-called M.

II

THE TEXT OF M

BETWEEN the portions of M, given below, we indicate the
nature of the intervening material—whether from Q or parallel to Mark. An important outcome of this study will be a sharper definition of Q and the other source material behind Matthew and of the compiler's editorial additions. For preliminary
purposes, however, the various strands of the Gospel must be
identified in a completely mechanical way. In the case of M,
we simply cull out from chapters 3–28 of Matthew every passage that has no parallel in Mark or Luke.[1] Similarly for Q we
list only the non-Markan parts that do have Lukan parallels.
The assignments to Q are virtually identical with those of Hawkins and Harnack.[2] Where the ascription to Q is uncertain, this
is shown by a question mark.

(1:1–17 Genealogy; 1:18–2:23 Infancy)

3:1 And in those days cometh John the Baptist, preaching in
the wilderness of Judea, saying, 2 Repent ye; for the kingdom
of heaven is at hand.

(3:3–5a Mark; 5b Q; 6 Mark; 7–10 Q; 11a Mark; 11b, 12 Q;
13a Mark)

3:13b . . . to the Jordan unto John, to be baptized of him. 14
But John would have hindered him, saying, I have need to be
baptized of thee, and comest thou to me? 15 But Jesus answering
said unto him, Suffer it now: for thus it becometh us to fulfil all
righteousness. Then he suffereth him.

(3:16–4:2a Mark; 2b–11a Q; 11b, 12 Mark)

---

1. Chapters 1 and 2 of Matthew, the Genealogy and Infancy, form a separate
problem which will be discussed in chap. xii, Sec. C.

2. John C. Hawkins, *Horae Synopticae: Contributions to the Study of the
Synoptic Problem* (2d ed.; Oxford, 1909), pp. 108 ff.; A. Harnack, *Sprüche und
Reden Jesu* (Leipzig, 1907), or English trans., *The Sayings of Jesus* (New
York: Putnam's Crown Theological Library, 1908).

4:13 and leaving Nazareth, he came and dwelt in Capernaum, which is by the sea, in the borders of Zebulun and Naphtali: 14 that it might be fulfilled which was spoken through Isaiah the prophet, saying, 15 The land of Zebulun and the land of Naphtali. Toward the sea, beyond the Jordan, Galilee of the Gentiles, The people that sat in darkness Saw a great light, And to them that sat in the region and shadow of death, To them did light spring up.

(4:17–23 Mark)

4:24 And the report of him went forth into all Syria: and they brought unto him all that were sick, holden with divers diseases and torments, possessed with demons, and epileptic, and palsied; and he healed them.

(4:25 Mark; 5:1 Q? 2–6 Q)

5:7 Blessed are the merciful: for they shall obtain mercy. 8 Blessed are the pure in heart: for they shall see God. 9 Blessed are the peacemakers: for they shall be called sons of God. 10 Blessed are they that have been persecuted for righteousness' sake: for theirs is the kingdom of heaven.

(5:11, 12 Q; 13a Q? 13b Q)

5:14 Ye are the light of the world. A city set on a hill cannot be hid.

(5:15 Q)

5:16 Even so let your light shine before men; that they may see your good works, and glorify your Father who is in heaven. 17 Think not that I came to destroy the law or the prophets: I came not to destroy, but to fulfil.

(5:18 Q)

5:19 Whosoever therefore shall break one of these least commandments, and shall teach men so, shall be called least in the kingdom of heaven: but whosoever shall do and teach them, he shall be called great in the kingdom of heaven. 20 For I say unto you, that except your righteousness shall exceed the righteousness of the scribes and Pharisees, ye shall in no wise enter into the kingdom of heaven. 21 Ye have heard that it was said to them of old time, Thou shalt not kill; and whosoever shall kill shall be in danger of the judgment: 22 but I say unto you, that every one who is angry with his brother shall be in danger

of the judgment; and whosoever shall say to his brother, Raca,
shall be in danger of the council; and whosoever shall say, Thou
fool, shall be in danger of the hell of fire. 23 If therefore thou
art offering thy gift at the altar, and there rememberest that thy
brother hath aught against thee, 24 leave there thy gift before
the altar, and go thy way, first be reconciled to thy brother, and
then come and offer thy gift.

(5:25, 26 Q)

5:27 Ye have heard that it was said, Thou shalt not commit
adultery: 28 but I say unto you, that every one that looketh
on a woman to lust after her hath committed adultery with
her already in his heart.

(5:29 Mark)

5:30 And if thy right hand causeth thee to stumble, cut it
off, and cast it from thee: for it is profitable for thee that one
of thy members should perish, and not thy whole body go into
hell. 31 It was said also, Whosoever shall put away his wife, let
him give her a writing of divorcement:

(5:32 Q?)

5:33 Again, ye have heard that it was said to them of old
time, Thou shalt not forswear thyself, but shalt perform unto
the Lord thine oaths: 34 but I say unto you, Swear not at all;
neither by the heaven, for it is the throne of God; 35 nor by
the earth, for it is the foot-stool of his feet; nor by Jerusalem,
for it is the city of the great King. 36 Neither shalt thou swear
by thy head, for thou canst not make one hair white or black.
37 But let your speech be, Yea, yea; Nay, nay: and whatsoever
is more than these is of the evil one. 38 Ye have heard that it was
said, An eye for an eye, and a tooth for a tooth:

(5:39 Q? 40 Q)

5:41 And whosoever shall compel thee to go one mile, go with
him two.

(5:42 Q)

5:43 Ye have heard that it was said, Thou shalt love thy
neighbor, and hate thine enemy:

(5:44 Q; 45 Q? 46–48 Q)

6:1 Take heed that ye do not your righteousness before men,
to be seen of them: else ye have no reward with your Father

who is in heaven. 2 When therefore thou doest alms, sound not a trumpet before thee, as the hypocrites do in the synagogues and in the streets, that they may have glory of men. Verily I say unto you, They have received their reward. 3 But when thou doest alms, let not thy left hand know what thy right hand doeth: 4 that thine alms may be in secret: and thy Father who seeth in secret shall recompense thee. 5 And when ye pray, ye shall not be as the hypocrites: for they love to stand and pray in the synagogues and in the corners of the streets, that they may be seen of men. Verily I say unto you, They have received their reward. 6 But thou, when thou prayest, enter into thine inner chamber, and having shut thy door, pray to thy Father who is in secret, and thy Father who seeth in secret shall recompense thee. 7 And in praying use not vain repetitions, as the Gentiles do: for they think that they shall be heard for their much speaking. 8 Be not therefore like unto them: for your Father knoweth what things ye have need of, before ye ask him.

(6:9 Q; 10 Q? 11–13a Q; 13b Q? 14 Mark)

6:15 But if ye forgive not men their trespasses, neither will your Father forgive your trespasses. 16 Moreover when ye fast, be not, as the hypocrites, of a sad countenance: for they disfigure their faces, that they may be seen of men to fast. Verily I say unto you, They have received their reward. 17 But thou, when thou fastest, anoint thy head, and wash thy face; 18 that thou be not seen of men to fast, but of thy Father who is in secret: and thy Father, who seeth in secret, shall recompense thee.

(6:19 Q? 20–7:5 Q)

7:6 Give not that which is holy unto the dogs, neither cast your pearls before the swine, lest haply they trample them under their feet, and turn and rend you.

(7:7–14 Q)

7:15 Beware of false prophets, who come to you in sheep's clothing, but inwardly are ravening wolves.

(7:16–18 Q? 19–22 Q; 23 Q? 24–28 Q; 29 Mark; 8:1 Q? 2–4 Mark; 5–12 Q; 13 Q? 14–16 Mark)

8:17 that it might be fulfilled which was spoken through Isaiah the prophet, saying, Himself took our infirmities, and bare our diseases.

(8:18 Mark; 19–22 Q; 23–9:12 Mark)

9:13a But go ye and learn what this meaneth, I desire mercy, and not sacrifice:

(9:13b–26 Mark)

9:27 And as Jesus passed by from thence, two blind men followed him, crying out, and saying, Have mercy on us, thou son of David. 28 And when he was come into the house, the blind men came to him: and Jesus saith unto them, Believe ye that I am able to do this? They say unto him, Yea, Lord. 29 Then touched he their eyes, saying, According to your faith be it done unto you. 30 And their eyes were opened. And Jesus strictly charged them, saying, See that no man know it. 31 But they went forth, and spread abroad his fame in all that land. 32 And as they went forth, behold, there was brought to him a dumb man possessed with a demon. 33 And when the demon was cast out, the dumb man spake: and the multitudes marvelled, saying, It was never so seen in Israel. 34 But the Pharisees said, By the prince of the demons casteth he out demons.

(9:35a Mark)

9:35b . . . in their synagogues, and preaching the gospel of the kingdom, and healing all manner of disease and all manner of sickness.

(9:36 Mark; 37, 38 Q; 10:1–4 Mark)

10:5 These twelve Jesus sent forth, and charged them, saying, Go not into any way of the Gentiles, and enter not into any city of the Samaritans: 6 but go rather to the lost sheep of the house of Israel.

(10:7, 8a Q)

10:8b . . . raise the dead, cleanse the lepers, cast out demons: freely ye received, freely give.

(10:9 Q; 10a Q? 10b Q; 11 Q? 12, 13 Q; 14 Q? 15, 16a Q)

10:16b . . . be ye therefore wise as serpents, and harmless as doves. 17 But beware of men: for they will deliver you up to councils, and in their synagogues they will scourge you;

(10:18, 19 Mark; 20 Q? 21, 22 Mark)

10:23 But when they persecute you in this city, flee into the next: for verily I say unto you, Ye shall not have gone through the cities of Israel, till the Son of man be come.

(10:24-40 Q)

10:41 He that receiveth a prophet in the name of a prophet shall receive a prophet's reward: and he that receiveth a righteous man in the name of a righteous man shall receive a righteous man's reward.

(10:42, 11:1 Mark; 2-19 Q)

11:20 Then began he to upbraid the cities wherein most of his mighty works were done, because they repented not.

(11:21-23 Q; 24 Q? 25-27 Q)

11:28 Come unto me, all ye that labor and are heavy laden, and I will give you rest. 29 Take my yoke upon you, and learn of me; for I am meek and lowly in heart: and ye shall find rest unto your souls. 30 For my yoke is easy, and my burden is light.

(12:1-4 Mark)

12:5 Or have ye not read in the law, that on the sabbath day the priests in the temple profane the sabbath, and are guiltless? 6 But I say unto you, that one greater than the temple is here. 7 But if ye had known what this meaneth, I desire mercy, and not sacrifice, ye would not have condemned the guiltless.

(12:8-10 Mark; 11 Q)

12:12a How much then is a man of more value than a sheep!

(12:12b-16 Mark)

12:17 that it might be fulfilled which was spoken through Isaiah the prophet, saying, 18 Behold, my servant whom I have chosen; My beloved in whom my soul is well pleased: I will put my Spirit upon him, And he shall declare judgment to the Gentiles. 19 He shall not strive, nor cry aloud; Neither shall any one hear his voice in the streets. 20 A bruised reed shall he not break, And smoking flax shall he not quench, Till he send forth judgment unto victory. 21 And in his name shall the Gentiles hope.

(12:22, 23 Q; 24-26 Q? 27, 28 Q; 29 Mark; 30 Q; 31 Mark; 32a Q; 32b, 33 Q? 34, 35 Q)

12:36 And I say unto you, that every idle word that men shall speak, they shall give account thereof in the day of judgment.

37 For by thy words thou shalt be justified, and by thy words thou shalt be condemned.

(12:38 Q? 39 Q; 40 Q? 41–45 Q; 46–13:13 Mark)

13:14 And unto them is fulfilled the prophecy of Isaiah, which saith, By hearing ye shall hear, and shall in no wise understand; And seeing ye shall see, and shall in no wise perceive: 15 For this people's heart is waxed gross, And their ears are dull of hearing, And their eyes they have closed; Lest haply they should perceive with their eyes, And hear with their ears, And understand with their heart, And should turn again, And I should heal them.

(13:16, 17 Q; 18–24 Mark)

13:25 but while men slept, his enemy came and sowed tares also among the wheat, and went away. 26 But when the blade sprang up and brought forth fruit, then appeared the tares also. 27 And the servants of the householder came and said unto him, Sir, didst thou not sow good seed in thy field? whence then hath it tares? 28 And he said unto them, An enemy hath done this. And the servants say unto him, Wilt thou then that we go and gather them up? 29 But he saith, Nay; lest haply while ye gather up the tares, ye root up the wheat with them. 30 Let both grow together until the harvest: and in the time of the harvest I will say to the reapers, Gather up first the tares, and bind them in bundles to burn them; but gather the wheat into my barn.

(13:31 Mark; 32 Q?? 33 Q; 34 Mark)

13:35 that it might be fulfilled which was spoken through the prophet, saying, I will open my mouth in parables; I will utter things hidden from the foundation of the world. 36 Then he left the multitudes and went into the house: and his disciples came unto him, saying, Explain unto us the parable of the tares of the field. 37 And he answered and said, He that soweth the good seed is the Son of man; 38 and the field is the world; and the good seed, these are the sons of the kingdom; and the tares are the sons of the evil one; 39 and the enemy that sowed them is the devil: and the harvest is the end of the world; and the reapers are angels. 40 As therefore the tares are gathered up and burned with fire; so shall it be in the end of the world. 41 The Son of man shall send forth his angels, and they shall gather out of his kingdom all things that cause stumbling, and them that do iniquity, 42 and shall cast them into the furnace of fire: there shall be the weeping and the gnashing of teeth. 43 Then shall the righteous shine forth as the sun in the kingdom of their Father. He that hath ears, let him hear. 44 The kingdom of heaven is like unto a treasure hidden in the field; which a man found, and hid; and in his joy he goeth and selleth all that he hath, and buyeth that field. 45 Again, the kingdom of heaven is like unto a man that is a merchant seeking goodly pearls: 46 and having found one pearl of great price, he went and sold all that he had, and bought it. 47 Again, the kingdom of heaven is like unto a net, that was cast into the sea, and gathered of every kind: 48 which, when it was filled, they drew up on the beach; and they sat down, and gathered the good into vessels, but the bad they cast away. 49 So shall it be in the end of the world: the angels shall come forth, and sever the wicked from among the righteous, 50 and shall cast them into the furnace of fire: there shall be the weeping and the gnashing of teeth. 51 Have ye understood all these things? They say unto him, Yea. 52 And he said unto them, Therefore every scribe who hath been made a disciple to the kingdom of heaven is like unto a man that is a householder, who bringeth forth out of his treasure things new and old.

(13:53—14:12a Mark)

14:12b . . . and they went and told Jesus.

(14:13, 14a Mark; 14b Q; 15–27 Mark)

14:28 And Peter answered him and said, Lord, if it be thou, bid me come unto thee upon the waters. 29 And he said, Come. And Peter went down from the boat, and walked upon the waters to come to Jesus. 30 But when he saw the wind, he was afraid; and beginning to sink, he cried out, saying, Lord save me. 31 And immediately Jesus stretched forth his hand, and took hold of him, and saith unto him, O thou of little faith, wherefore didst thou doubt?

(14:32—15:11 Mark)

15:12 Then came the disciples, and said unto him, Knowest thou that the Pharisees were offended, when they heard this saying? 13 But he answered and said, Every plant which my heavenly Father planted not, shall be rooted up. 14a Let them alone:

(15:14*b* Q; 15–22 Mark)

15:23 But he answered her not a word. And his disciples came and besought him, saying, Send her away; for she crieth after us. 24 But he answered and said, I was not sent but unto the lost sheep of the house of Israel.

(15:25–31*a* Mark)

15:31*b* . . . and they glorified the God of Israel.

(15:32—16:2*a* Mark; 2*b*, 3 Q; 4–10 Mark)

16:11*a* How is it that ye do not perceive that I spake not to you concerning bread?

(16:11*b* Q)

16:12 Then understood they that he bade them not beware of the leaven of bread, but of the teaching of the Pharisees and Sadducees.

(16:13–16 Mark)

16:17 And Jesus answered and said unto him, Blessed art thou, Simon Bar-Jonah: for flesh and blood hath not revealed it unto thee, but my Father who is in heaven. 18 And I also say unto thee, that thou art Peter, and upon this rock I will build my church; and the gates of Hades shall not prevail against it. 19 I will give unto thee the keys of the kingdom of heaven: and whatsoever thou shalt bind on earth shall be bound in heaven; and whatsoever thou shalt loose on earth shall be loosed in heaven.

(16:20–23*a* Mark)

16:23*b* . . . thou art a stumbling-block unto me:

(16:23*c*–27*a* Mark)

16:27*b* . . . and then shall he render unto every man according to his deeds.

(16:28—17:6 Mark)

17:7 And Jesus came and touched them and said, Arise, and be not afraid.

(17:8–12 Mark)

17:13 Then understood the disciples that he spake unto them of John the Baptist.

(17:14–19 Mark; 20, 21 Q; 22, 23 Mark)

17:24 And when they were come to Capernaum, they that received the half-shekel came to Peter, and said, Doth not your teacher pay the half-shekel? 25 He saith, Yea. And when he came into the house, Jesus spake first to him, saying, What thinkest thou, Simon? the kings of the earth, from whom do they receive toll or tribute? from their sons, or from strangers? 26 And when he said, From strangers, Jesus said unto him, Therefore the sons are free. 27 But lest we cause them to stumble, go thou to the sea, and cast a hook, and take up the fish that first cometh up; and when thou hast opened his mouth, thou shalt find a shekel: that take, and give unto them for me and thee.

(18:1–3 Mark)

18:4 Whosoever therefore shall humble himself as this little child, the same is the greatest in the kingdom of heaven.

(18:5, 6 Mark; 7 Q; 8, 9 Mark)

18:10 See that ye despise not one of these little ones: for I say unto you, that in heaven their angels do always behold the face of my Father who is in heaven.

(18:11 Q, if authentic; 12, 13 Q; 14, 15 Q?)

18:16 But if he hear thee not, take with thee one or two more, that at the mouth of two witnesses or three every word may be established. 17 And if he refuse to hear them, tell it unto the church: and if he refuse to hear the church also, let him be unto thee as the Gentile and the publican. 18 Verily I say unto you, What things soever ye shall bind on earth shall be bound in heaven; and what things soever ye shall loose on earth shall be loosed in heaven. 19 Again I say unto you, that if two of you shall agree on earth as touching anything that they shall ask, it shall be done for them of my Father who is in heaven. 20 For where two or three are gathered together in my name, there am I in the midst of them.

(18:21, 22 Q?)

18:23 Therefore is the kingdom of heaven likened unto a certain king, who would make a reckoning with his servants. 24 And when he had begun to reckon, one was brought unto him, that owed him ten thousand talents. 25 But forasmuch as he had not wherewith to pay, his lord commanded him to be sold, and his wife, and children, and all that he had, and payment to be made. 26 The servant therefore fell down and worshipped him, saying, Lord, have patience with me, and I will pay thee all.

27 And the lord of that servant, being moved with compassion, released him, and forgave him the debt. 28 But that servant went out, and found one of his fellow-servants, who owed him a hundred shillings: and he laid hold on him, and took him by the throat, saying, Pay what thou owest. 29 So his fellow-servant fell down and besought him, saying, Have patience with me, and I will pay thee. 30 And he would not: but went and cast him into prison, till he should pay that which was due. 31 So when his fellow-servants saw what was done, they were exceeding sorry, and came and told unto their lord all that was done. 32 Then his lord called him unto him, and saith to him, Thou wicked servant, I forgave thee all that debt, because thou besoughtest me: 33 shouldest not thou also have had mercy on thy fellow-servant, even as I had mercy on thee? 34 And his lord was wroth, and delivered him to the tormentors, till he should pay all that was due. 35 So shall also my heavenly Father do unto you, if ye forgive not every one his brother from your hearts.

(19:1–6 Mark)

19:7 They say unto him, Why then did Moses command to give a bill of divorcement, and to put her away? 8 He saith unto them, Moses for your hardness of heart suffered you to put away your wives: but from the beginning it hath not been so.

(19:9 Mark)

19:10 The disciples say unto him, If the case of the man is so with his wife, it is not expedient to marry. 11 But he said unto them, Not all men can receive this saying, but they to whom it is given. 12 For there are eunuchs, that were so born from their mother's womb: and there are eunuchs, that were made eunuchs by men: and there are eunuchs, that made themselves eunuchs for the kingdom of heaven's sake. He that is able to receive it, let him receive it.

(19:13–28a Mark; 28b Q; 29, 30 Mark)

20:1 For the kingdom of heaven is like unto a man that was a householder, who went out early in the morning to hire laborers into his vineyard. 2 And when he had agreed with the laborers for a shilling a day, he sent them into his vineyard. 3 And he went out about the third hour, and saw others standing in the marketplace idle; 4 and to them he said, Go ye also into the vineyard, and whatsoever is right I will give you. And they went their way. 5 Again he went out about the sixth and the ninth hour, and did likewise. 6 And about the eleventh hour he went out, and found others standing; and he saith unto them, Why stand ye here all the day idle? 7 They say unto him, Because no man hath hired us. He saith unto them, Go ye also into the vineyard. 8 And when even was come, the lord of the vineyard saith unto his steward, Call the laborers, and pay them their hire, beginning from the last unto the first. 9 And when they came that were hired about the eleventh hour, they received every man a shilling. 10 And when the first came, they supposed that they would receive more; and they likewise received every man a shilling. 11 And when they received it, they murmured against the householder, 12 saying, These last have spent but one hour, and thou hast made them equal unto us, who have borne the burden of the day and the scorching heat. 13 But he answered and said to one of them, Friend, I do thee no wrong: didst not thou agree with me for a shilling? 14 Take up that which is thine, and go thy way; it is my will to give unto this last, even as unto thee. 15 Is it not lawful for me to do what I will with mine own? or is thine eye evil, because I am good?

(20:16 Q? 20:17—21:3 Mark)

21:4 Now this is come to pass, that it might be fulfilled which was spoken through the prophet, saying, 5 Tell ye the daughter of Zion, Behold, thy King cometh unto thee, Meek, and riding upon an ass, And upon a colt the foal of an ass.

(21:6—10a Mark)

21:10b . . . all the city was stirred, saying, Who is this? 11 And the multitudes said, This is the prophet, Jesus, from Nazareth of Galilee.

(21:12, 13 Mark)

21:14 And the blind and the lame came to him in the temple; and he healed them. 15 But when the chief priests and the scribes saw the wonderful things that he did, and the children that were crying in the temple and saying, Hosanna to the son of David; they were moved with indignation, 16 and said unto him, Hearest thou what these are saying? And Jesus saith unto them, Yea:

did ye never read, Out of the mouth of babes and sucklings thou hast perfected praise?

(21:17–27 Mark)

21:28 But what think ye? A man had two sons; and he came to the first, and said, Son, go work to-day in the vineyard. 29 And he answered and said, I will not: but afterward he repented himself, and went. 30 And he came to the second, and said likewise. And he answered and said, I go, sir: and went not. 31 Which of the two did the will of his father? They say, The first.

(21:31*b*, 32 Q? 33–42 Mark)

21:43 Therefore say I unto you, The kingdom of God shall be taken away from you, and shall be given to a nation bringing forth the fruits thereof.

(21:44 Q, if authentic)

21:45 And when the chief priests and the Pharisees heard his parables, they perceived that he spake of them.

(21:46 Mark; 22:1–10 Q?)

22:11 But when the king came in to behold the guests, he saw there a man who had not on a wedding-garment: 12 and he saith unto him, Friend, how camest thou in hither not having a wedding-garment? And he was speechless. 13 Then the king said to the servants, Bind him hand and foot, and cast him out into the outer darkness; there shall be the weeping and the gnashing of teeth. 14 For many are called, but few chosen.

(22:15—23:1*a* Mark)

23:1*b* . . . and to his disciples, 2 saying, The scribes and the Pharisees sit on Moses' seat: 3 all things therefore whatsoever they bid you, these do and observe: but do not ye after their works; for they say, and do not.

(23:4 Q)

23:5 But all their works they do to be seen of men: for they make broad their phylacteries, and enlarge the borders of their garments,

(23:6 Q? 7*a* Mark)

23:7*b* . . . and to be called of men, Rabbi. 8 But be not ye called Rabbi: for one is your teacher, and all ye are brethren. 9 And call no man your father on the earth: for one is your

Father, even he who is in heaven. 10 Neither be ye called masters: for one is your master, even the Christ.

(23:11 Mark; 12, 13Q; 14 Mark, if authentic)

23:15 Woe unto you, scribes and Pharisees, hypocrites! for ye
compass sea and land to make one proselyte; and when he is
become so, ye make him twofold more a son of hell than yourselves. 16 Woe unto you, ye blind guides, that say, Whosoever
shall swear by the temple, it is nothing; but whosoever shall
swear by the gold of the temple, he is a debtor. 17 Ye fools and
blind: for which is greater, the gold, or the temple that hath
sanctified the gold? 18 And, Whosoever shall swear by the altar,
it is nothing; but whosoever shall swear by the gift that is upon
it, he is a debtor. 19 Ye blind: for which is greater, the gift, or
the altar that sanctifieth the gift? 20 He therefore that sweareth
by the altar, sweareth by it, and by all things thereon. 21 And he
that sweareth by the temple, sweareth by it, and by him that
dwelleth therein. 22 And he that sweareth by the heaven, sweareth by the throne of God, and by him that sitteth thereon.

(23:23 Q)

23:24 Ye blind guides, that strain out the gnat, and swallow
the camel!

(23:25–27 Q)

23:28 Even so ye also outwardly appear righteous unto men,
but inwardly ye are full of hypocrisy and iniquity.

(23:29–31 Q; 32 Q?)

23:33 Ye serpents, ye off-spring of vipers, how shall ye escape
the judgment of hell?

(23:34–39 Q; 24:1–9 Mark)

24:10 And then shall many stumble, and shall deliver up one
another, and shall hate one another. 11 And many false prophets
shall arise, and shall lead many astray. 12 And because iniquity
shall be multiplied, the love of the many shall wax cold.

(24:13–20a Mark)

24:20b . . . neither on a sabbath:

(24:21–25 Mark; 26 Q? 27, 28 Q; 29, 30a Mark)

24:30b . . . shall appear the sign of the Son of man in heaven:
and then shall all the tribes of the earth mourn, and . . .

(24:30c–36 Mark; 37–41 Q)

24:42 Watch therefore: for ye know not on what day your Lord cometh.

(24:43-51a Q; 51b Q?)

25:1 Then shall the kingdom of heaven be likened unto ten virgins, who took their lamps, and went forth to meet the bridegroom. 2 And five of them were foolish, and five were wise. 3 For the foolish, when they took their lamps, took no oil with them: 4 but the wise took oil in their vessels with their lamps. 5 Now while the bridegroom tarried, they all slumbered and slept. 6 But at midnight there is a cry, Behold, the bridegroom! Come ye forth to meet him. 7 Then all those virgins arose, and trimmed their lamps. 8 And the foolish said unto the wise, Give us of your oil; for our lamps are going out. 9 But the wise answered, saying, Peradventure there will not be enough for us and you: go ye rather to them that sell, and buy for yourselves. 10 And while they went away to buy, the bridegroom came; and they that were ready went in with him to the marriage feast: and the door was shut. 11 Afterward came also the other virgins, saying, Lord, Lord, open to us. 12 But he answered and said, Verily I say unto you, I know you not.

(25:13-28 Q? 29 Q; 30 Q?)

25:31 But when the Son of man shall come in his glory, and all the angels with him, then shall he sit on the throne of his glory: 32 and before him shall be gathered all the nations: and he shall separate them one from another, as the shepherd separateth the sheep from the goats; 33 and he shall set the sheep on his right hand, but the goats on the left. 34 Then shall the King say unto them on his right hand, Come, ye blessed of my Father, inherit the kingdom prepared for you from the foundation of the world: 35 for I was hungry, and ye gave me to eat; I was thirsty, and ye gave me drink; I was a stranger, and ye took me in; 36 naked, and ye clothed me; I was sick, and ye visited me; I was in prison, and ye came unto me. 37 Then shall the righteous answer him, saying, Lord, when saw we the hungry, and fed thee or athirst, and gave thee drink? 38 And when saw we thee a stranger, and took thee in? or naked, and clothed thee? 39 And when saw we thee sick, or in prison, and came unto thee? 40 And the King shall answer and say unto them, Verily I say unto you, Inasmuch as ye did it unto one of these my brethren, even these least, ye did it unto me. 41 Then shall he say also unto them on the left hand, Depart from me, ye cursed, into the eternal fire which is prepared for the devil and his angels: 42 for I was hungry, and ye did not give me to eat; I was thirsty, and ye gave me no drink; 43 I was a stranger, and ye took me not in; naked, and ye clothed me not; sick, and in prison, and ye visited me not. 44 Then shall they also answer, saying, Lord, when saw we thee hungry, or athirst, or a stranger, or naked, or sick, or in prison, and did not minister unto thee? 45 Then shall he answer them, saying, Verily I say unto you, Inasmuch as ye did it not unto one of these least, ye did it not unto me. 46 And these shall go away into eternal punishment: but the righteous into eternal life. 26:1 And it came to pass, when Jesus had finished all these words, he said unto his disciples,

(26:2, 3a Mark)

26:3b . . . and the elders of the people, unto the court of the high priest, who was called Caiaphas;

(26:4–15a Mark)

26:15b . . . And they weighed unto him thirty pieces of silver.

(26:16–24 Mark)

26:25 And Judas, who betrayed him, answered and said, Is it I, Rabbi? He saith unto him, Thou hast said.

(26:26–49 Mark)

26:50a And Jesus said unto him, Friend, do that for which thou art come.

(26:50b, 51 Mark)

26:52 Then saith Jesus unto him, Put up again thy sword into its place: for all they that take the sword shall perish with the sword. 53 Or thinkest thou that I cannot beseech my Father, and he shall even now send me more than twelve legions of angels? 54 How then should the scriptures be fulfilled, that thus it must be?

(26:55—27:2 Mark)

27:3 Then Judas, who betrayed him, when he saw that he was condemned, repented himself, and brought back the thirty pieces of silver to the chief priests and elders, 4 saying, I have sinned in that I betrayed innocent blood. But they said, What is that to us?

see thou to it. 5 And he cast down the pieces of silver into the sanctuary, and departed; and he went away and hanged himself. 6 And the chief priests took the pieces of silver, and said, It is not lawful to put them into the treasury, since it is the price of blood. 7 And they took counsel, and bought with them the potter's field, to bury strangers in. 8 Wherefore that field was called, The field of blood, unto this day. 9 Then was fulfilled that which was spoken through Jeremiah the prophet, saying, And they took the thirty pieces of silver, the price of him that was priced, whom certain of the children of Israel did price; 10 and they gave them for the potter's field, as the Lord appointed me. 11 Now Jesus stood before the governor:

(27:11b–18 Mark)

27:19 And while he was sitting on the judgment-seat, his wife sent unto him, saying, Have thou nothing to do with that righteous man; for I have suffered many things this day in a dream because of him.

(27:20–23 Mark)

27:24 So when Pilate saw that he prevailed nothing, but rather that a tumult was arising, he took water, and washed his hands before the multitude, saying, I am innocent of the blood of this righteous man; see ye to it. 25 And all the people answered and said, His blood be on us, and on our children.

(27:26–35 Mark)

27:36 and they sat and watched him there.

(27:37–42 Mark)

27:43 He trusteth on God; let him deliver him now, if he desireth him; for he said, I am the Son of God.

(27:44–51a Mark)

27:51b . . . and the earth did quake; and the rocks were rent; 52 and the tombs were opened; and many bodies of the saints that had fallen asleep were raised; 53 and coming forth out of the tombs after his resurrection they entered into the holy city and appeared unto many.

(27:54–61 Mark)

27:62 Now on the morrow, which is the day after the Preparation, the chief priests and the Pharisees were gathered together unto Pilate, 63 saying, Sir, we remember that that deceiver said while he was yet alive, After three days I rise again. 64 Command therefore that the sepulchre be made sure until the third day, lest haply his disciples come and steal him away, and say unto the people, He is risen from the dead: and the last error will be worse than the first. 65 Pilate said unto them, Ye have a guard: go, make it as sure as ye can. 66 So they went, and made the sepulchre sure, sealing the stone, the guard being with them.

(28:1 Mark)

28:2 And behold, there was a great earthquake; for an angel of the Lord descended from heaven, and came and rolled away the stone, and sat upon it. 3 His appearance was as lightning, and his raiment white as snow: 4 and for fear of him the watchers did quake, and became as dead men.

(28:5–8 Mark)

28:9 And behold, Jesus met them, saying, All hail. And they came and took hold of his feet, and worshipped him. 10 Then saith Jesus unto them, Fear not: go tell my brethren that they depart into Galilee, and there shall they see me. 11 Now while they were going, behold, some of the guards came into the city, and told unto the chief priests all the things that were come to pass. 12 And when they were assembled with the elders, and had taken counsel, they gave much money unto the soldiers, 13 saying, Say ye, His disciples came by night, and stole him away while we slept. 14 And if this come to the governor's ears, we will persuade him, and rid you of care. 15 So they took the money, and did as they were taught: and this saying was spread abroad among the Jews, and continueth until this day. 16 But the eleven disciples went into Galilee, unto the mountain where Jesus had appointed them. 17 And when they saw him, they worshipped him; but some doubted. 18 And Jesus came to them and spake unto them, saying, All authority hath been given unto me in heaven and earth. 19 Go ye therefore, and make disciples of all the nations, baptizing them into the name of the Father and of the Son and of the Holy Spirit: 20 teaching them to observe all things whatsoever I commanded you: and lo, I am with you always, even unto the end of the world.

Part I
EVIDENCE FROM LANGUAGE AND STYLE

III

THE LANGUAGE OF M AND Q COMPARED

IN HAWKINS' *Horae Synopticae* are listed 95 expressions that distinguish the style of the Gospel of Matthew.[1] Each of these words and phrases occurs at least four times in Matthew and at least twice as often there as in Mark and Luke put together. Hawkins thought that 16 of them were due to the subject matter and therefore not really distinctive of Matthew. However, only 5 of the expressions are confined to single contexts in Matthew (*gumnos*, naked; *zizanion*, darnel; *lampas*, lamp; *magos*, "wise man"; *metoikesia*, change of abode),[2] and the remaining 90 will all be considered in this study. A search of the concordances[3] reveals 12 additional items that come under Hawkins' principle: *allos* (other) with article, *anemoi* (winds) pl., *archiereis kai presbuteroi* (chief priests and elders), *dia prophētou/-tōn* (through the prophet/s), *eutheōs* (straightway), *Iēsous Christos* (Jesus Christ), *katoikeō* (dwell), *kruptos* (hidden), *peri* (about) with accusative of time, *puros* (of fire) after *geenna* (Gehenna) or *kaminos* (furnace), *skandalon* (offense/stumbling-block), *psuchē . . . sōma* (soul . . . body)—making 102 in all.

A. DISTRIBUTION OF THE MATTHEAN EXPRESSIONS

These 102 expressions provide a good starting point for investigating the style of Matthew and particularly the relation

1. John C. Hawkins, *Horae Synopticae: Contributions to the Study of the Synoptic Problem* (2d ed.; Oxford, 1909), pp. 3 ff.
2. Perhaps those not familiar with Greek should be warned that nearly every Greek word has several shades of meaning and that the translations given here may not be identical with those found in a particular passage of an English New Testament. Of course it is the Greek that is significant in studying the style of Matthew and its sources.
3. Both the concordance by W. F. Moulton and A. S. Geden and that by A. S. Bruder have been used. Each of these reveals certain phenomena that are not apparent in the other.

of M to Q. With respect to their occurrence in M they fall naturally into four groups, as seen in Tables I–IV of the Appendix. The tables show how often each of the expressions occurs in M, in Matthew's Q, its parallels to Mark, and its Genealogy and Infancy. The results need only be summarized here.

I. *Expressions which in M are confined to teachings of Jesus.* —There are 54 of these, with 449 occurrences throughout Matthew, or an average of 8.2 each. All 54 occur in M, with 207 instances; 35 in parallels to Mark, with 76 instances; 6 in the Genealogy and Infancy, with 47 instances; and 40 in Q (including doubtful Q), with 119 instances.

II. *Expressions which in M occur both in sayings of Jesus and in narrative or editorial matter.*—These 16 items occur 287 times in Matthew, or on an average of 18 each. They occur 115 times in M (63 in discourse, 52 in narrative and editorial); 11 of them are found in parallels to Mark, with 106 instances; 8 in the Genealogy and Infancy, with 19 instances; 11 in Q, with 47 instances.

III. *Expressions which in M occur only in narrative or editorial.*—These 15 items occur 130 times throughout Matthew, or an average of 8.7 each. They occur 37 times in M; 13 of them appear also in parallels to Mark, with 62 instances; 6 in the Genealogy and Infancy, with 23 instances; 5 in Q, with 8 instances.

IV. *Matthean expressions that do not appear in M.*—There are 17 of these, with 102 occurrences in the Gospel, or an average of 6 each. Of the 17, 14 appear in parallels to Mark, with 46 instances; 5 in Genealogy and Infancy, with 17 instances; and 13 in Q, with 39 instances.

It will be seen that the expressions of the second group are, on the average, the most distinctive of Matthean usage; those in the fourth group, the least.

We can now give the first part of an answer to the question whether M and Q can be parts of a single source. Roughly half of Matthew consists of parallels to Mark, one-fourth is M, and one-fourth is Q, with M slightly longer than Q. The Markan material is mostly narrative, whereas M and Q are both mostly discourse. If, then, M and Q are from the same document, they ought to exhibit much the same kind of language.

Now, of the 102 expressions, 85 occur in M, with a total of 357 instances. Yet only 23 of them appear in Matthew's Q with frequencies at all comparable to those in M: (I) *allos* (other) with article, *arti* (just now), *brugmos tōn odontōn* (gnashing of teeth), *dikaiosunē* (righteousness), *diōkō* (persecute/pursue), *heis* (one) for *tis* (a certain), *klauthmos* (weeping), *homoioō* (liken/compare), *hosos an/ean* (who/whatsoever), *Patēr hēmōn/humōn/sou/autōn* (our/your/thy/their Father), *Patēr ho en ouranois* (Father in heaven), *Patēr ho ouranios* (heavenly Father), *ho ponēros/to ponēron* (the evil one), *tuphlos* (blind) used metaphorically, *husteron* (afterward), *phoneuō* (kill), *hōsper* (as); (II) *kruptō* (hide), *proskuneō* (worship/do obeisance), *sunagō* (gather); (III) *eutheōs* (straightway), *kleptō* (steal), *taphos* (sepulcher)—M 80 times, Q 73 times.

The other 62 items in the first three groups appear in M 279 times, in Q only 102. The expressions (I) *anomia* (evil-doing), *apodidōmi* (pay/render/recompense), *dipsaō* (thirst), *thusiastērion* (altar), *kruptos* (hidden/secret), *misthos* (wages/reward), *mōros* (fool/foolish), *sullegō* (gather), *sundoulos* (fellow-servant/slave), (II) *phainomai* (appear), (III) *arguria* (money) occur in M more than 5 times as often as in Matthew's Q. The particle *hopōs* (because/how) is found in M 9 times, Q 3; *pros to* with infinitive (in order to), M 4 times, Q none; *tote* (then), which characterizes Matthean style more than almost any other word, appearing 30 times in M and 45 times in parallels to Mark, occurs only 13 times in Q; and 27 other expressions (17 of which fall in M's discourse material), with 89 occurrences in M, do not appear in Q at all.

B. DISTINCTIVE STYLE OF Q

It is to be expected, of course, that expressions distinctive of one Gospel will fall most frequently in passages peculiar to that Gospel. There are two reasons, however, why that does not cover the wide discrepancy between M and Q.

In the first place, Matthean language does pervade the Markan parts of Matthew to a degree much greater than we should antecedently expect. This will be more fully brought out in the next chapter. Here we simply call attention to the figures for the second group, which, as we saw, contains the most distinctively Matthean words: M, 115 instances; parallels to Mark, 106; Q, 47.

In the second place, Q has a positive vocabulary of its own which is not shared by the rest of Matthew.

Q is so short that, in deciding what to recognize as distinctive of it, we cannot use the same criteria as for a complete Gospel. Also, no questions must be begged as to the relation of Q to M. We therefore take as characteristic of Q any expression that occurs at least 3 times in Matthew's Q, 3 in Luke's Q, and oftener in each of these than in either Mark or John. Thirty-two such expressions have been found—a surprising number, considering that Q covers less than three hundred verses. They are listed in Table V of the Appendix.[4]

Here is conclusive proof that Q does have its own independent linguistic usage. Our definition, which did not prejudge the relationship between Q and M, yields 200 instances in Matthew's Q and 187 in Luke's Q, but only 61 in M. Fourteen of the Q expressions are entirely absent from M, while 6 others occur in M but once each. Yet those 20 include four grammatical particles, *ara* (then/so), *hos* (who/which), *plēn* (than/except), and *hupo* with accusative (under).

C. CONCLUSIONS

We now have the basis for three conclusions:

1. Since the style of M does not pervade Q, and the style of Q does not pervade M, therefore Q and M have different origins.

2. Since Q has not been assimilated to Matthean types of expression, and since Q's own distinctive language differs from the rest of the Gospel, therefore Q is really from an autonomous

4. In this table it will be noticed that the total for Matthew's parallels to Mark is greater than that for Mark itself. This is due entirely to the presence of *idou* (behold) the figures for which include those of Table III. The frequency of this word elsewhere in the New Testament suggests that it is characteristic of M and Mark to omit it rather than of Q to use it.

source. Moreover, the compiler of Matthew has evidently treated the language of Q with a great deal of respect.

3. Among the distinctively "Matthean" terms of Tables I and IV, several are actually frequent in Q and infrequent in the rest of the Gospel: (I) *diōkō* (persecute/pursue), *hēmera kriseōs* (day of judgment), *skandalon* (stumbling block/offense), (IV) *homologeō* (confess), *parousia, trophē* (food), *psuchē . . . sōma* (soul . . . body). These, then, are really Q-type expressions. They distinguish Matthew only because Luke did not keep them. Furthermore, the other 32 Q expressions occur more frequently in Matthew's Q than in Luke's; yet they appear oftener in the rest of Luke than in the rest of Matthew. This could be because Luke used more of Q than Matthew did, or because Luke more fully assimilated his sources to each other. In any case, the pristine vocabulary of Q is more fully reflected in Matthew than in Luke.

Two further characteristics of the Q vocabulary may have caught the reader's eye: their ethical interest (bear fruit, evil, good, reap, worthy, etc.) and their generally non-Jewish nature. These features will concern us when we come to examine the content of Matthew's sources.

IV

THE LANGUAGE OF M AND MATTHEW'S MARKAN MATERIAL

THE distinctive Matthean expressions considered in the last chapter (Tables I–IV) were selected in such a way as to stress the differences between Matthew and Mark or Luke. These differences will, of course, show up most frequently in passages peculiar to Matthew. It follows that Tables I, II, and III contain a fair listing of the vocabulary characteristics of M.[1]

It also follows that similarities of M to Q or Mark are depressed in Tables I–III. This is far more true for Mark than for Q. (If, for example, Luke repeats a Q word twice, Matthew must have it 8 times for it to get into Tables I–IV; but if Luke twice shares a word with Mark, Matthew must have it 16 times for it to get counted.) In Tables I–IV, then, relationships between M and the Markan material will be less evident than those between M and Q. Any resemblances they do show of M to the Markan material will be the more impressive.

A. M VOCABULARY PERVADES MATTHEW'S MARKAN PARTS

Here, in addition to what has just been said, two points must be kept in mind.

1. Matthew's parallels to Mark, as listed in chapter ii, cover about 485 verses, and its Q about 259 verses. Given a sufficiently large number of expressions, then, pure chance would put these into the Markan passages, and into Matthew's Q, in the proportion of about 15 to 8. If other things were equal, we should ex-

---

1. A somewhat purer list could be got by ignoring Hawkins' data altogether and taking the M words direct from the concordances. The Hawkins list is, however, sufficiently representative of M's nature for practical purposes; e.g., of his 95 words, 26 occur more often in M alone than in all of John, Acts, the Epistles, and Revelation together.

pect the M vocabulary to reappear in Matthew's Markan parts about 15 times for every 8 times in Q.[2]

2. But other things are not equal. Q resembles M in dealing mainly with Jesus' teachings. The Markan portions differ greatly from M in dealing chiefly with events and descriptions. This, by itself, would lead us to expect very little of M's distinctive vocabulary to appear in the Markan material. However often M words fall in Q, they should, on this account, fall much less often in parallels to Mark.

This second consideration greatly offsets the previous one. So far as the first principle may be held to apply, it will be to items that reflect an author's narrative style and his linguistic mannerisms—his choice from among synonyms and especially his use of adverbs and particles. When M expressions are not dictated by the subject matter, then if they appear in the Markan parts much more than twice as often as in Q, this will show that M is closer in language to the Markan matter than to Q.

The second principle will apply chiefly to expressions that reflect content and emphasis. Thus if the vocabulary of M's discourse reappears at all extensively in the Markan portions, this again will point to a closer relationship between M and the Markan portions than between M and Q.

Now, of the Matthean expressions discussed in the last chapter, Groups I and II comprise those that occur in the teaching material of M. Here, according to the above principles, we should expect a considerably lower total for the Markan matter than for Q. Yet the actual totals are: M, 322; Q, 166; parallels to Mark, 182. The style of M's discourse reappears not less but more frequently in Matthew's Markan portions than it does in Q.

More striking still is the combination of Groups II and III, which together exhibit the narrative and editorial usage of M. These 31 words and phrases occur 152 times in M, of which 89 are in editorial or narrative. Only 16 of them appear in Q, with 55 instances. Yet 24 of the 31 appear in parallels to Mark, with

2. Of course these figures should not be applied with mathematical rigor. It is because the facts depart so far from these normal expectations that they are significant.

168 instances. The ratio in comparison with Q is not less than 2 to 1, as we should have expected, but more than 3 to 1.

An author's choice of verbs will usually be dictated by the subject matter, but at one point a clear-cut test of style can be made. Greek affords many ways of expressing the idea of "go" or "come." Including compound words, more than a dozen terms would have been at the disposal of any New Testament writer. Notice, then, the distribution of the following words in Matthew:

	M	Parallels to Mark	Q
anachōreō	1	5	0
deute	2	3	1
paragō	1	2	0
proserchomai	14	29	9
hupagete	4	2	0
Total	22	41	10

Yet *hēxo* and *exerchomai* with purpose clause, which appear 6 times in Q, fall only once in M and twice in parallels to Mark (*exerchomai* in all three cases).

However, the way in which the style of M pervades the Markan parts of Matthew is most clearly seen when we isolate the adverbs and particles of these lists; for those are the expressions that would be least controlled by the subject matter and therefore are most indicative of stylistic tendencies:

	M	Parallels to Mark	Q
I. a certain (*heis* for *tis*), about (with accus. of time), afterward/last, as/even/like, exceedingly, in order to (*pros to*), just now, other (*allos*) with art., whosoever/whatsoever	24	24	14
II. because/how, then	39	49	16
III. thence (*ekeithen*) in narr., straightway, behold (*idou*) after gen. abs.	5	24	1
Total	68	97	31

Even the particles of the first group, which in M are confined to discourse, recur in parallels to Mark nearly twice as often as in Q. The particles as a whole appear more than three times as often in parallels to Mark as in Q. This is far in excess of the proportionate lengths of these two groups of material.

Thus every test, based on the vocabulary of M, points in the same direction. Where we should have expected the Markan parts to have fewer M expressions than Q has, we found more than in Q. Where we should have expected less than twice as many in the Markan parts as in Q, we found more than three times as many—the latter ratio appearing in three separate tests. M vocabulary appears in the Markan parts of Matthew much more heavily than normal expectations would allow. The converse is likewise true.

B. LANGUAGE OF MATTHEW'S MARKAN PARTS PERVADES M MUCH MORE HEAVILY THAN Q

Here the data must be gathered in such a way as not to obscure, in the least, the relation of Matthew's Markan parts either to Q, or to M, or to canonical Mark. We take, as characterizing Matthew's Markan portions, any expression that occurs 4 times in Matthew's parallels to Mark and oftener there than in John, Acts, the Epistles, and Revelation together. The 51 items fitting this definition are listed in Table VI of the Appendix. They fall 322 times in Matthew's Markan material.

Now, the manner in which this list was formed did not prejudge the relation of Matthew's Markan parts either to M or to Q. Since, then, M and Q are similar in length (M is, roughly, 7 per cent longer than Q) and in content (teachings of Jesus), these expressions ought, from an a priori viewpoint, to fall almost equally in the two strands. Instead, M has 33 of the items, with 97 instances, and Q only 18 items, with 59 instances. The ratio is about 5 to 3 in favor of M.

From one standpoint it would be better to focus attention on those items in Table VI which occur more often in Matthew's Markan parts than in Mark itself, for these cannot be due solely to supposed copying from Mark: behold (*idou*) after genitive absolute, brother (*adelphos*) of Jesus, chief priests and elders (*archiereis kai presbuteroi*), come near/approach (*proscho-mai*), depart (*anachōreō*), do . . . with (*poieō . . . en*), exceedingly (*sphodra*), fig-tree (*sukē*), governor (*hegemōn*), heal (*therapeuō*), kingdom of heaven (*basileia tōn ouranōn*), have mercy (*eleeō*), miserably/evilly (*kakōs*), mock (*empaizō*), offend/cause to stumble (*skandalizō*), son of David (*huios/huie Daueid*), stretch out (*ekteinō*), take bread (*arton lambanō*), that hour (*hōra ekeinē*), thence (*ekeithen*), Zebedee (*Zebedaios*). To these may be added the following, which occur three times each in Matthew's Markan passages and oftener than in Mark or in John-through-Revelation: baptist (*baptistēs*), be of good courage (*tharseō*), elders of the people (*presbuteroi tou laou*), go . . . thence (*metabainō . . . ekeithen*), just now (*arti*), the left (*euōnumos*), take counsel (*sumboulion lambanō*), what thinkest thou?/what think ye? (*ti soi/humin dokei*), who/what then (*tis/ti ara*). The expressions just named occur in Matthew as follows:

TOTAL MATTHEW	31 items,	295 instances
M	23 items,	65 instances
Parallels to Mark	31 items,	185 instances
Genealogy, Infancy	6 items,	13 instances
Q	12 items,	32 instances

—more than twice as many instances in M as in Q.

Here, then, is a most interesting set of circumstances. Q, which resembles M in length and subject matter, differs radically from it in language. Yet M and the Markan sections of Matthew, which differ greatly in both respects, seem, allowing for these differences, to be heavily pervaded each with the language of the other. How is this to be accounted for? Just three possibilities suggest themselves:

1. In adapting Mark and his M source together, the compiler of Matthew followed his own editorial proclivities—as Luke did in the case of Mark, Q, and Luke's special source L. The two cases are not really comparable, however. (*a*) L contains a great deal of narrative, so that Luke might readily fuse its language with that of Mark. M, on the contrary, records the words of the Lord, and we should expect the Matthean compiler to show greater respect than to adapt these to Markan style. (*b*) Yet the

Matthean revision, and integration of Mark and M, would actually have been much more extensive than Luke's treatment of Mark and L.[3] (c) There is the stubborn fact that the Matthean compiler has respected the language of Q—more than Luke has done—and has not rephrased Q with the wordings of Mark or M. Is it credible that he would show greater reverence toward Q than toward his own discourse material?

2. M and Mark were combined first, and Q was added later by a different hand. That is to say, grant the prior unity of M and the Markan matter, but suppose that at some still earlier date they were separate. Certainly this would explain the differences in the handling of M and Q in Matthew. Still, we should be faced with the circumstance that somebody treated the language of M more cavalierly than either Luke or the compiler of Matthew has treated Q.

3. M and Mark are from the same original source. This accounts for all the linguistic phenomena we have been studying. It avoids the difficulties of the first two suggestions. And there is further evidence in its favor. Indeed, one further piece of evidence comes under the heading of First Gospel language.

C. POSSIBLE ARAMAISMS IN MATTHEW

During the thirties and forties of the twentieth century much ink was spilled over the question whether the New Testament Gospels were originally composed in Greek or are translations from Aramaic. (Aramaic is the language Jesus and his followers spoke in Palestine.) Professor C. C. Torrey, the chief American advocate for the translation theory, has contended that all the Gospels show mistranslations from Aramaic into Greek, thus proving their Aramaic origin.[4] Now it is not our purpose to engage in this controversy. One point, however, is worth calling attention to. In his notes on Matthew,[5] Torrey adduces 90 cases where, he thinks, an Aramaic original is plainly to be seen. Of

3. See chap. xvi, Sec. A.

4. *Our Translated Gospels* (New York: Harper & Bros., 1936); *Documents of the Primitive Church* (New York: Harper & Bros., 1941); *The Four Gospels* (2d ed.; New York: Harper & Bros., 1947).

5. *The Four Gospels*, pp. 289 ff.

these 90, as it turns out, 11 are in the Genealogy and Infancy; 20 are in M, 36 in parallels to Mark, and just 13 in Q. Whatever be the estimate of Torrey's own conclusions, these figures underscore the difference between Q and the rest of Matthew and the similarity of M to the Markan portions.

In most cases, New Testament scholars generally feel, it is precarious to try to identify "translation Greek." Often what is attributed to translation in the New Testament turns out to be simply colloquial Greek such as is commonly found in the papyri. There is one feature in Matthew, however, that has a good deal of weight. It is the use of *tote* (then).

For those not versed in biblical languages, a few prefatory remarks may help to make the following discussion clear. Most of the Old Testament was written originally in Hebrew; but two rather long sections (Ezra 4:23—6:13 and Dan. 2:14—7:19) were composed in Aramaic. Now, there is an ancient Greek translation of the Old Testament, called the "Septuagint" (Latin *septuaginta*, "seventy") because it was supposed to have been done by seventy translators. "Septuagint" is usually abbreviated to "LXX." By comparing the LXX with the original, we can often get very good evidence of how ancient translators were accustomed to render various terms from Hebrew and Aramaic into Greek.

In the LXX, outside of Daniel and Ezra, *tote* is rare. For example, it occurs only 4 times each in Genesis and Leviticus, once in Numbers, and not at all in Exodus or Deuteronomy. Yet in Ezra 4:23—6:13 and Dan. 2:14—7:19 *tote* appears 37 times. Here it renders the very common Aramaic particle *edayin*, "then," "thereupon." Of 19 other occurrences of *edayin* in these books, 17 are translated by *kai* (and), 1 by *tade* (thus, so; Ezra 4:9) and once the word is omitted (Dan. 5:24). Thus *tote* in the LXX corresponds closely to this common Aramaic conjunction.

In the New Testament the figures for *tote* are: Matthew, 91; Mark, 6; Luke, 15; Acts, 21; Paul, 14; John, 10; others, 5. Of Mark's six occurrences (Mark 2:20; 3:27; 13:14, 21, 26, 27), the first four are where Matthew has *tote* also, and the fifth where Matthew has it in the preceding verse (Matt. 24:30).

Of Matthew's occurrences, on the other hand, 45 are in parallels to Mark. At these points Mark itself reads: nothing, 6 times; *tote*, 4 times; *kai* (and), 28 times, of which 26 are before Mark 14:51; and *de* (but), 7 times, of which 6 are in Mark 14:63– 15:44. Thus, where Matthew uses *tote*, Mark through 14:50 nearly always has *kai*, which is the next most frequent rendering of *edayin* in the LXX. Beyond 14:50 Mark regularly reads *de*. This high consistency cannot be accidental. It is hard to explain if, as is usually held, Matthew copied direct from our Mark (particularly since *tote*, as Matthew uses it, is poorer Greek than Mark's *kai* and *de*). It is easy to explain if both Matthew and Mark are based on a common source.

This evidence does not prove that the source, as it came to the authors of Matthew and Mark, was in Aramaic. It could, so far as these data show, have been in a rough Greek form which the canonical authors changed in different ways. What the evidence does show—unmistakably, we think—is that there was some literary phenomenon behind these two Gospels.

In the switch from *kai* to *de* can we see the Markan author dropping his work and picking it up again, perhaps with a different helper? It is an interesting coincidence that the change occurs at the point (Mark 14:51–52) where the young man flees naked. The young man is commonly supposed to have been John Mark himself.

V

LANGUAGE AND STYLE IN CANONICAL MARK

THE vocabularies hitherto considered represent the separate usages of M, Q, and Matthew's Markan material, and the question asked was, "To what extent does the distinctive phrasing of each of these pervade the other two?" It has become apparent that Q usage is really independent but that M and Matthew's Markan parts are so infused each with the language of the other as to suggest that they are from one source. Now, if that is true, there ought to be a usage common to both M and the Markan matter, while being clearly distinct from the rest of the New Testament. Furthermore, if canonical Mark is abridged from this earlier, longer K, then K usage ought to pervade Mark too.

A. DISTINCTIVE VOCABULARY SHARED WITH M

Here we cannot proceed as in the case of a single strand of material. Instead, we deliberately pick out from the concordances any expressions that do fall heavily in Mark and throughout Matthew's K, while being infrequent in Q and elsewhere. Specifically, we have searched for items that appear at least twice as heavily in each of these as in the rest of the New Testament.[1]

The value of the following list depends on two things: (a) the number of items and (b) their relative frequency. One might by chance find a few words and phrases that distinguish almost any two or three books. The more we find, however, the less likely are they to be due to chance. If the expressions fall in all three areas, Mark, M, and Matthew's Markan parts, far more heavily than elsewhere, the probability is increased that they are due to Matthew's and Mark's common debt to K.

1. As always, we ignore forms confined to single contexts and forms appearing less than three times in Mark, M, or Matthew's parallels to Mark.

about: *peri* with accus.
bind: *deō*
boat: *ploion*
borders/coasts: *horia*
bridegroom: *numphios*
brother: *adelphos* (of Jesus)
come together: *sunagomai*
come ye: *deute*
compassion, be moved with: *splagchnizomai*
cry: *krazō*
demons, be possessed of: *daimoni-zomai*
denarius: *dēnarion*
depart into: *aperchomai eis*
destroy: *kataluō*
evening: *opsia*
fare, to/to be: *echō* with adv.
fast, to: *nēsteuō*
fire: *pur*, metaph.
flee, to: *pheugō*
honor, to: *timaō*
how long: *pote*
how much: *posos*, other than in *posō mallon*

Jordan: *Iordanēs*
lawful, it is: *exestin*
left, on the: *euōnumos*
miserably/evilly: *kakōs*
offend/cause to stumble: *skandalizō*
other side: *peran*
perceive/think: *noeō*
preach (the Gospel): *kerussō* (*to euaggelion*)
rabbi: *hrabbei*
right hand, on the: *ek dexiōn*
sea: *thalassa*
sleep: *katheudō*
Son of David: *huios, huie Daueid*
stretch forth: *ekteinō*
seize/lay hold of: *krateō*
summoned, having: *proskalesame-nos*
swine: *choiros*
thence: ekeithen
understand: *suniēmi*
whole: *holos*
wish: *thelō* with fin. vb.

In Westcott and Hort's Greek Testament[2] Matthew takes up 70 pages, so that its parallels to Mark would occupy about 33 pages if printed continuously; M, 17 pages; Q, 16 pages. From

	Items	Instances	Instances per Page
CANONICAL MARK	43	266	6.4
MATTHEW, parallels to Mark	43	220	6.7
MATTHEW, M	43	104	6.1
MATTHEW, Genealogy, Infancy	4	5	1.3
MATTHEW, Q	11	14	0.9
LUKE	36	121	1.7
Other New Testament	38	353	1.1

this we can calculate the relative frequency per page of the above expressions in the various parts of Matthew. This is given in the third column of the accompanying tabulation.

This tabulation exhibits some striking features. (*a*) There are

2. *The New Testament in the Original Greek* (New York: Macmillan Co., 1941).

not a half-dozen or so but 43 expressions on the list.[3] (*b*) We sought expressions that occur in Mark and in Matthew's K at least twice as often per page as elsewhere in the New Testament. Yet the resulting expressions occur, as a whole, about six times as intensively in the former as in the latter. (*c*) They fall in Mark, in Matthew's parallels to Mark, and in M, with about the same frequency per page. It seems, therefore, that the above list does genuinely represent, on the whole, the distinctive language of K.

It is not surprising, of course, that Mark should share a vocabulary with its parallels in Matthew. What is surprising—astonishing, under previous Synoptic solutions—is that this same, highly distinctive vocabulary is shared just as fully with M. This strongly reinforces the conclusion that Mark comes from the same K document that M comes from.

The reader will notice certain dominant interests reflected in the foregoing word list. The expressions have largely to do with healing and exorcism of demons and with social, religious, and especially geographical circumstances in Palestine. These, and particularly the latter, will concern us at a later point.[4]

B. ROUGHNESS IN THE GREEK

There is another matter that bears on the derivative nature of Mark's language and style. In Matthew the Greek is usually smoother, and passages are frequently shorter, than at corresponding points in Mark.[5] So far as these conditions hold, they indicate that Matthew has at many points polished the source material more than Mark has done. It does not follow, from this, that Mark was itself Matthew's source. Precisely the same situation would arise if two editors handled the same document independently. Furthermore, the inference that Matthew did the greater editing is open to two serious qualifications:

   1. Matthew's smoother flow may not always be due to polish-

3. A slight relaxing of the requirements, say, to 1¾ times in K for 1 in John-through-Revelation, would more than double the length of the list.
   4. See, especially, chap. x.
   5. For an analysis of the harshnesses in Mark's language and style see John C. Hawkins, *Horae Synopticae: Contributions to the Study of the Synoptic Problem* (2d ed., Oxford, 1909), pp. 131 ff.

ing. If Mark left out parts of K, these omissions would be almost certain to produce roughness.[6]

2. Matthew does not always show more editorial finish than Mark. Consider Matthew's constant use of *tote* where Mark has the smoother *kai* and *de*. The Matthew-Mark vocabulary, listed above, occurs somewhat more intensively in Matthew's Markan parts (6.7 per page) than in Mark (6.4), suggesting that here Matthew is, if anything, somewhat closer to the original. Consider, finally, the following passages, wherein Matthew averages about 17 per cent more words than Mark while adding little or nothing to the content—in several of them Mark actually tells more than Matthew does:

> Mark: 1:10, 11; 2:14; 2:22; 2:24; 3:32*b*–35; 4:20; 6:14;
>
> ---
>
> Matt.: 3:16, 17; 9:9; 9:17; 12:2; 12:47–50; 13:23; 14:1, 2;
>
> Mark: 8:4, 5;   8:8; 9:11, 12*a;* 9:19; 9:42; 11:8; 11:29–31;
>
> ---
>
> Matt.: 15:33, 34*a;* 15:37; 17:10, 11; 17:17; 18:6; 21:8; 21:24, 25;
>
> Mark: 12:1–3;   12:15*b*–17; 13:2; 14:47; 15:3, 4; 15:32*b;*
>
> ---
>
> Matt.: 21:33–35; 22:18–21; 24:2; 26:51; 27:12–14; 27:44;
>
> Mark: 15:34–36; 15:37, 38; 16:7.
>
> ---
>
> Matt.: 27:46–49; 27:50, 51*a;* 28:7.

Thus while Mark's Greek is usually the rougher, sometimes Matthew's is. Mark is usually more discursive, but often Matthew is. This is hard to explain if Matthew copied direct from Mark. It is easy to explain if both authors worked independently upon a common source.

6. As, in fact, they have. See chap. vii.

Part II
EVIDENCE FROM STRUCTURE

VI

THE GAPS IN M

EARLY in this study mention was made of the incompletenesses and lack of structure in the so-called M. These are plainly visible when one reads the text of M (chap. ii, above). Now, in considering the structural characteristics of a book, one important feature would be its outline or arrangement. M is so short, however, and so largely devoted to sayings of Jesus, that its order will tell us little about where it came from. This subject is better deferred until we consider the arrangements of Matthew and Mark as wholes.

In this chapter we shall examine the structure of M from two standpoints: (A) the transitions from one M passage to the next and the character of the intervening material and (B) those sections that are incomplete in themselves.

If the transition is smooth, this again will not tell us very much. The intervening material may be an insertion from another source; or it may not, since it is often possible to skip a sentence, or a whole paragraph, and still "make sense." However, smooth transitions will more often accompany the removal of insertions than they will real gaps in the original book.

If the transition is rough, on the other hand, and does not make even tolerably good sense, then something is missing. Sometimes bad transitions might be due, of course, to displacements in M or to editorial additions by the compiler of the Gospel. But if we consistently find one type of material, and not the other, between these disjunctures, then the presumption will be that part, at least, of that intervening material belonged with M originally.

Still more positive evidence comes from those sections of M that are incomplete in themselves—those which demand a context, which M does not give, to make them intelligible. What contexts do they actually have in Matthew?

If M and Q were from the same source, "M" would just be

47

parts of Q that Luke left out. Then the incomplete passages ought, in Matthew, to fall extensively in Q contexts.

If M were simply editorial expansions by the compiler, he would have been free to put these in anywhere he chose. We could expect them to fall in Markan and Q contexts in the proportion of about 2 to 1. (Additions to narratives might perhaps fall more heavily in Markan contexts, additions to sayings in Q contexts.)

If M were selections from a separate book, there ought to be very few of these incomplete passages at all. Such as there are ought to appear in Markan and Q contexts in the proportion of roughly 2 to 1.

If, however, M and the Markan matter are from the same source, M is simply parts of that source (K) that Mark left out. Then the incomplete M passages will fall very largely in Markan contexts.

A. TRANSITIONS BETWEEN M PASSAGES

1. If the reader will examine the text of M (chap. ii), he will probably agree that the following transitions, from one M passage to the next, are smooth—or at least no rougher than one meets frequently in a complete Gospel. The passages are grouped according to the nature of the intervening material, the intervening material being indicated by ellipses:

Begins and ends with parallels to Mark:[1] 4:16 . . . 4:24; 9:13*a* . . . 9:27; 10:17 . . . 10:23; 17:13 . . . 17:24; 18:4 . . . 18:10; 19:8 . . . 19:10; 19:12 . . . 20:1; 21:11 . . . 21:14; 21:16 . . . 21:28; 23:10 . . . 23:15;[2] 26:54 . . . 27:3; 27:53 . . . 27:62; 27:66 . . . 28:2.
Begins with parallels to Mark and ends with Q: 10:41 . . . 11:20.
Begins and ends with Q: 5:10 . . . 5:14 . . . 5:16; 5:17 . . . 5:19; 5:24 . . . 5:27; 5:41 . . . 5:43; 6:18 . . . 7:6 . . . 7:15; 10:6 . . . 10:8*b*; 10:23 . . . 10:41; 16:11*a* . . . 16:12; 18:20 . . . 18:23; 21:43 . . . 21:45; 23:3 . . . 23:5; 23:22 . . . 23:24 . . . 23:28 . . . 23:33; 24:42 . . . 25:1; 25:12 . . . 25:31.

Thus, where the transition is smooth, the intervening matter begins and ends with parallels to Mark 13 times (or 12, if Matt.

1. Of course it is only the beginning and end of the intervening matter that is helpful in considering transitions from one M passage to the next. Within the intervening matter there might, theoretically, have been insertions from extraneous sources.
2. If 23:14 is authentic. Otherwise the gap ends with Q material.

23:14 is unauthentic). Once (or twice) it begins with Markan but ends with Q material. It both begins and ends with Q 18 times, of which 5 contain doubtful Q assignments. As was to be expected, the evidence from smooth transitions is inconclusive. So far as it goes, it suggests that Q is more likely than the Markan portions to have been inserted from a separate source.

2. The reader will probably agree that the following transitions are not smooth:

Begins and ends with parallels to Mark: 3:2 . . . 3:13b; 3:15 . . . 4:13; 5:28 . . . 5:30; 8:17 . . . 9:13a; 9:34 . . . 9:35b . . . 10:5; 11:29 . . . 12:5; 12:12a . . . 12:17; 13:30 . . . 13:35; 13:52 . . . 14:12b . . . 14:28; 14:31 . . . 15:12; 15:24 . . . 15:31b . . . 16:11a; 16:12 . . . 16:17; 16:19 . . . 16:23b . . . 16:27b . . . 17:7 . . . 17:13; 17:27 . . . 18:4; 18:35 . . . 19:7; 21:5 . . . 21.10b; 22:14 . . . 23:1b; 24:12 . . . 24:20b . . . 24:30b; 26:1 . . . 26:3b . . . 26:15b . . . 26:25 . . . 26:50a . . . 26:52; 27:11a . . . 27:19 . . . 27:24; 27:25 . . . 27:36 . . . 27:43 . . . 27:51b; 28:4 . . . 28:9.
Begins with parallels to Mark and ends with Q: 4:24 . . . 5:7; 12:7 . . . 12:12a; 21:45 . . . 22:11; 24:30b . . . 24:42.
Begins with Q and ends with parallels to Mark: 6:8 . . . 6:15; 7:15 . . . 8:17; 13:15 . . . 13:25; 15:14a . . . 15:23; 20:15 . . . 21:4; 21:31a . . . 21:43; 23:5 . . . 23:7b; 23:33 . . . 24:10.
Begins and ends with Q: 5:31 . . . 5:33; 5:38 . . . 5:41; 5:43 . . . 6:1; 10:8b . . . 10:16b; 11:20 . . . 11:28; 12:21 . . . 12:36; 18:10 . . . 18:16.

Where the transition between M passages is rough, the intervening material begins and ends with parallels to Mark 36 times and with Q 7 times (in 3 of which the assignment to Q is dubious). It begins with one strand and ends with the other 12 times (in 7 of which the assignment to Q is dubious). Thus, where the transition is bad, the intervening material is Markan by very large proportions. This strongly suggests that the Markan material in these gaps was not originally separate from M.

B. INCOMPLETE PASSAGES IN M

Sometimes a transition between two M passages is bad because one or both passages are themselves incomplete. Of all the structural shortcomings, these incompletenesses afford the most decisive evidence regarding the nature of M.

As they appear in M, these passages need a preceding context to make them intelligible: 3:13b-15; 6:15-18; 8:17; 9:13a;

9:35*b;* 10:5, 6; 12:5–7; 12:17–21; 13:14, 15; 13:25–30; 13:35–52; 14:12*b;* 14:28–31; 15:12–14*a;* 15:23, 24; 15:31*b;* 16:11*a;* 16:17–19; 16:23*b;* 16:27*b;* 17:13; *18:16–20;* 19:7, 8; 21:4, 5; *22:11–14;* 23:1*b*–3; 23:7*b*–10; 24:10–12; 24:20*b;* 24:30*b;* 26:15*b;* 26:25; 26:52–54; 27:24, 25; 27:36; 27:43; 27:51*b*–53; 28:9–20. The two italicized passages are preceded, in Matthew, by Q material (dubious Q in both cases). All 36 of the others are preceded by Markan material.

These passages require both preceding and following context to make them intelligible: 17:7; 26:3*b;* 26:50*a;* 27:3–11*a.* All four are both preceded and followed, in Matthew, by Markan material.

These passages need a following context to make them intelligible: *5:30, 31; 5:33–38; 5:43.* All three are followed by Q material (dubious Q in the first two cases).

Occasionally an M passage itself is intelligible enough, but the presence of a connective word implies that something else has immediately preceded. Here, of course, we could be dealing merely with rewordings by the final compiler: 3:1, 2 ("And in *those* days"); *5:41* ("and"); *12:12a* ("then"); 18:4 ("as *this* child"); 21:43 ("therefore"); 24:10–12 ("and then"); *24:42* ("therefore"); 27:19 ("he" would be unclear from the preceding M passage). The first of these follows the Infancy story. The three italicized ones come immediately after Q material. The other four come after Markan material.

Disregarding the connective phrasings just mentioned, we have, in this M text of less than three hundred verses, 45 passages so defective as to be unintelligible by themselves. Structurally the text of M consistently demands some larger context, such as Matthew actually gives it. Moreover, of these 45 half-told sayings and incidents, 40 are completed in Matthew by Markan matter, 4 by dubious Q, and just 1 by matter assigned positively to Q. This would be an inexplicable situation had M and Q come from the same source or had the compiler been free to juxtapose his M material with Mark or Q indifferently.

The last point is so significant that it is well to look at it in another way. It is when Markan passages are removed that M so often looks broken and disjointed. When Q passages are removed, on the contrary, M remains nearly always smooth and free-flowing.[3] Here is strong evidence that Q was added, chiefly through simple juxtaposition, to an already existing, highly integrated body of material.

Here is evidence, also, for our previous description of M. M looks like the parings that would have been left after a task of abridgment and excision of unwanted passages.

3. So consistent is this that the few apparent exceptions probably are not exceptions at all. Probably at those points we have not M passages but introductions to Q material from the final compiler.

VII

SIGNS OF ABRIDGMENT IN MARK

IT IS not enough to say that M looks like parings. If canonical Mark was formed largely by omitting M material from a parent Gospel, the structure of Mark should, like its language, give signs of what has happened. For example, Matthew and Mark differ somewhat in arrangement. If Matthew copied from Mark, then Mark's order must always be the more primitive. But if both copied from a third book, then Matthew's order could on occasion be more primitive than Mark's. The latter is, indeed, the case; but proof of it is most easily presented when we come to consider the probable arrangement of K itself.[1]

There is, however, another and even more striking structural indication. Canonical Mark shows numerous signs of abridgment and condensation. These always occur at points where Matthew has M material.[2]

A. AUTHOR DECLARES THERE IS MATERIAL
HE HAS NOT USED

Several times the Markan author says, quite clearly, that he is aware of material which he has not used. Mark 4:2 reads, "He WAS SAYING (*elegen*) to them AMONGST HIS TEACHING (*en tē didachē autou*)." There follow three parables. Then Mark concludes (4:33), "And WITH MANY SUCH PARABLES (*toiautais parabolais pollais*) he spake the word unto them."

Matthew at this point gives seven parables (Matt. 13:3-34),

1. See chap. xviii, Sec. A.

2. The author's attention was first drawn to these Markan signs of revision by Dom John Chapman, *Matthew, Mark and Luke* (London: Longmans, 1937), pp. 1-19. Of the sixteen cases here cited, Chapman gave seven. He noted two others which are less obvious (at Mark 8:13-21 and 10:31), though they likewise fall opposite material peculiar to Matthew. Chapman did not notice that Mark's abridgments fall consistently opposite M or that Luke was unable to fill Mark's gaps. He could thus draw the prescribed conclusion that canonical Matthew underlies both Mark and Luke.

and the author concludes with the words, "ALL THESE THINGS (*tauta panta*) he said." Of Matthew's four additional stories, three are M. The other, assigned to Q, is given by Luke at a different point (Matt. 13:33 = Luke 13:20, 21), suggesting that this one did not belong to the group originally. In the present passage, Luke 8:4-18 has no more than Mark 4:2-25, and Luke omits Mark's two phrases.

Mark 12:1 reads, "And he began to speak unto them in PARABLES (pl., *parabolais*)" yet gives only one parable. Luke also has just this one, but he smooths the introduction: "He began to say this parable (sing., *parabolēn*)." In Matthew, however, it is the second of three stories and is called "ANOTHER (*allēn*) parable."

Mark 12:38 ff. gives one short saying against the scribes. It is introduced with the words, "And AMONGST HIS TEACHING HE WAS SAYING"—the same formula as at 4:2. At this point Matt. 23:1 ff. has an entire discourse, and it is introduced with, "Then Jesus SPAKE (*elalēsen*) to the multitudes and to his disciples." Luke has only the Markan saying. He omits "amongst his teaching," and for "he was saying" reads "he said (*eipen*)."

Mark 13:5-37 gives, in comparison with Matthew, only the first part of Jesus' apocalyptic discourse, through Matt. 24:42. This Mark introduces with, "He BEGAN (*ērxato*) to say to them."[3] Matthew's discourse, however, runs from 24:4 to 26:1. It is introduced with, "Jesus SAID to them (*eipen autois*)," and concludes with, "Jesus FINISHED ALL THESE WORDS (*etelesen pantas tous logous toutous*)." Luke has only through Mark 13:21 (though with Mark 13:22-37 compare Luke 21:34-36). He replaces "he began to say" with "he said" and has nothing to correspond to Matt. 26:1.

B. AWARE OF ADDITIONAL MATERIAL

Mark implies knowledge of events which he does not give and which M does give. Mark 4:34 reads, "But privately to his own disciples he expounded all things," yet gives no teaching. Neither does Luke, who omits Mark's statement. But Matthew's M does give the teaching (Matt. 13:36-43). Note that in both Mark and

3. On Mark's use of *ērxato* see below, pp. 56 ff.

Matthew this follows the above-mentioned passage (Mark 4:2–33; Matt. 13:3–34) without a break.

Mark 6:7, "He began to send them forth by two and two," does not tell whither the disciples were sent. Luke likewise fails to tell and again omits Mark's phrase. Matt. 10:5–7 does tell: "Go not into any way of the Gentiles, and enter not into any city of the Samaritans: but go rather to the lost sheep of the house of Israel."

C. ECHOES M PASSAGES

Mark sometimes echoes the phrasing of a passage found only in Matthew. Mark has not Matthew's story of Peter and the tribute payment; yet at the corresponding point Mark has reminiscences of Matthew's description:

Matt. 17:24–25. And when they were come to Capernaum they that received the half-shekel came to Peter and said, Doth not your teacher pay the half-shekel? He saith, Yea.	Mark 9:33. And they came to Capernaum
And when he came into the house Jesus spake first to him, saying, What thinkest thou . . . ?	and when he was in the house he asked them, What were ye reasoning?

Mark 13:26 (also Luke 21:27) has the preposition *en* (in) and the typically Matthean expression *kai tote* (and then). In Matthew both of these are in the preceding verse (24:30) which is M.

D. SUMMARIZES M PASSAGES

Sometimes the Markan passage reads like a summary of the Matthean one. Mark 1:4 summarizes what is found in Matt. 3:1, 2. Matthew quotes the Baptist's preaching directly, but Mark gives an indirect paraphrase. Luke 3:3*b* follows Mark exactly.

Mark 15:15*a*, "wishing to satisfy the multitude," reads like a summary paraphrase of Matt. 27:24, 25. (Luke omits here too, but this is less significant, since Luke is mainly following L at this point.)

E. CONDENSATIONS IN MARK

In at least two cases the Markan condensations are hardly intelligible until they are compared with Matthew. Mark 9:50, "and be at peace one with another (*kai eirēneuete en allēlois*)," is so awkward that it has perplexed commentators for generations. Luke omits it. Yet it is a short but exact summary of M at that point (Matt. 18:15–20; vs. 14 is dubious Q).

The Parable of the Two Sons (Matt. 21:28 ff.) completes Jesus' condemnation of Pharisees who, after going out to John the Baptist, rejected him. The condemnation at Mark 11:27 ff. and at Luke 20:1 ff. is correspondingly incomplete.

F. TRANSITIONS IN MARK

On three occasions the transition in Mark would certainly seem awkward to anyone not familiar with the whole Gospel story. We indicate by ellipsis the place where something is needed—there is nothing there in Mark.

Mark 1:1, 2. "The beginning of the gospel of Jesus Christ . . . even as it is written in Isaiah &c." Mark then quotes a prophecy which he applies to nothing at all, and his incomplete sentence has troubled every commentator on his Gospel. Just possibly, as we shall see later, Mark's Gospel got mutilated here.[4] At all events, Matt. 3:1–3 does apply the prophecy to a description of John the Baptist. The latter is M. Luke applies it too, having supplemented Mark from his own source L (Luke 3:1 ff.).

Mark 5:42, 43a. "And straightway the damsel rose up and walked; for she was twelve years old. And they were amazed with a great amazement. . . . And he charged them much that no man should know this." Now, how could the little girl's parents keep secret the fact that she was brought back from death? In Matthew there is no such awkwardness, for Jesus' charge comes at the end of the following healing (Matt. 9:27–31), which is M. Luke follows Mark here.

Mark 14:47, 48. "One of them that stood by drew his *sword*, and smote the servant of the high priest, and struck off his ear. . . . And Jesus answered and said unto them, Are ye come out, as

4. Below, pp. 120 ff.

against a robber, with *swords* and staves to seize me?" The clumsy junction does not occur in Matthew, for an extended M passage intervenes. In Luke there is a brief statement that Jesus healed the wounded man; it is hard to say whether it is from L or, as seems more likely, represents Luke's own editing (Luke 22:51).

The last three cases, taken by themselves, could be seen as Matthew's and Luke's separate efforts to get around Mark's maladroitness. In the light of the other thirteen cases, however, they look like real transitional breaks in Mark, owing to his omission of material.

Here, then, are sixteen cases where abridgment or summary seems clearly indicated in the text of Mark, often with a good deal of awkwardness.[5] That Luke felt this awkwardness is shown by the fact that, in every case, he either omits Mark's transitional phrase entirely or else sutures the gap with smoother-flowing Greek. In only two cases has Luke filled the Markan break (Luke 3:1 ff. and 22:51) and in only the first of these does he seem to have used a source—his own L. Yet in every instance Matthew has at the corresponding point an extended passage from M. Shall we say that Matthew was just extraordinarily fortunate in being able to bridge Mark's gaps from his own material—and with such finesse as to make them disappear altogether?

G. MARK'S USE OF "ĒRXATO"

It is well known that the form *ērxato* (he/she/it began) occurs much more frequently in Mark and Luke than elsewhere in the New Testament. The figures are: Mark, 18; Luke, 11; Matthew, 7; Acts, 4; John, 1; rest of New Testament, 0. Of the many instances in Mark and Luke, only two are in passages common to these two Gospels (Mark 11:15 = Luke 19:45; Mark 12:1 = Luke 20:9). Evidently Luke's usage was on a different basis from Mark's. We are here concerned only with the Markan uses.

1. Of the eighteen occurrences of *ērxato* in Mark, three introduce acts of Jesus:

6:7, "He began to send them forth by two and two." This is one of the instances of abridgment noticed above.

5. There are others. See pp. 63, 68, 93–94, 95, 106–7, 116, 179.

11:15, "He began to cast out them that sold and bought in the temple." Compared with Matthew's story, Mark and Luke both lack the healings, the rejoicing of the people, and the discussion by the Sanhedrin (Matt. 21:14-16).

14:33-34, "He began to be greatly amazed and sore troubled," is about like Matt. 26:37-38, and Matthew too reads *ērxato*. Luke omits this passage.

2. Seven times Mark uses *ērxato* to introduce sayings of Jesus:

4:1, "He began to teach by the sea side," prefaces the discourse in which, as we saw previously, Mark gives several clear signs of abridgment (4:2, 33, 34). While Mark stops at 4:34 = Matt. 13:34, Matthew continues for nineteen more verses. Luke follows Mark but omits Mark 4:1, 26-34 and revises 4:2.

6:2, "He began to teach in the synagogue." Matthew has no more here than Mark has. In this passage, interestingly enough, Mark varies from Matthew in two notes about our Lord's family.

Matt. 13:55. Is not this the *carpenter's son?*	Mark 6:3. Is not this the *carpenter,*
is not his mother called Mary?	the son of Mary . . . ?
57. A prophet is not without honor, save in his own country,	4. A prophet is not without honor, save in his own country, *and among his own kin,*
and in his own house.	and in his own house.[6]

6:34, "He began to teach them many things," does not give the teaching; but neither does Matthew, which in fact mentions no teaching at all (Matt. 14:14a). It is hard to say whether both Mark and Matthew have omitted a passage from the source, or Mark has substituted this for Matt. 14:14b (which we placed in dubious Q), or whether 6:34 is simply due to the Markan redactor. In any case, Luke has once more felt Mark's awkwardness, for he substitutes the general statement, "He spake to them of the kingdom of God" (Luke 9:11).

8:31, "He began to teach them, that the Son of man must suffer many things . . . ," is about like Matt. 16:21, and Matthew too reads *ērxato*. Note that Matthew, but not Mark, says that the teaching was specifically to the disciples. Luke 9:22 follows Mark, with improved Greek.

6. These variants are by no means unimportant. See below, pp. 104 ff., 120 ff.

10:32*b*, "He began to tell them the things that were to happen," is about the same as Matt. 20:17*b*. Neither Matthew nor Luke has *ērxato*.

12:1, "He began to speak unto them in parables" (plural). This is another of the cases of abridgment discussed above.

13:5, "Jesus began to say unto them . . . ," introduces the apocalyptic discourse. As previously noticed, Mark has only the first part of the discourse as it appears in Matt. 24:4 ff.

3. In five cases *ērxato* in Mark introduces sayings by or to Peter. We shall hereafter notice a significant difference in the treatment of Peter in these two Gospels.[7]

8:32, "Peter began to rebuke him," does not give Peter's words. Matt. 16:22 does so. Luke omits. This looks like another instance of Markan abridgment, similar to those considered above. On the other hand, Matthew may also have read *ērxato* (the textual evidence is conflicting), while, as we shall see later,[8] Matt. 16:22 may be from Q.

10:28, "Peter began to say unto him . . . ," gives, in comparison with Matt. 19:27-28, only part of Peter's question and part of Jesus' reply. In Matthew only, Peter asks, "What then shall *we* get?" and Jesus assures him that the Twelve shall judge the tribes of Israel.

14:69, "The maid began to say. . . ." The maid's words are given more briefly in Mark than in Matthew. Mark does not quote Peter's reply, but Matthew does (Matt. 26:71-72).

14:71, Peter "began to curse." Here Matt. 26:74 also reads *ērxato* and is slightly *less* complete than Mark.

4. The remaining instances of *ērxato* in Mark preface sayings by others. At Mark 1:45 and 5:20 healed persons "began" to proclaim what Jesus had done for them. Both stories are absent from Matthew. At Mark 10:47 a blind man "began" to ask for healing. The passage is about like Matt. 20:30 ff., though the latter has two blind men. At Mark 15:8, "The crowd began to ask Pilate." Mark 15:7-10 is close to Matt. 27:16-18, but Mark lacks Matt. 27:19, 24, 25 which describe the reactions of Pilate and his wife.

Thus, of eighteen instances of *ērxato* in Mark, nine (or ten if we include Mark 8:32) fall at points where Mark has less mate-

7. Below, chap. xi, Sec. C.   8. P. 83.

rial than Matthew. In all these cases (except perhaps 8:32) the additional Matthean matter is M, while in three passages (4:1, 6:7, 12:1) Mark has other positive signs that it has abridged. Mark's *ērxato* is twice associated with other important differences from Matthew (Mark 6:2, 34), and the second of these also looks like an abridgment. Twice, *ērxato* introduces Markan stories lacking in Matthew—both of them about healed persons proclaiming Jesus. These are thirteen of the eighteen cases. In two others (or three, with Mark 8:32*b*) Matthew has the word too, so that there *ērxato* may have been in the source.

It is evident that *ērxato* in Mark is more than a linguistic habit. It is one more positive sign that Mark has revised, and especially that it has abridged, the source which it shared with canonical Matthew.

Now these internal signs of abridgment in Mark simply do not square with previous solutions to the Synoptic Problem. Did the author of Matthew combine three separate documents, Mark, Q, and M? Had he done that, he could have used either Q or M to fill those sixteen gaps in Mark. He always uses M.

Does M comprise merely an author's late editorial expansions? Consider that, at least four times, Mark virtually declares that there is material which he has not used and that at every one of those points Matthew has the material.

Did Mark abridge from canonical Matthew, as Roman and some other scholars say, and did Luke base his Gospel on both Matthew and Mark? How is it, on that theory, that Luke did not know how to fill these Markan gaps, since plainly he was embarrassed by them? And what would be the probability that Mark would always (not usually, but always) abridge at points where Luke would later decide to omit Matthean matter?

Are M and Q from the same source "S"? Then how, and *why*, did Matthew always select for these breaks material which Luke discarded from S?

Here, the more familiar solutions to the Synoptic Problem break against improbabilities of almost astronomical proportions. There is just one remaining explanation. The mathematical probabilities, weighing so heavily against the others, weigh in favor of this one in exactly the same measure. Mark and Matthew are founded upon a document, K, that antedates them both.

VIII

MATTHEW'S METHOD WITH Q

THERE are many further reasons for believing in the K Gospel, and we shall note them as we proceed. The evidence that is already in is, however, so strong that we may at this point turn to a different structural problem, viz., Matthew's treatment of Q. This involves two topics: (*a*) how Matthew used Q (we shall see that the author inserted selections from Q piecemeal into the already existing K document) and (*b*) how much of Q Matthew used. This will lead to a sharper definition of Matthew's Q material than was employed above in chapter ii. The further question—why the author used Q as he did—will be considered when we come to the content of the first two Gospels.

In this chapter we shall examine four rather long passages from Matthew whose assignment to Q raises some problems.

A. ADDITIONAL LINGUISTIC CRITERIA

The word lists previously used to show the relationship of M to Matthew's Markan parts furnish important criteria for the following study. It will be helpful, however, to have more extended lists of expressions, first, for Q and, second, for distinctive items that Matthew shares with Mark.

Additional Q expressions.—The following forms occur in Q at least as often as in all the rest of Matthew. Those starred occur frequently elsewhere in Luke; still they are probably Q-type expressions, since Luke used more of Q than Matthew did, and the style of Q has affected the rest of Luke more than it has the rest of Matthew:[1] *aiteō* (ask) accus., **autoi* (they) pl., *diabolos* (devil), **eirēnē* (peace), **mē* (not) with ppl., **ouchi* (not, is not?), *ō* (be) subj.

The following occur in Q slightly less often than in all the rest of Matthew: *dia touto* (therefore, for this reason), *empros-*

1. See below, pp. 157 ff.

then (before, in the presence of), *oude* (neither, nor), *ophthalmos* (eye), *toutōn* (of these) gen. pl.

The following Matthean expressions, as we have seen, really characterize Q rather than M or the parallels to Mark: *diōkō* (persecute, pursue), *hēmera kriseōs* (day of judgment), *homologeō* (confess), *parousia, skandalon* (offense, stumbling block), *trophē* (food), *psuchē . . . sōma* (soul . . . body).

Matthew-Mark expressions.—The following occur at least three times in Matthew, three in Mark; and in Mark, and in Matthew's parallels to Mark, as often as in Luke-John-Acts combined:[2] *apoluō gunaika* (put away one's wife), *geenna* (Gehenna, hell), *grēgoreō* (be vigilant), *lian* (very), *hopou an/ean* (wherever), *paralutikos* (paralytic), *peritithēmi* (set about), *planaō* (lead astray), *proagō* (bring), *speirō* (sow), *hupagete* (go your way).

The following occur three times in Matthew, three in Mark, and as often in each of these as in Luke and John combined: *hepta* (seven), *hēlios* (sun), *kakei* (and there), *parakaleō* (entreat), *peirazō* (tempt), *presbuteros* (elder), *prōi/prōia* (at early morn), *tois sabbasin* (on the Sabbath), *sperma* (seed; not including "seed of Abraham" which occurs frequently in John), *teleutaō* (bring to an end, die), *hupage* (go thy way), *hōste* (as).

In deciding how Matthew treated a passage, or in determining its source, language is but one of many factors to be considered. It would be absurd, of course, to essay a final decision from an isolated word here or there. When a typical vocabulary is obviously preponderant, however, or when (as is usually the case) other weighty considerations point in the same direction, then linguistic criteria may be used with confidence.

B. THE TEMPTATION (MATT. 4:3 FF.; LUKE 4:3 FF.)

Why are the second and third temptations in different order in Matthew and Luke? And how is it that the order of Matthew, which is the most eschatologically minded of the Four Gospels,

---

2. The lists in this and the next paragraph are not complete but give only those expressions that are referred to in the following study. For complete listing see the Appendix.

is eschatologically inferior to Luke's?[3] Light is thrown on this situation when we examine the language of Matthew and Luke.

	No. of Words in Matthew	No. of Words in Luke	No. of Words in Common
a) Stones to Bread	38	32	19½
Matt. 4:3, 4			
Luke 4:3, 4			
b) Jerusalem Temple	62	64	50
Matt. 4:5–7			
Luke 4:9–12			
c) Vision of Nations	50	62	31
Matt. 4:8–10			
Luke 4:5–8			

Here is a remarkable difference of treatment by Matthew and Luke as between (b), on the one hand, and (a) and (c), on the other. In (a) Matthew has about 19 per cent more words than Luke, and the two Gospels have roughly 55 per cent of their words in common. In (c) Matthew uses about 19 per cent fewer words than Luke, and the two again have about 55 per cent of their words in common. But in (b), which is the *longest* of the three, the two Gospels are nearly identical in length and have about 80 per cent of their words in common.

Furthermore, while the differences in (b) are mostly trivial, those in (a) and (c) extend to important discrepancies in content. In (a) Matthew reads "these stones"; Luke, "this stone." Matthew quotes the latter part of Deut. 8:3,.but Luke does not. In (c) only Matthew has "unto an exceeding high mountain"; only Luke has "this authority," "for it hath been delivered unto me and to whomsoever I will I give it," and "it shall all be thine"; while "and the glory of them" is placed by Luke in the Devil's speech, but by Matthew in his own description.

Finally, Matthew's vocabulary in (a) and (c) differs not only from Luke but also from Matthew's own (b). To be sure, neither Matthew nor Luke shows a marked Q style in any of these narratives (*devil; shall be*, Luke 4:7); but in (a) and (c), the portions

3. On the superiority of Luke's arrangement from the eschatological standpoint see C. C. McCown, "The Temptation of Jesus Eschatologically and Socially Interpreted," *Biblical World*, LIII (1919), 402 ff.

that differ most from Luke, Matthew uses terms that are normally distinctive of K. In these and later quotations from Matthew we shall indicate by SMALL CAPITALS EXPRESSIONS TYPICAL OF K and by *italics expressions typical of Q*.

a) And the TEMPTER CAME (proselthōn) . . . ,

c) Again, the *devil* taketh him unto an EXCEEDING high mountain, and sheweth him all the kingdoms of the world, and the glory of them; and he said unto him, All these things will I give thee, if thou wilt fall down and WORSHIP me. THEN Jesus saith unto him, GET THEE HENCE, Satan: for it is written, Thou shalt WORSHIP the Lord thy God, and him only shalt thou serve.

Yet a single THEN (*tote*) is the only K characteristic in Matthew's much longer (*b*)!

These considerations, taken together, suggest that both Gospels cannot have used a single source for all three narratives. Whereas Luke got them all from Q, Matthew took only the Jerusalem Temple one from that source, his first and third temptation stories coming from K. He conflated the three on a topical scheme (Jesus alone, over the city, over the world), whereas Luke's is the Q order. Assignment: to Q, Luke 4:3-12 but Matt. only 4:5-7; to K, Matt. 4:3, 4, 8-11*a*.

This analysis of the Matthean passage explains Mark 1:13, which, as many have noticed, reads like a summary. As so frequently elsewhere, canonical Mark here abbreviated a source which did contain a detailed account of the Temptation.

c. THE CENTURION'S BOY (MATT. 8:5 FF.; LUKE 7:1 FF.)

As with the temptation stories, we have here what seems to be a clear case of conflation by the compiler of Matthew. To show this, it is necessary to consider the story in sections.

a) Matt. 8:5 And when he was entered into Capernaum, THERE CAME unto him a centurion, BESEECHING him, 6 and saying, Lord, my servant lieth in the house SICK OF THE PALSY, grievously tormented.

b) 7 And he saith unto him, I will come and heal him. 8 And the centurion answered and said, Lord, I am not worthy that thou shouldst come *under my roof:* but only say the word, and my servant shall be healed. 9 For I also am a man *under authority*, having *under myself* soldiers: and I say to this one, Go, and he goeth; and to another, Come and he cometh; and to my *servant*, Do this, and he doeth it. 10 And when Jesus heard it, he marvelled, and said to them that followed, Verily I say unto you, I have not found so great faith, *no, not* in Israel.

c) 11 And I say unto you, that many *shall come* from the east and the west, and shall sit down with Abraham, and Isaac, and Jacob, in the kingdom of heaven: 12 but the sons of the kingdom shall be cast forth into the outer darkness: there *shall be* weeping and gnashing of teeth.

d) 13 And Jesus said unto the centurion, GO THY WAY; as thou hast believed, SO BE IT DONE unto thee. And the servant was healed IN THAT HOUR.

We comment on each of these portions in turn. (*a*) Out of 23 (Greek) words in Matthew and 72 in Luke 7:1-5, only 6 are even partly common to both. In Matthew the centurion's child (*pais*) is ill; in Luke, his slave. In Matthew the centurion comes to Jesus; in Luke he sends Jewish leaders. Matthew has a marked K vocabulary, with no Q words at all; but Luke has *doulos* (slave) and the typically Q word *axios* (worthy). (*b*) Unlike the preceding, this is almost identical with Luke 7:6-9; and here Matthew has a strong Q vocabulary. (*c*) This is found in Luke at another place (Luke 13:28, 29). Here again Matthew uses typical Q expressions. (*d*) But in a passage that has *no* parallel in Luke, Matthew reverts to K vocabulary again, with expressions that are most unlike Q. Thus, where Luke has a marked Q style throughout, Matthew has it only in the part (vss. 7-12) that is actually paralleled in the Third Gospel. Elsewhere his usage is strongly K.

Now note that at Matt. 8:7 Jesus says, "I will come and heal him," but only in Luke (7:6) does he actually set out. Indeed, Matthew's verse 13 contradicts verse 7! Still more significantly, note that Matt. 8:5, 6, 13 forms a complete story by itself:

And when he was entered into Capernaum, there came unto him a centurion, beseeching him, and saying, Lord, my child lieth in the house sick of the palsy, grievously tormented. And Jesus said unto the centurion, Go thy way; as thou hast believed, so be it done unto thee. And the child was healed in that hour.

It is remarkable that this shorter narrative carries all the features that have caused the longer passage to be likened to John 4:46 ff.:

And there was a certain nobleman, whose son was sick at Capernaum. When he heard that Jesus was come . . . he went unto him, and besought him that he would come down, and heal his son . . . Jesus saith unto him, Go thy way; thy son liveth. The man believed . . . his son lived . . . the fever left him . . . at that hour.

Equally striking in many respects is the similarity to Matt.
15:21 ff. (cf. Mark 7:24 ff.):

And Jesus . . . withdrew into the parts of Tyre and Sidon. And behold,
a Canaanitish woman came out from those borders, and cried, saying,
Have mercy on me . . . my daughter is grievously vexed with a devil. . . .
Then Jesus answered and said unto her, O woman, great is thy faith: be
it done unto thee even as thou wilt. And her daughter was healed from
that hour.

In each case, Jesus arrives at a destination. A parent (Matthew:
a gentile parent) comes seeking aid for his child who is grievously ill. Jesus speaks the word. The parent has faith. The child is
healed, at a distance, in the same hour.

Thus Matt. 8:5, 6, 13 is complete and homogeneous by itself.
It lacks the Q usage that appears in the rest of the passage and
throughout the Lukan story. It is very unlike Luke, whereas
verses 7–12 are closely paralleled in Luke. And, unlike verses 7–
12, verses 5, 6, and 13 exhibit a strong, positive K vocabulary.
The true Q account of the centurion's slave is in Luke. Matthew
has expanded an originally independent K story, about a centurion's child, by two additions from Q (7–10; 11, 12). Matthew's ambiguous *pais* may have been chosen by the editor to
cover both K's *huios* (son) and Q's *doulos* (slave). Assignment:
to Q, Matt. 8:7–12, but Luke 7:1–10; to K, Matt. 8:5, 6, 13.

In both John 4:46 ff. and Matt. 15:21 ff. the lacuna is filled by
an objection from Jesus, which is overruled by the importunity
of the parent. The original K story may have contained a similar
dialogue.

D. PARABLE OF THE WEDDING FEAST (MATT. 22:1–14; LUKE 14:16–24)

Matt. 22:1 And Jesus answered and spake again in parables unto them,
saying, 2 The kingdom of heaven IS LIKENED unto a certain king, who
made a MARRIAGE FEAST for his son, 3 and sent forth his *slaves* to call them
that were bidden to the MARRIAGE FEAST: and they would not come.
4 Again he sent forth other *slaves*, saying, Tell them that are bidden, *Behold*, I have made ready my dinner; my oxen and my fatlings are killed,
and all things are ready: COME to the MARRIAGE FEAST. 5 But they made
light of it, and went their ways, one to his own farm, another to his merchandise; 6 and the rest LAID HOLD ON his *slaves*, and treated them shamefully, and killed them. 7 But the king was wroth; and he sent his armies,
and destroyed those murderers, and burned their city.
8 THEN saith he to his *slaves*, The WEDDING is ready, but they that were

bidden were not *worthy*. 9 Go ye therefore unto the partings of the high-ways, and AS MANY AS ye shall find, bid to the MARRIAGE FEAST. 10 And those *slaves* went out into the highways, and GATHERED TOGETHER all as many as they found, both *bad* and *good:* and the WEDDING was filled with guests.

11 But when the king came in to behold the guests, he saw there a man who had not on a WEDDING GARMENT: 12 and he saith unto him, Friend, how camest thou in hither not having a WEDDING GARMENT? And he was speechless. 13 THEN the king said to the ministers, BIND him hand and foot, and cast him out into the outer darkness; there shall be the WEEPING and the GNASHING OF TEETH. 14 For many are called, but few are chosen.

Verses 11–14 are peculiar to Matthew. Heavy with K expressions, and lacking any Q ones, they seem to be definitely from K. Yet they are not intelligible without at least part of what precedes.

But 1–10 were assigned to Q (doubtfully) in chapter ii. Moreover, besides some resemblance to the Lukan parable, they contain expressions highly typical of Q and unlike either M or the parallels to Mark. On the other hand, they lack some Q expressions that Luke has: *heteros* (other) twice, *exerchomai* (go forth) with purpose clause, *dia touto* (for this cause); while with all their Q expressions, they contain even more K ones. Finally, the Lukan passage is very differently worded from Matthew's and has nothing to correspond, for example, to Matt. 22:6, 7. Thus the indications, as to the source of Matt. 22:1–10, are contradictory.

But now consider that (*a*) Matt. 22:1 speaks of *parables* (pl., *parabolais*), yet, as it stands, 22:1–14 is all one story. (*b*) This story is, however, very disjointed, and has no less than *three denouements*, at verses 7, 10, and 13–14. (*c*) In Matthew the majority of the Q expressions are concentrated at two points, verses 4 and 8–10. Finally, (*d*) verses 2, 3*a*, and 5–7 make by themselves a single, straightforward parable:

The kingdom of heaven is likened unto a certain king, who made a marriage feast for his son, and sent forth his servants to call them that were called to the marriage feast. But they made light of it, and went their ways, one to his own farm, another to his merchandise; and the rest laid hold on his servants, and treated them shamefully, and killed them. But the king was wroth; and he sent his armies, and destroyed those murderers, and burned their city.

Here "them that were called" points unmistakably to the Jewish nation; "sent forth his servants" and "treated them shamefully and killed them," to the experiences of Jewish Christian missioners; while "burned their city" sounds like a prediction of the destruction of Jerusalem. There is nothing here about bringing in Q's more "worthy" Gentiles (cf. vs. 8).

Hence it looks as though the compiler of Matthew has once more been conflating. He had as basis the K parable of verses 2, 3*a*, and 5–7, and possibly a second one represented now by verses 11–14, though it seems more likely that 11–13 came from the redactor himself. These K passages have been fused and expanded on the basis of the Q story which Luke preserves. Assignment: to Q, Matt. 22:3*b*, 4, 8–10, but Luke 14:16–24; to K, Matt. 22:1–3*a*, 5–7, 14; to the redactor, probably 11–13.

E. PARABLE OF THE TALENTS (MATT. 25:14–28; CF. LUKE 19:12–25)

Matthew's Parable of the Ten Virgins, which immediately precedes this, is replete with K expressions: *mōros* (foolish) three times, *homoioō* (liken), *husteron* (afterward), *phronimos* (wise) four times, *tote* (then) twice, *gamos* (marriage), *grēgoreō* (be watchful), *katheudō* (sleep). K usage appears still more heavily in the Parable of the Talents, but in the latter there are also numerous Q expressions. To be sure, Luke has a greater variety of them, adding *heteros* (other) and *idou* (behold). Unlike the other passages we have analyzed, however, the points in Matt. 25:14 ff. where K and Q expressions fall are not clearly distinct from one another:

Matt. 25:14 For IT IS AS when a man, going into another country, called his *slaves*, and delivered unto them his goods. 15 And unto one he gave five TALENTS, to another two, to another one; to each according to his several ability; and he went on his journey. 16 STRAIGHTWAY he that received the five TALENTS went and traded with them, and made other five TALENTS. 17 In like manner he also that received the two GAINED other two. 18 But he that received the one went away and digged in the earth, and HID his lord's money. 19 Now after a long time the lord of those *slaves* cometh, and maketh a reckoning with them. 20 And he that received the five TALENTS CAME and BROUGHT other five TALENTS, saying, Lord, thou deliveredst unto me five TALENTS: lo, I HAVE GAINED other five TALENTS. 21 His lord said unto him, Well done, *good* and faithful *slave*:

thou hast been faithful over a few things, I will set thee over many things; enter thou into the joy of thy lord. 22 And he also that received the two TALENTS CAME and said, Lord, thou deliveredst unto me the two TALENTS: lo, I HAVE GAINED other two TALENTS. 23 His lord said unto him, Well done, *good* and faithful *slave:* thou hast been faithful over a few things, I will set thee over many things; enter thou into the joy of thy lord. 24 And he also that had received the one TALENT CAME and said, Lord, I knew thee that thou art a hard man, *reaping* where thou didst not sow, and GATHER-ING WHERE thou didst not scatter; 25 and I was afraid, and went away and HID thy TALENT in the earth: lo, thou hast thine own. 26 But his Lord answered and said unto him, Thou *wicked* and slothful *slave*, thou knewest that I *reap* where I SOWED not, and GATHER WHERE I did not scatter; 27 thou oughtest therefore to have put my MONEY to the bankers, and at my coming I should have received back mine own with interest. 28 Take ye away therefore the TALENT from him, and give it unto him that hath the ten TALENTS.

Now Mark has important contacts with both of the Matthean parables:

a) Matt. 25:5 Now while the bridegroom tarried, they all slumbered and slept. 6 But at midnight there is a cry, Behold, the bridegroom! Come ye forth to meet him.

Mark 13:35 . . . at even, or at midnight, or at cockcrowing, or in the morning; 36 lest coming suddenly he find you sleeping.

b) 13 Watch therefore, for ye know not the day nor the hour.

33 Stay awake (*agrupneite*), watch; for ye know not when the time is.

Here Mark's "stay awake" carries the same thought as Matt. 25:5.

c) 14 As when a man going into another country, called his own servants, and delivered unto them his goods. 15 . . . to each according to his several ability; and he went on his journey.

34 As when a man, sojourning in another country, having left his house, and given authority to his servants, to each one his work. . . .

d) 19 Now after a long time the lord of those servants cometh.

35 . . . for ye know not when the lord of the house cometh.

Note that (*b*), (*c*), and (*d*), are in the same order in both Gospels.

These contacts cannot be accidental, and they furnish one more case where canonical Mark appears to have abridged his source. But whereas in Matthew's second parable, as it now stands, the lesson is trustworthiness, the lesson in Mark is watchfulness. Yet the latter is the point of Matthew's first story, and it is certainly implied in verse 19*a* of the second.

Now consider that Luke's parable is almost entirely devoted to the accounting, whereas Matthew has much besides. Nevertheless, in Matthew the majority of the Q expressions likewise fall in the accounting and especially in the replies of the lord.

Matthew's contacts with Mark, its mixed vocabulary, and the greater concentration of Q expressions in that part of the story that is paralleled in Luke all point to the same conclusion. K contained the Parable of the Ten Virgins and a second parable about the departure and return of a lord (the word is in Mark). In its original form, the second K parable taught watchfulness, as did the first, and may have concluded at some such point as Matt. 25:19a ("after a long time the lord cometh") or this plus 30b ("there shall be weeping and gnashing of teeth"). This story the compiler of Matthew fused with one from Q on trustworthiness but which also told of the departure and return of a lord. The substance of the Q parable is better preserved in Luke.

It is now almost impossible to disentangle the strands of the Matthean passage, since the integration has gone further than in the other examples we have studied. The following assignments are approximate: Matt. 25:13, 14, 19 to K; 25:15–18, 20–28 to Q in substance, though the original Q form is better seen at Luke 19:12 ff.

The foregoing analyses provide important indications about how Matthew handled the Sayings Source:

1. The compiler's procedure cannot properly be described as a putting-together of two or more documents on equal terms.

2. Instead, he has added Q to other material, and the latter is basic in every case that we have examined. This is precisely the conclusion which we previously reached on other grounds, viz., that, while removal of Markan matter often leaves M disintegrated, removal of Q leaves M intact.[4]

3. Both the choice and the arrangement of Q material in Matthew seem to have been dictated partly by superficial similarities of circumstance or of wording.

4. Yet the Q additions have served to alter, at times quite markedly, the sense of the basic document. The nature of this last effect, and its significance in the formation of the Gospel tradition, will be discussed under the heading of the content of the First Gospel.

4. Above, pp. 50–51.

IX

THE EXTENT OF Q IN MATTHEW

WHILE considering the methods that the compiler of Matthew used with Q, we were led, in the four passages studied, to modify our conception of the extent to which that document had been employed in the First Gospel. We shall now try to delimit, with greater precision than hitherto, the extent of Q material throughout the Gospel. To do this, it is necessary to examine every remaining passage about which doubt arises. We shall again mark with SMALL CAPITALS TYPICAL K EXPRESSIONS and with *italics typical Q expressions.*

A. Q PASSAGES PROVISIONALLY MARKED DUBIOUS

Matt. 5:1. And seeing the multitudes, he went up into the mountain: and when he had sat down, his disciples CAME UNTO him.

The verse is utterly unlike Luke 6:20 and reads like a succinct equivalent of Mark 3:13 ff. Assignment: K.

5:5. Blessed are the meek: for they shall inherit the earth.

The only linguistic indication is *praüs* (meek), which occurs three times in Matthew (5:5, 11:29, 21:5) and only once elsewhere in the New Testament (I Pet. 3:4). The verse may be due to the redactor.

5:13. Ye are the salt of the earth: but if the salt have lost its savor, wherewith shall it be salted? it is thenceforth good for nothing, but to be cast out and trodden under foot of men.

This is Matthew's only parallel to Mark 9:50a. Compare Luke 14:34-35. Assignment: K.

5:32. But I say unto you, that every one that PUTTETH AWAY HIS WIFE, saving for the cause of fornication, maketh her an adulteress: and whosoever shall marry HER WHEN SHE IS PUT AWAY committeth adultery.

This is closer to Luke 16:18 than to Mark 10:11-12, whereas Matt. 19:9 is closer to the Markan passage. But Luke, who has the saying only once, has contacts with both Matt. 5:32 (*pas ho apoluon*) and with Mark (*kai gamōn heteran*). K and Q seem to have overlapped. Matthew has kept both, while Luke has conflated. Matt. 5:32*b* has the balance of textual evidence in its favor. Assignment: Q.

5:39. But I say unto you, Resist not HIM THAT IS EVIL: but whosoever smiteth thee on thy right cheek, turn to him THE OTHER also.

The verse is necessary to complete 5:38 which is M (i.e., K). It is very different from Luke 6:27 ff. The confusion of pronominal cases sounds Semitic. Assignment: K.

5:44. But I say unto you, Love your enemies, and pray for *them that persecute* you;

At least the first part of this is necessary to complete verse 43, which is M—yet that is the part closest to Luke 6:27. K and Q may have overlapped again. Assignment: 44*a*, doubtful K; 44*b*, Q.

5:45 THAT ye may be sons OF YOUR FATHER WHO IS IN HEAVEN: for he maketh his SUN to rise on the *evil* and the *good*, and sendeth rain on the just and the unjust.

The italicized constructions are infrequent in M, so that the language points both ways. The passage is, however, quite unlike Luke 6:35. Assignment: doubtful K.

6:10. Thy kingdom come. Thy will BE DONE, as *in heaven, so on earth.*

If 10*b* stood in Q, it is hard to see why Luke omitted it; yet it needs its present Q context to make it intelligible. The verse remains dubious Q.

6:13*b*. But deliver us from THE EVIL ONE.

The words in small capitals are not infrequent in Q. (One papyrus, Aeg. 954, reads *tēs ponērias*, "from wickedness," which would fit Q's ethical interest.) It seems best to keep the verse in Q.

6:19. *Treasure* not up for yourselves *treasures* upon the earth, where moth and rust consume, and where STEALERS break through and STEAL.

The pleonasms, here transliterated literally, are not in Q's style. The passage is very different from Luke 12:33*a*. Assignment: K.

6:34. *Be* not therefore *anxious* for the morrow: for the morrow *will be anxious* for itself. Sufficient unto the day is the evil thereof.

Luke has no exact parallel (though cf. Luke 12:32), but "to be anxious" does not appear in M and only once in parallels to Mark. Assignment: Q.

7:16. By their fruits ye shall know them. DO MEN GATHER grapes of thorns, or figs of thistles?

The expression in small capitals is frequent in M and does not appear elsewhere in Q. The verse is not necessarily connected with the next two. There is no parallel in Luke. Assignment: K.

7:17, 18. Even so every *good tree bringeth forth* good *fruit;* but the CORRUPT *tree bringeth forth evil fruit. A good tree* cannot *bring forth evil fruit, neither* can a CORRUPT *tree bring forth* good *fruit.*

The parallel at Luke 6:43 is close enough. Assignment: Q.

7:23. And THEN *will I profess* unto them, I never knew you: depart from me, YE THAT WORK LAWLESSNESS.

The parallel at Luke 13:27 is similar in meaning but differently worded and may be from L. If the last part of the saying is a quotation from Ps. 6:9, Luke and Matthew are equally, though differently, at variance with the LXX. Assignment: doubtful K.

8:1. And when he was come down from the mountain, great multitudes followed him.

The only reason for placing this in Q was that it follows a Q passage. It has no parallel in Luke. Furthermore, it seems correlative to 5:1, which we have placed in K. The present verse may be from K or else from the redactor.

9:34. But the Pharisees said, *By* the prince of demons *casteth he out* demons.

12:24. But when the Pharisees heard it, they said, This man *doth* not *cast out* demons, but *by Beelzebub* the prince of demons.

Matt. 9:34 is probably authentic, its omission from D and a few other manuscripts being because it is like 12:24. Matt. 9:34*b* = Luke 11:15*b* is identical with Mark 3:22*b*, whereas Matt. 12:24*b* differs somewhat in phrasing and order. The name "Beelzebub" is in Mark; it may have been omitted from Matt. 9:34 by the compiler. Similarly, *ekballō en* (cast out . . . by) appears in all four passages. Matt. 12:24 has, with Luke, *de* (but) and *eipon* (they said; Luke, *eipan*). K and Q again seem to have overlapped. Luke has combined the Q saying with Mark 3:22*b*, while Matthew has kept both, allowing reminiscences of 9:34 to lead him to introduce "Pharisees" in 12:24. Perhaps Q originally read, "But some of them, when they heard it, said," etc., with Matt. 12:24. Assignment: 9:34 to K; 12:24 to Q.

10:9, 10*a*. Get you no GOLD, nor silver, nor brass in your purses; no wallet for your journey, neither two coats, nor shoes, nor staff.

"Gold" is not mentioned elsewhere in Q. The passage is much like Mark 6:8–9 and very different from Luke 10:4. Assignment: K.

10:11*a*. And into whatsoever city or village ye shall enter, search out in it who is *worthy*.

In Matthew, "worthy" (*axios*) appears only in Q. This is in the midst of a Q context, verses 10*b*, 12, and 13. Assignment: Q.

10:11*b*. AND THERE abide till ye go forth.

Kakei does not occur elsewhere in Q, and the passage is like Mark 6:10*b*. Matthew is conflating through here. Assignment: K.

10:14. And whosoever shall not receive you, nor hear your words, as ye go forth out of that house or that city, shake off the dust of your feet.

This is closer to Mark 6:11 = Luke 9:5 than to Luke 10:10–11. The mixture of pronouns sounds Semitic. Assignment: K.

10:20. For it is not ye that speak, but the Spirit of YOUR FATHER that speaketh in you.

This is much closer to Mark 13:11 than to either Luke 12:11–12 or Luke 21:15. Assignment: K.

11:14. And if ye are willing to receive it, this is Elijah that is to come.

Luke has no parallel, and the name "Elijah" does not occur elsewhere in Q. But the verse needs its present Q context to make it intelligible, and the true parallel to Mark 9:13 is Matt. 17:12. Q seems the more probable source for 11:14.

11:24. But I say unto you that *it shall be more* tolerable for the land of Sodom in *the day of judgment, than* for thee.

Note how this continues the anti-Jewishness of verses 21–23. Assignment: Q.

12:24. (Discussed under 9:34 above; assigned to Q.)

12:25, 26. And knowing their thoughts he said unto them, Every kingdom divided against itself is brought to desolation; and every city or house divided against itself shall not stand: and if Satan casteth out Satan, he is divided against himself; how therefore shall his kingdom stand?

The agreements of Matthew and Luke against Mark all have to do with the first and last parts of the saying, their central portions being quite Markan. It seems that both Matthew and Luke have conflated a Q and a K saying (Luke getting it through Mark). The language of Luke 11:18b is typically Q (*Beezeboul*, *ekballein en*). The original Q passage probably ran something like this:

But knowing their thoughts he said [to them], Every kingdom divided against itself is brought to desolation. But if [Beelzebub] cast out [Beelzebub] how shall his kingdom stand? for ye say that by Beelzebub I cast out demons.

12:33. Either *make* the *tree* good, and its *fruit* good; or *make* the *tree* CORRUPT, and its *fruit* CORRUPT: for the *tree* is known by its fruit.

The true parallel to Luke 6:43 is Matt. 7:18. The present verse, however, is in the midst of a Q context (vss. 32–35), and its point is sufficiently different from that of Matt. 7:18 so that Q could easily have had both. Assignment: Q.

12:38. THEN certain of the SCRIBES and Pharisees answered him, saying, TEACHER, we would see a sign from thee.

The true parallel to Mark 8:11 is Matt. 16:1, and the latter has an even more pronounced K vocabulary (*proselthontes*, *Saddoukaioi*, *peirazontes*). We therefore retain 12:38 in Q.

12:40. For JUST AS Jonah was three days and three nights in the belly of the whale; so *shall* the Son of man *be* three days and three nights in the heart of the earth.

The entire Q passage, 12:39–42, has a strong gentile interest, with the sole exception of this verse. In the Lukan parallel, Luke 11:30 maintains the gentile bias. It seems probable that Matthew substituted this for the Q saying that Luke gives. With some hesitation we place Matt. 12:40 in K.

13:31, 32. Another PARABLE set he before them, saying, THE KINGDOM OF HEAVEN is like unto a grain of mustard SEED, which a man took, and SOWED in his field: which indeed is less than all SEEDS; but when it is grown, it is greater than the herbs, and becometh a *tree*, SO THAT the *birds* of the heaven come and lodge in the branches thereof.

Q's typical *tree* occurs also at Luke 13:19 but not at Luke 4:31–32. Similarly Matt. 13:31 and Luke 13:18 read "which a man took" and "his" (Matt., *autou;* Luke, *heautou*). Both complete the quotation from chapter 4 of Daniel. Yet Luke *omits* most of the central part of the parable. This seems to be another clear case where Luke has preserved a Q parable which Matthew has conflated with one from K. Assignment: Matt. 13:31*a*, 32*b*, Q in the main; 13:31*b*, 32*a*, K.

14:14*b*. . . . and healed their sick.

This falls opposite one of those points where *ērxato* in Mark may indicate Markan abridgment,[1] thus with a slight suggestion that Matt. 14:14*b* is from K. On the other hand, *therapeuō* (heal) occurs also at Luke 9:11, and there are no other linguistic signs. The passage may well be from the redactor.

18:14. Even so it is not the will of YOUR FATHER WHO IS IN HEAVEN, that one of these little ones should perish.

The words in small capitals are not sufficiently distinctive of K, and the passage remains doubtful Q.

18:15. And if thy brother sin against thee, GO, show him his fault between thee and him alone: if he hear thee, THOU HAST GAINED thy brother.

This is very different from Luke 17:3 and is a necessary part of the whole K passage, verses 15–17. Assignment: K.

18:21, 22. THEN CAME Peter and said to him, Lord, how oft shall my brother sin against me, and I forgive him? until SEVEN TIMES? Jesus saith unto him, I say not unto thee, Until SEVEN TIMES; but, Until seventy times [and] SEVEN.

The idea recalls Luke 17:4, but the expression of it and the situation are very different. With the marked K vocabulary, there can be little hesitation in assigning the passage to that source.

1. Above, p. 57.

21:31*b*, 32. Jesus saith unto them, Verily I say unto you, that the publicans and the harlots GO into the kingdom of God BEFORE you. For John came unto you in the way of RIGHTEOUSNESS, and ye believed him not; but the publicans and the harlots believed him: and ye, when ye saw it, did *not even* repent yourselves AFTERWARD, that ye might believe him.

B, etc., read *oude* (*not even*) but C, etc., read *ou* (not). There is no real similarity to Luke 7:29–30, and the passage has a definite K style. Assignment: K.

23:6, 7. and love the chief place at feasts, and the chief seats in the synagogues, and the salutations in the market places, and to be called of men, Rabbi.

Verses 6 and 7*a* are about equally close to Mark 12:38, 39 = Luke 20:46 and to Luke 11:43. The latter reads *ouai* (woe), a frequent Q word. Matthew seems to be conflating. Verses 6 and 7*a* are dubious; 7*b* is almost certainly K.

23:32. Fill ye up then the measure of your fathers.

The sense goes better with what precedes (23:29–31, Q) than with what follows. Assignment: Q.

24:26. If therefore they shall say unto you, *Behold*, he is in the wilderness; *go* not *forth: Behold*, he is in the inner chambers; believe it not.

Assignment: Q.

24:51*b*. There *shall be* the WEEPING and the GNASHING OF TEETH.

This saying occurs about equally often in M and in Matthew's Q. Luke nearly always omits it (though see Luke 13:28). The present saying concludes a long Q section, 24:37–41, 43 ff. Assignment: Q.

25:30. And cast ye out the unprofitable *slave* into the outer darkness: there *shall be* the WEEPING and the GNASHING OF TEETH.

From our previous analysis of Matt. 25:14 ff.,[2] verse 30 seems to fit better the Q part of that parable.

B. OTHER Q PASSAGES ABOUT WHICH DOUBT ARISES

In a few cases Q passages, not marked dubious in the preliminary definition, show on investigation characteristics which raise doubt about their inclusion in that source.

2. Above, pp. 67 ff.

Matt. 5:18. For verily I say unto you, Till *heaven and earth* pass away, one jot or one tittle shall in no wise pass away from the law, till all things be acomplished.

In its Matthean context this verse seems to exalt the Torah in a manner that is unusual in Q as a whole. In the parallel at Luke 16:17, however, the Torah is not thus exalted: Jesus says that the Torah was in force "until John" and that it is not easily dislodged. Matthew has expanded a K passage in praise of the Torah by means of a Q verse apparently taken out of context. Assignment: Q.

5:26. Verily I say unto thee, By no means *shalt thou come out* THENCE, till THOU HAVE PAID the last farthing.

This is very close to Luke 12:59 and is unintelligible apart from the Q context. Assignment: Q.

5:48. Therefore *ye shall be* perfect, AS YOUR HEAVENLY FATHER is perfect.

For *hōsper* (as) many manuscripts read *hōs*. Like 5:45, this verse differs widely from the Lukan parallel (Luke 6:36) and has conflicting vocabulary indications. On the whole, the more likely source seems to be Q, though with some doubt.

6:26. Behold the *birds* of the heaven, that THEY SOW not, *neither do they reap, nor* GATHER into barns; and YOUR HEAVENLY FATHER feedeth them. Are not ye of much more value than they?

None of the K words occurs in the parallel at Luke 12:24. There seems to have been conflation here, or at least redaction by the compiler. We keep the passage in Q.

8:19. And THERE CAME ONE SCRIBE, and said unto him, TEACHER, I will follow thee WHITHERSOEVER thou goest.

The first part of this verse is unlike Luke 9:57. The man's words, however, are part of a Q passage which is almost identical in the two Gospels (Matt. 8:19*b*–22 = Luke 9:57–60). The whole of Matt. 8:19 ff. is an interruption, and it is possible that 19*a* is part of a K story now lost. Assignment: Matt. 8:19*a*, dubious K; 19*b*, Q.

11:12. And from the days of John the Baptist until NOW, THE KINGDOM OF HEAVEN suffereth violence, and men of violence take it by force.

There is no parallel at the corresponding point, Luke 7:24 ff., and the supposed parallel at Luke 16:16 is very different. Note the suggestion that John the Baptist shared in the Kingdom, which contradicts the preceding verse. Assignment: K.

12:11. And he said unto them, What man *shall there be* of you, that shall have one SHEEP, and if this fall into a pit ON THE SABBATH DAY, WILL HE *not* LAY HOLD on it, and lift it out?

"Lay hold" (*krateō*) is listed by Hawkins as a distinctively Markan word.[3] There is hardly a word in common with Luke 14:5. Assignment: dubious K.

12:22, 23. THEN WAS BROUGHT unto him ONE POSSESSED WITH A DEMON, blind and dumb: and he healed him, INSOMUCH THAT the dumb man spake and saw. And all the multitudes were amazed, and said, Can this be the SON OF DAVID?

Not this but 9:32–33 is the true parallel to Luke 11:14. Unlike 9:32–33, the present passage is devoid of Q usage. Verse 23 is very Jewish in tone. Assignment: K.

15:14b. . . . They are BLIND guides. And if the blind guide the blind, both shall fall into a pit.

The first of these sentences uses "blind" metaphorically. Such usage is common in M but is not repeated elsewhere in Q, and Luke has no parallel. The second sentence is not a metaphor but a true parable. Assignment: first sentence to K; second to Q.

16:2b, 3. When it is EVENING, ye say, It will be fair weather: for the heaven is red. And IN THE MORNING, It will be foul weather to-day: for the heaven is red and lowering. [YE HYPOCRITES,] ye know how to discern the face of the heaven; but ye cannot discern the signs of the times.

Neutral manuscripts omit this passage, while Western and Caesarean ones retain it. It shows no Q usage and is very different from Luke 12:54–56. If authentic, it would belong with K.

16:11b. But beware of the leaven of the Pharisees and SADDUCEES.

"Sadducees" is absent from Luke 12:1 and occurs but once elsewhere in Q (Matt. 3:7). It may be redactorial, drawn back from the M verse 12. In other respects the passage is close to Luke and is retained in Q.

3. John C. Hawkins, *Horae Synopticae: Contributions to the Study of the Synoptic Problem* (2d ed.; Oxford, 1909), p. 13.

17:20. And he saith unto them, Because of your LITTLE FAITH: for verily I say unto you, If ye have faith as a grain of mustard seed, *ye shall say* unto this mountain, REMOVE hence to yonder place; and IT SHALL REMOVE; and nothing shall be impossible unto you.

Except for "faith as a grain of mustard seed," which must have been frequently quoted by early Christians, there is nothing to connect this with Luke 17:6. Even the lone Q word *ereite* is absent from Luke. Assignment: K.

18:12, 13. HOW THINK YE? if any man have a hundred SHEEP, and one of them BE GONE ASTRAY, *doth* he *not* leave the ninety and nine, and go unto the mountains, and seek that WHICH GOETH ASTRAY? And if so be that he find it, verily I say unto you, he rejoiceth over it more than over the ninety and nine which HAVE *not* GONE ASTRAY.

The forms for "not" are *ouchi* and *mē* with participle, the latter occurring in Q as often as in all the rest of Matthew together. In the parallel at Luke 15:4 ff. the only K-type expression is "sheep," which is required by the context. In other respects Matthew and Luke differ greatly, though Luke's most important variations are in the form of additional matter. Possibly this is another place where K and Q overlapped and Matthew conflated. Assignment: dubious Q.

24:27. For JUST AS the lightning *cometh forth* from THE EAST and is SEEN even unto the west; so *shall be* the *coming* of the Son of man.

The K expressions all occur elsewhere in Q. Verses 26 and 27 belong together and are parallel, respectively, to Luke 17:23 and 24. We keep the verse in Q.

C. M PASSAGES ABOUT WHICH DOUBT ARISES

Matthew must have used some parts of Q that Luke omitted, and Luke many parts that Matthew omitted. Hitherto there has been no reliable method whereby to isolate Q material occurring in only one Gospel. The distinctive Q vocabulary, which has now been identified, does provide a lens through which a number of additional passages from the Q source come into view.

Matt. 5:7–10. *Blessed* are the merciful: for they shall obtain mercy. *Blessed* are the pure in heart: for they shall see God. *Blessed* are the peacemakers: for they shall be called sons of God. *Blessed* are *they that have been persecuted* for RIGHTEOUSNESS' sake: for theirs is the KINGDOM OF HEAVEN.

Both the K expressions occur elsewhere in Q. Verses 7–9 have no K expressions at all. Assignment: Q.

5:31. It was said also, Whosoever SHALL PUT AWAY his WIFE, let him give her a writing of divorcement.

The K-type expression is in an Old Testament quotation. Throughout Matt. 5:21–44 the repeated formula is, "Ye have heard that it was said (*ēkousate hoti errethē*)." The sole exception is at this point, where it changes to *errethē de*. Moreover, verse 31 needs the Q verse 32 to complete it. Possibly 5:31 is Q; more likely, it was introduced by the redactor to prepare for verse 32.

5:37. But *let* your speech *be*, Yea, yea; Nay, nay: and whatsoever is more *than these* is OF THE EVIL ONE.

There is no necessary connection between this and the very Jewish passage preceding. The adjective "evil" (*ponēros*) is common in Q; and the only other occurrence of *perisson* (more) in the Synoptic Gospels is at Matt. 5:47, which is Q. There can be little hesitation in assigning the present verse to that document.

9:32, 33. And as they *went forth*, BEHOLD, THERE WAS BROUGHT to him a dumb man POSSESSED WITH A DEMON. And when the demon was cast out, the dumb man spake: and the multitudes marvelled, saying, IT WAS never so SEEN in Israel.

While the first part of verse 32 is not paralleled in Luke, *exerchomenōn* is typically Q. The true parallel to verses 32*b* and 33 is not Markan; it is Luke 11:14, which is almost identical. Assignment: Q. (Compare 12:22–23, which is K, not Q.) Is there an aspersion against the Jews in 33*b*?

10:16*b*. Be ye therefore WISE as serpents, and harmless as doves.

While this follows a Q saying (vss. 15, 16*a*), the two are not necessarily connected. Indeed, 16*b* would go well with several K portions of this discourse, for example, after 14 (which we have concluded is K) or after 6. We keep the passage in K.

10:23. But when *they persecute* you in this city, flee into *the next* (*tēn heteran*): for verily I say unto you, Ye shall not have gone through the cities of Israel, till the Son of man be come.

Tēn heteran is better supported than *tēn allēn* (DΘ, etc.), which would be more like K. Both Q expressions are in the first part of the verse, and that is not necessarily connected with the second part. Assignment: 10:23*a*, dubious Q; 23*b*, K.

11:20. THEN began he to upbraid the cities wherein most of his mighty works were done, because they repented not.

This introduces a long Q passage. It might itself be Q but is more likely to be from the redactor.

12:12*a*. How much then is a man of more value than a SHEEP.

This is preceded by a passage which we have, with some hesitation, assigned to K. It is followed by K material. It may be redactorial. Assignment: dubious K.

20:1–16. For the KINGDOM OF HEAVEN is like unto a man that was a householder, who *went out* early IN THE MORNING *to* hire laborers into his VINEYARD. 2 And when he had agreed with the laborers for a DENARIUS a day, he sent them into his VINEYARD. 3 And he went out ABOUT THE THIRD HOUR, and saw others standing in the marketplace idle; 4 and to them he said, GO YE also into the VINEYARD, and whatsoever is right I will give you. And they went their way. 5 Again he went out ABOUT THE SIXTH and THE NINTH HOUR, and did likewise. 6 And ABOUT THE ELEVENTH he went out, and found others standing; and he saith unto them, Why stand ye here all the day idle? 7 They say unto him, Because no man hath hired us. He saith unto them, GO YE also into the VINEYARD. 8 And when EVEN was come, the lord of the VINEYARD saith unto his steward, Call the laborers, and PAY them their HIRE, beginning from the last unto the first. 9 And when they came that were hired ABOUT THE ELEVENTH HOUR, they received every man a DENARIUS. 10 And when the first came, they supposed that they should receive *more;* and they likewise received every man a DENARIUS. 11 And when they received it, they murmured against the householder, 12 saying, These have spent but one hour, and thou hast made them equal unto us, who have borne the burden of the day and the scorching heat. 13 But he answered and said to one of them, Friend, I do thee no wrong: *didst not* thou agree with me for a DENARIUS? 14 Take up that which is thine, and GO THY WAY; it is my will to give unto this last, even as unto thee. 15 IS IT not LAWFUL for me to do what I will with mine own? or is thine eye *evil*, because I am *good?* 16 So the last *shall be* first, and the first last.

Notice that (*a*) most of the Q expressions fall in verses 13–16. (*b*) Except for "denarius," which is required by the context, the heaviest concentration of K expressions is in verses 1–8. (*c*) Again except for "denarius," verses 9–12 have very few expressions of either type. (*d*) Verse 16, while it has the lone Q word *esontai* (shall be), provides a not unnatural sequel to verse 8:

Call the laborers and pay them their hire, beginning from the last unto the first. . . . So the last shall be first, and the first last.

In the previous chapter several Matthew-Luke parallels were considered, in which the First Gospel has plainly conflated Q with K material. The present passage, which has no Lukan counterpart, looks in other respects very much like those previously examined. The chief objection to associating verse 16 with verse 8 is that 16 is Matthew's only possible parallel to Luke 14:30 (Matt. 19:30 plainly = Mark 10:31) and that the Lukan verse comes at the end of a long Q passage. Assignment: 20:1–8, K; 9–16, doubtful Q. There is a strong possibility that the latter, and particularly verses 9–13, are an expansion by the Matthean redactor himself.

21:43. *Therefore* say I unto you, The kingdom of God shall be taken away from you, and shall be given to a nation *bringing forth the fruits* thereof.

Note the un-Matthean "of God" for "of heaven." There is no close connection with the K passage immediately preceding. The next verse, if retained on the authority of Neutral and Caesarean manuscripts and many versions, would be Q (cf. Luke 20:18). We may safely assign the present verse to the Q source.

23:33. Ye serpents, ye offspring of vipers, how shall ye escape the JUDGMENT of GEHENNA?

This is in the midst of a Q context and resembles the accusation which Q puts on the lips of John the Baptist (Matt. 3:7*b* = Luke 3:7*b*). These are not, however, sufficient reason for disallowing the present verse to K, particularly since Q does not elsewhere speak of Gehenna.

D. APPARENT MARKAN PASSAGES ABOUT WHICH DOUBT ARISES

At Matt. 13:31–32 = Mark 4:30 ff. we have seen that Matthew has probably conflated a K and a Q parable. At Matt. 16:16*b*, Peter's confession is, "Thou art the Christ, *the Son of the living God*." Luke 9:20 reads, "The Christ *of God*." Since Mark 8:29 lacks the italicized words, they might represent a Q passage.

Again, Matt. 16:22*b* gives Peter's words, "Be it far from thee, Lord: this shall never be unto thee." They are absent from Mark, and *estai* (shall be) sounds rather more like Q than K. Now, if Q told of Peter's confession, this could explain the completely different setting of it in Luke from that in Matthew and Mark. This is only a possibility, however, and cannot be verified. Many readers will prefer Canon Streeter's suggestion that Luke failed to mention Caesarea Philippi because his copy of Mark was defective and lacked the name.[4]

E. SUMMARY

1. Of the passages studied in this and the preceding chapters, we have made the following assignments to Q. From Q passages marked doubtful in the preliminary definition: 5:32, 44*b*; 6:13*b*, 34; 7:17, 18; 10:11*a*; 11:14, 24; 12:24, 25*a*, 26*b*, 33, 38; 13:31*a*, 32*b*; 23:32; 24:26, 51*b*; 25:30. The following remain doubtful: 6:10; 18:14; 23:6, 7*a*. From other Q passages studied: 4:5-7; 5:18, 26; 8:7-12, 19*b*; 13:33; 15:14*b*; 16:11*b*; 22:3*b*, 4, 8-10; 24:27; 25:15-18, 20-28. Also, but doubtfully: 5:48; 18:12, 13. From M: 5:7-10, 37; 9:32, 33; 21:43. Also, doubtfully: 10:23*a*; 20:14-16. From parallels to Mark, doubtfully: 16:16*b*, 22*b*.

2. We have assigned the following to K. From Q passages previously marked dubious: 5:1, 13, 39; 6:19; 7:16; 9:34; 10:9, 10*a*, 11*b*, 14, 20; 12:25*b*, 26*a*; 13:31*b*, 32*a*; 18:15, 21, 22; 21:31*b*, 32; 23:7*b*. Less certainly: 5:44*a*, 45; 7:23; 12:40. From other Q passages studied: 4:3, 4, 8-11*a*; 8:5, 6, 13; 11:12; 12:22, 23; 15:14*a*; 16:2, 3; 17:20; 22:1-3*a*, 5-7, 14; 25:13, 14, 19. Less certainly: 8:19*a*; 12:11. From M: 10:16*b*, 23*b*; 20:1-8; 23:33. From parallels to Mark: 13:31-32.

3. Assignments to the redactor of Matthew, in the foregoing analyses, were based of course upon our effort to identify Q material in Matthew. Hereafter we shall find additional passages ascribable to him for different reasons. So far, the following have with more or less assurance been attributed to the final compiler: from dubious Q: 5:5; 8:1; 14:14*b*; from other Q: 6:26 if authentic: 22:11-13; and from M: 5:31; 11:20; 12:12*a*; 20:9-13.

4. B. H. Streeter, *The Four Gospels* (2d ed.; London: Macmillan & Co., 1930), pp. 176 ff.

Examination of Matthew's Q has confirmed, in the strongest terms, the conclusions reached on other grounds earlier in this book. Again and again the solution to a tangled problem has proved to be that the Matthean compiler added Q to a basic document already in existence—a document, moreover, that must certainly have included more than our present Mark. Matthew's procedure with Q can most readily be accounted for by assuming the prior unity of Mark and M.

Part III

EVIDENCE FROM CONTENT

X

MARK AND JEWISH CHRISTIANITY

ASSUMING that there was a K document from which canonical Mark was abstracted, then why did the abridgment
occur? If we are able to answer that question, the case for K itself will be greatly strengthened. The answer must come from a
comparison, passage by passage, of Mark with the K portions of
Matthew. This will cover, of course, the passages common to the
two Gospels. Far more importantly, it requires study of the
materials which the author of Mark discarded as unsuitable.

Two prefatory notes must be made, one practical, the other of
more theoretical nature:

1. The text of M, given in chapter ii, was admittedly provi-
sional. We have since seen reason to modify its extent somewhat,
and some readers may wish to make further changes here and
there. However, such variations have to do only with details
and do not affect the over-all character of M.[1] In fact, the conclusions here reached will be based on passages about which
there is little or no doubt whatever. The words of B. S. Easton
are nowhere more germane than here: "In work of this sort, only
bulk counts."[2]

2. In considering the differences of emphasis, as between K
and Mark, we must perforce examine the motives which underlay the formation of these documents. This involves a discipline
recalling, in some respects, the discipline of Form Criticism.
There are, however, important differences between that approach and the present one. (*a*) We are not primarily concerned
with independent units such as are supposed to have circulated
in oral tradition. Our chief concern is with the written docu-

1. While the separate existence of an M source is denied, it is convenient
to retain the symbol M, with the meaning, "those parts of Matt. 3–28 that have
no parallel in Mark or Luke."

2. *The Gospel According to St. Luke: A Critical and Exegetical Commentary*
(New York: Scribner's, 1926), Introd., p. xxv.

ments considered as wholes. (*b*) The particular forms or stereo-
types, which the various sections are thought to have assumed in
early preaching, will have little or no bearing on the present investigation. (*c*) It is by no means necessary to assume that there
were "creative communities" producing gospel lore out of their
own imaginations or from the exigencies of their own, post-
Resurrectional "seats in life."

In fact, what is here assumed is only what no one could legiti-
mately deny: (*a*) that each evangelist did select from the materials at his disposal; (*b*) that he often paraphrased his sources;
and (*c*) that in such selecting and paraphrasing he was motivated,
at least in part, by his own controlling interests in writing.

Yet, if these be granted, the reason for the Markan abridgment
suggests itself at once. M, which no longer means a separate
document, does embrace those recoverable parts of K that were
not used in Mark. Now M is Jewish, or rather, Jewish Christian.
In rejecting this material, therefore, the compiler of Mark has
gentilized what had been an earlier Jewish Christian tradition.
We think it can be shown that the desire to conform the Gospel
to gentile Christianity did, in fact, underlie almost the whole of
the Markan revision. For while M is so disjointed in structure as
to preclude the belief that it ever stood alone, it nonetheless has,
in its religious and social outlook, a homogeneous and quite remarkable character.

A. K, BUT NOT MARK, ASSUMES A PALESTINIAN MILIEU

M assumes that its readers dwell in Palestine, and it deals with
religious and secular practices that could concern almost no one
but a Jew living in that country. Pharisaism is treated as though
it were a living issue confronting the reader. One must be on
guard about the Pharisees' teaching (Matt. 16:11*a*, 12; 11*b* is Q
and is not necessary to the connection). One must obey them
(23:2-3) but do more than they do (5:20)—the real meaning of
perisseuō is "abound in," "do more fully." One deprecates the
Pharisees' broad phylacteries (23:5). These men are stupid
(23:24). They reject Jesus' conception of ceremonial cleanliness
(15:12-13). They proselytize (23:15). One must not take their
title of Rabbi (23:7*b*, 8).

One is expected to worship at the Temple (5:23), clearly implying that the Temple was standing when this was first written. There is the same implication at 12:7, 8, where priestly activities are described and indorsed by appeal to the Torah. The high priest and his court are mentioned (26:3b) yet so briefly as to suggest that they are familiar to the reader. The reader is expected to know the regulations that govern the Temple treasury (27:6) and what the Day of Preparation is (27:62).

Further, it is assumed that the reader will wish to make Jewish religious oaths (5:33-37; 23:16-22), and warning is given against swearing either by Jerusalem or by its Temple. The latter injunction, taken literally, would have been ridiculous after A.D. 70. Also one should avoid the epithets *mōre* and *raka* sometimes used by Jews (5:21, 22).[3]

In praying or fasting, one should not make public displays such as are commonly seen in the synagogues or on the streets (6:1-6, 16-18). Long journeys on the Sabbath would be disastrous (24:20b). One is in danger of being impressed by a Roman soldier (5:41). It is assumed that one knows the geography of Syria (4:24a) and the differences among Palestinian dialects (26:73b).

Now of what possible concern could all this have been to a gentile Christian anywhere? To be sure, the historic Church has used many of these passages as parables of Christian behavior or as biographical material about its Lord. But they are not so treated in Matthew's K. If Matthew has reoriented much of this material, the material itself constantly and everywhere takes for granted that Palestinian life is familiar, and orthodox Palestinian Judaism a live option, to the reader.

Mark makes no such assumptions. Occasionally it clarifies a point which, plain enough to a Palestinian Jew, might be obscure to Gentiles:

---

3. That speakers of Aramaic should occasionally pick up a Greek expression like *mōre* (fool) would be only natural. This very word is used in Midrash. Cf. A. H. McNeile, *The Gospel According to St. Matthew* (London: Macmillan & Co., 1915), p. 62 and attendant references. Cf. below, p. 149.

Matt. 4:24. All Syria.	Mark 3:8. Idumaea . . . and about Tyre and Sidon.
15:22. A Canaanitish woman.	7:26. The woman was a Greek, a Syrophoenician by race.
22:31, 32. Have ye not read that which was spoken unto you by God, saying	12:26. Have ye not read in the book of Moses, in the place concerning the Bush, how God spake unto him, saying. . . .
26:73. Of a truth thou also art one of them, for thy speech betrayeth thee.	14:70. Of a truth thou also art one of them, for thou art a Galilaean.
27:62. The Preparation	15:42. The Preparation, that is, the day before the sabbath.

At Mark 7:3, 4 is an explanation, obviously for Gentiles, of Jewish purification customs. It is wanting in Matthew:

> For the Pharisees, and all the Jews, except they wash their hands diligently, eat not, holding the tradition of the elders: and when they come from the marketplace, except they wash themselves, they eat not: and many other things there be, which they have received to hold, washings of cups, and pots, and brasen vessels.

Once Mark positively assumes a gentile audience by giving a teaching against women divorcing their husbands (Mark 10:12) —a practice quite unknown in Palestine. For the most part, however, Mark simply omits those sections where K speaks to a Palestinian Jewish religious situation.

B. USE OF TESTIMONIA

M draws heavily on the Old Testament, particularly for "testimonia" or prophecies of Jesus. It is frequently remarked that in passages having Markan or Lukan parallels Matthew follows the LXX closely, whereas the Old Testament quotations peculiar to the First Gospel depart widely from the LXX and are reminiscent of the Hebrew. This is not, however, a quite adequate description of the facts. The truth is that, with one apparent exception, Matthew follows the LXX in quotations placed on the lips of Jesus but departs from it elsewhere; and this is true whether there are parallels in the other Gospels or not.

Matthean OT Quotations Attributed to Jesus	Total Words	Words in Common with LXX	Per Cent
Having parallels in Mark: 15:4, 8–9; 19:5–6, 18–19; 21:31, 42; 22:32, 37, 39, 44; 24:15; 26:31; 27:46	193	162	84
Paralleled in Luke only: 4:4, 6, 7, 10	48	47	97
Peculiar to Matthew: 9:13; 12:7; 13:14–15; 21:16	65	60	92
Total	306	269	88

Matthean OT Quotations *not* Attributed to Jesus			
Having parallels in Mark: 3:3; 11:10; 22:24	49	29	59
Peculiar to Matthew:* 1:23; 2:6, 15, 18; 4:15, 16; 8:17; 12:18–21; 13:35; 21:5; 27:9, 10	200	99	50
Total	249	128	51

* There are none with parallels in Luke only.

In both the above groups the treatment of the Old Testament is virtually identical in M and in parallels to Mark. The real variation is as between discourse and narrative or editorial. Now this seems susceptible of a very natural explanation. The compiler of Matthew, or the author or translator of K, has done just what any writer would be likely to do. In his own comment he has depended on his own recollection of the Jewish Bible. (The ancients had no easy way to look up references.) In quotations made by our Lord, however, he has resorted to a "pony," the standard Greek translation of the Hebrew Scriptures. The same condition obtains, though less extremely, in the Gospel of Mark: Old Testament quotations attributed to Jesus (Mark 7:6, 10; 9:48; 10:6–9; 11:17; 12:26, 29–30, 31, 36; 13:14; 14:27; 15:34) are 85 per cent like the LXX, others (1:2, 3; 12:19, 32–33) only 75 per cent.

To the foregoing rule there is, as we said, one seeming exception. Within Matt. 5:19 ff. are six Old Testament citations, totaling 38 words, of which only 19 are like the LXX. However, this passage has other striking features that set it apart. (*a*) The word *errethē* occurs six times here (five from M, once probably from the redactor) and nowhere else in the Synoptic Gospels. It occurs just four more times in the New Testament, of which only one introduces an Old Testament quotation (Rom. 9:12). (*b*) While these quotations differ from the LXX, they differ almost as widely from the Hebrew, and this is not true of Matthew's other Old Testament passages. (*c*) *Errethē* represents *itmar*, a formula used frequently in rabbinic writings to introduce biblical passages for comment. Thus we seem to have here, not a set of Old Testament quotations on a level with the others, but a bit of rabbinic exegesis, made by our Lord on the basis of rabbinic tradition or an Aramaic targum. Therefore it is not a real exception to the treatment of the Old Testament elsewhere in the Gospel.

This discussion has been necessary in order to show that the use of the Old Testament is consistent throughout Matthew's K material. Hence it is highly probable that the Matthean testimonia do come from K—or at least many of them—and are not contributions by the compiler. But, if that is true, we have another point where K reflects a custom special to the Palestinian Church. In Acts, too, we find the Jewish Christian leaders adducing testimonia for events in the gospel story: Jesus' advent (Acts 3:25; 13:33), his ministry (3:22; 10:34 ff.), his passion (2:25; 4:11, 25 ff.; 8:32–33), the death of Judas (1:20), the Resurrection (2:31; 13:34–35), the Ascension (2:34–35). It is plain that Luke is here recording, objectively, a habit of the Palestinian Christians themselves; for in his own Gospel, where he can follow his own editorial bent, he makes almost no independent use of testimonia.

Now note that only two of the Acts testimonia are placed on the lips of Paul (13:33, 34–35); that all the testimonia come in the first part of the book, which deals with the Palestinian Church; in fact, that they all occur before the point (13:46) where Paul turns to the Gentiles. Elsewhere the New Testament does, of course, use the Old for a variety of purposes: to defend a chosen course of action (Paul), to support a particular Christology (e.g., Hebrews), and generally as a dominant religious and literary influence. Indeed, Paul recognizes, a bit cryptically, that events of the Passion and Resurrection were "according to the scriptures" (I Cor. 15:3, 4; cf. Acts 13:27)—though we cannot be quite sure what he meant by "scriptures." Yet the adducing of particular Old Testament prophecies as corresponding to particular events in the life of its Lord seems to have been especially the practice of Jewish Christianity. No doubt a chief reason was that this type of proof was more congenial to the Jewish than to the gentile mind.

Mark has eliminated K's testimonia. Sometimes Mark echoes the omitted quotation.

Matt. 8:17 = Isa. 53:4. Himself took our infirmities and bare our *diseases*.	Mark 1:34. He healed many that were sick with divers *diseases*.
13:14–15 = Isa. 6:9–10. By hearing ye shall hear, and in no wise understand; And seeing ye shall see, and shall in no wise perceive. . . . Lest haply they should perceive with their eyes, And hear with their ears, And understand with their heart, And should turn again, And I should heal them.	4:12. That seeing they may see, and not perceive; and hearing they may hear, and not understand lest haply they should turn again, and it should be forgiven them.[4]
13:35: = Ps. 78:2. I will open my mouth in parables. . . .	[This is part of the passage, Matt. 13:35–43, which Mark summarizes at 4:34.]

Twice, where K cites testimonia to support Jesus' claim, Mark uses instead the recognition of him by unseen spirits.

8:17. That it might be fulfilled which was spoken by Isaiah the prophet, saying. . . .	1:34. And he suffered not the demons to speak, because they knew him.
12:17 ff. [Same formula as at 8:17.]	3:11. And the unclean spirits, whensoever they beheld him, fell down before him, and cried, saying, Thou art the Son of God.

Elsewhere the K story seems actually to have been built upon, or at least affected by, the Old Testament citation. The mention of Zebulun and Naphtali (Matt. 4:13) is evidently based on the

---

4. Note that Mark is much closer to the Isaianic quotation than to the preceding verse, Matt. 13:13.

quotation from Isaiah in verses 15-16. The implication that Jesus sat on both the ass and the colt (Matt. 21:4-7) is certainly due to the quotations from Isaiah and Zechariah; in Mark, which has not the quotations, the story is straight. Only Matthew tells about the thirty pieces of silver and Judas' death (Matt. 26:15; 27:3-10); the form of these narratives may be due to the testimonium, attributed to Jeremiah but actually, in part, from Zechariah. Where Matthew's stories are thus conformed to Old Testament passages, it has been customary to ascribe them to the final redactor. Yet they are entirely in the spirit of the primitive Jewish Christian community, which delighted in finding fulfilments of ancient predictions. In particular, the story of Judas' death was early Jewish Christian, for a variant of it appears in Acts 1:17 ff.

In the following cases Mark has left out Old Testament quotations that are not testimonia: Matt. 12:7 and its doublet 9:13*a*; the former concludes a passage in which appeal is made to the Torah. Matt. 24:30*a* = Zech. 12:12; the first part of this is hardly more than a variant of verse 30*b* = Mark 13:26. Matt. 21:14-16 = Ps. 8:2, and Matt. 27:43 = Ps. 22:8. These instances are so few, and relatively so unimportant, that the conclusion seems evident. It was K's testimonia that the compiler of Mark found unavailing for his own purposes.[5]

We come now to a feature, visible in Matthew but not in Mark, that is hard to evaluate but is, without doubt, of very great significance.

C. ATTITUDE TOWARD JOHN THE BAPTIST

M suggests, more than does any other Synoptic material, that Jesus' movement was intimately related to the movement of John the Baptist. The preaching of Jesus (Matt. 4:17) is identical with that of the Baptist (Matt. 3:2); at corresponding points Mark quotes Jesus' words but merely summarizes John's (Mark 1:15, 4). In M Jesus condemns Jewish leaders for hypocritical treatment of John (Matt. 21:28 ff.); as was seen in chapter vii, this is

5. Mark has an interesting error, "Abiathar" for "Ahimelech," at 2:26. Q makes a similar mistake, "Barachiah" for "Jehoiadah" (Matt. 23:35) which was corrected in the Gospel of the Hebrews (Jerome *Comm. in Matth.*). Both sound like gentile rather than Jewish lapses; but a Jew would have had nearly as much trouble as a Gentile in looking up texts.

the necessary completion of Matt. 21:23-27 = Mark 11:27-33, so that Mark here is incomplete. In M the identification of John as Elijah *redivivus* is made explicit (Matt. 17:13; cf. 11:14); it is not explicit in Mark (see Mark 9:11-13). In M, moreover, John actually shares in the Kingdom (Matt. 11:12).

Matt. 14:12b, 13a makes the death of John the occasion for Jesus' and the disciples' retirement. Mark 6:29 ff. omits these two clauses and explains the retirement by the disciples' need for rest. Note the awkward break between Mark 6:29 and 30. (Also note "apostles" in Mark. Is this a slip?)

Matthew's account of the Baptism has remarkable contacts with a story preserved, in our own day, by the Mandeans. These are a religious sect in Mesopotamia which traces its origin to John the Baptist. Its followers call themselves "Nazoreans." Their sacred books, which are in a peculiar dialect of Babylonian Aramaic, record the baptism of Jesus by John in the Jordan. John is at first reluctant (because he detects that Jesus is an imposter) but is overruled by a heavenly voice. So he baptizes Jesus, first pledging him to strict obedience to his teaching.[6] Note how readily this story could be a perversion of Matthew but not of Mark (or Luke or John): Matthew also says that John recognized who Jesus was, was reluctant to baptize him, and was overruled (Matt. 3:14-15). Indeed, Matt. 3:14a, c, 15 itself reads almost like a deliberate submission on Jesus' part:

But John would have hindered him, saying, . . . Comest thou to me? But Jesus answering said unto him, Suffer it now: for thus it becometh us to fulfil all righteousness.

Again suggesting submission, where Mark 1:9 reads simply, "He came and was baptized," Matt. 3:13 says that Jesus came to John in order to be baptized (*paraginetai . . . tou baptisthēnai*). In fact, the only Matthean phrase which contradicts the Mandean story is the words of John, "I have need to be baptized of thee." This may well have been added by a later hand, perhaps by the final redactor, to avoid the anti-Christian interpretation.

A further contact between K, the Jewish Christians, and the sect of the Baptist appears in the treatment of the words "Nazo-

6. Cf. B. S. Easton, *Christ in the Gospels* (New York: Scribner's, 1930), p. 70.

rean" and "Nazarene" in the Synoptic Gospels. To derive "Nazorean" from the name "Nazareth" is not quite impossible.[7] Certainly, however, "Nazarene" would be far more natural as designating one from that village. Yet (a) Nazorean, not Nazarene, was, if we may believe Acts, a common designation of Jesus among early Jewish Christians (Acts 2:22; 3:6; 4:10; 6:14; 22:8; 26:9); (b) Jewish Christians themselves were called Nazoreans from the first century (Acts 24:5) at least until the time of Jerome;[8] and (c) "Nazorean" is likewise a self-designation of followers of the Mandean sect to this day.

In the light of the above facts the situation in the Synoptic Gospels becomes exceedingly interesting:

Matthew		Mark		Luke	
—		1:24	Nazarene	4:34	Nazarene
20:30	—	10:47	Nazarene	18:37	Nazorean*
26:69	Galilean	14:67	Nazarene	22:56	him
28:5	—	16:6	Nazarene	24:5	—
2:23	Nazorean	—		—	
26:71	Nazorean	14:69	—	22:58	—
21:11	the one from Nazareth†	—		—	
		—		24:19	Nazarene

* D and a few others read "Nazarene."
† ho apo Nazaret, also used of Jesus in Acts 10:38.

Matthew twice says "Nazorean," never "Nazarene." Where in Matt. 26:71 the accusation against Peter is, "This fellow was with Jesus the Nazorean," Mark 14:69 (also Luke) has, "This is one of *them*," strongly suggesting a group or sect. On the other hand, Mark four times says "Nazarene" but never "Nazo-

7. The problem has been widely discussed, and we mention but two or three recent studies. In favor of the derivation of Nazōraios from Nazaret see H. M. Shires, "The Meaning of the Term 'Nazarene,'" Anglican Theological Review, XXIX (1947), 19 ff.; W. F. Albright, "The Names Nazareth and Nazorean," Journal of Biblical Literature, LXV (1946), 397 ff. For an opposing view see J. Spencer Kennard, "Was Capernaum the Home of Jesus?" Journal of Biblical Literature, LXV (1946), 131 ff., and "Nazorean and Nazareth," ibid., LXVI (1947), 79 ff.

8. Jerome De Vir. Inl. iii; Comm. in Is. preface and notes on Isa. 11:2, 40:9 ff.; Comm. in Ezech. 16:3, 18:7; Comm. in Matth. 12:13, 23:35. Once, however, Jerome called them "Nazarenes" (Adv. Pelag. iii. 2) and once "the Nazarene sect" (Comm. in Matth. 27:9).

rean." At these four points Matthew thrice omits the title and once reads "the Galilean." The most probable conclusion from all this seems to be that K read "Nazorean" everywhere; that Mark sometimes omitted the designation but more frequently changed it to "Nazarene"; and that the compiler of Matthew dealt with the term in various ways, retaining it once in what was evidently the mark of a group, and once[9] in a supposed Old Testament quotation.

The best text makes Luke read "Nazorean" once, and this where Mark has "Nazarene." This suggests that for Luke there was no problem. He wrote it, probably, under influence of his source for Acts. Luke affords no independent evidence on the K reading.[10]

Now, for lack of information, the relation between early Jewish Christianity and the sect of John the Baptist is very obscure. Josephus has a good deal to say about John but next to nothing about Christianity. Mandean records are mixed and late, and interpretation of them is too little advanced to afford dependable data. We are therefore thrown back on a series of passages in Acts. Here, too, the information is meager enough.

Acts 18:24. Now a certain Jew named Apollos, an Alexandrian by race, an eloquent man, came to Ephesus; and he was mighty in the scriptures. 25 This man had been instructed in the way of the Lord; and being fervent in spirit, he spake and taught accurately the things concerning Jesus, knowing only the baptism of John: 26 and he began to speak boldly in the synagogue. But when Priscilla and Aquila heard him, they took him unto them, and expounded unto him the way of God more accurately. . . . [Thereafter] 28 he powerfully confuted the Jews, and that publicly, showing by the scriptures that Jesus was the Messiah.

It appears that (a) Apollos had known a good deal about Jesus. (b) This he must have learned through contact with the "baptism of John," i.e., through those who, like himself, had come under John's baptism. It seems to follow (c) that there was a movement or sect of John the Baptist at this time and (d) that Jesus was well known within that movement. But (e) Apollos did not know, until taught "more accurately" by Priscilla and Aquila, that Christians held that Jesus was himself the

9. If K had the Infancy section; see below, pp. 120 ff.
10. See below, pp. 159 ff.

Messiah. (*f*) On accepting this teaching, Apollos apparently was not required to be baptized again. If that is a true inference, then (*g*) Priscilla and Aquila regarded John's baptism as sufficient for admission into the Christian fold. Note that Paul was not present on this occasion (Acts 18:23; 19:1).[11]

Acts 10:36. The word which he sent unto the children of Israel, preaching good tidings of peace by Jesus Christ (he is Lord of all) 37 that saying ye yourselves know, which was published throughout all Judaea, beginning from Galilee, after the baptism which John preached.

If this really means Judea, and not Palestine generally, it may imply that, prior to his ministry in Galilee, Jesus had a Judean ministry which overlapped that of John. This is, of course, explicitly asserted in the Fourth Gospel.

Acts 1:21. Of the men therefore that have companied with us all the time that the Lord Jesus went in and went out among us, 22 beginning from the baptism of John, unto the day that he was received up from us, of these must one become a witness with us of his resurrection.

This defines the sort of person who would be acceptable as one of the Twelve. It seems to say that Jesus and the disciples had first been associated together under the aegis of John and, further, that only one with a like experience was fit for the inner circle.

Acts 1:4. And, being assembled together with them, he charged them not to depart from Jerusalem, but to wait for the promise of the Father, which, said he, ye heard from me: 5 for John inded baptized with water; but ye shall be baptized in the Holy Spirit not many days hence.

To appreciate the force of his passage, let the reader ask himself, "Why, in the context of a Resurrection appearance, should the baptism of John be mentioned at all?" The only possible inference seems to be that, even under those circumstances, John's baptism carried definitive import to the apostles. (*a*) Here, again, we have the implication that not only Jesus but the Twelve had partaken of John's movement. It is further implied (*b*) that water baptism was distinctively John's, while (*c*) the feature which set Christianity apart from the movement of John

11. Cf. William Manson, *Jesus the Messiah* (Philadelphia: Westminster Press, 1946), pp. 18, 227 ff. If, as we suggest, early Jewish Christians thought John's baptism sufficient, this disposes of Richard Reitzenstein's notion (*Das Iranische Erlösungs-mysterium* [Bonn, 1921]) that by not being baptized Apollos remained in John's group.

was the additional baptism by the Spirit. This additional feature is, in fact, recorded for nearly every baptism in the first part of Acts (2:38-41; 8:12-17; 10:44-47; also 19:5, 6), the only exceptions in that part being 8:36-39, where the Spirit catches away the baptizer himself, and 9:18, Paul's baptism. Moreover, this baptism of the Spirit is again and again said to be the designative mark of the follower of Jesus (5:32; 10:44-47; 11:15-17; 15:8-9; 19:2 ff.).

Consider further that, although the Twelve required baptism of all their converts, there is no record that they themselves received Christian baptism. Why not, unless they were already adequately baptized?

Consider, finally, that not one of the foregoing passages gives the slightest hint that John subordinated himself to Jesus. That contention is reserved, in Acts, for a sermon by Paul![12] Only Paul is said to have required the rebaptism of converts who had had John's baptism (19:1-7). That Paul elsewhere minimizes his own baptizing activities (I Cor. 1:14-17) may be a further sign of his difference of viewpoint from the Twelve. As with other Jewish Christian features we have noticed, Luke points here implicitly to a real variance between Paul and his predecessors.

Thus the frequent references to John, in the first part of Acts, comprise no mere dating of Jesus' ministry. Here, as at numerous other points, Luke's description conflicts with his own preferences as shown in his own Gospel. His evidence must therefore have come from his sources and is plainly a trustworthy indication of actual conditions in Jewish Christianity. This evidence constantly implies that Jesus' work somehow stemmed from John's; that there was a real, organic connection between John's movement and the earliest Christian stirrings in Palestine; indeed, that, long after the Resurrection, John's baptism continued to be of definitive significance for the Palestinian Church.

Therefore K, in likewise reflecting this relationship, has once more been faithful to the religion of Christian Judaism. And Mark, by not reflecting it, has aligned itself with Paul and the gentile Church.

---

12. Acts 13:25. A similar assertion appears, of course, in Mark 1:7-8 and parallels. But K's original intent seems to have been different and less adverse to John. See below, p. 147.

XI

MARK AND THE JUDAIZING CONTROVERSY

WE HAVE found three areas in which the K Gospel differed from its daughter Gospel of Mark: (1) K assumed that its readers dwelt in Palestine, and it concerned itself with problems that were peculiar to a Palestinian environment. (2) K made heavy use of the Old Testament, especially in adducing testimonia of Jesus. (3) K hinted strongly at a close, organic relationship between the movements of Jesus and of John the Baptist. All these elements pervade both M and Matthew's parallels to Mark. All of them set K within the framework of Palestinian Jewish Christianity and place it at wide remove from the attitudes of canonical Mark.

We have now to consider a series of K characteristics which not only are Jewish Christian but which relate that document to the first great schism within the Christian Church. In regard to the Judaizing controversy, K took a stand which, if not polemical in itself, must at least have given strong support to the pro-Jewish polemicists. Contrary to the procedure in the last chapter, it will here be convenient first to summarize the controversy, especially as it appears in Acts and Galatians, and then see how K and Mark were related to it.

A. NATURE OF THE CONTROVERSY

That the Palestinian Church was face to face with Judaism, that authority lay with the Jerusalem Church and centered among those who "had been with Jesus," and that chief authority resided at one time with Peter, and later with James, are points so evident from Acts and Galatians as to need no proof. But that these Jewish Christian leaders were loyal to the Torah and opposed the admission of uncircumcised Gentiles seems at first to contradict some widely familiar stories in Acts:

1. The charge against Stephen was that he had violated the Torah (Acts 6:11-14).

2. Peter's vision (Acts 10:9–16) and his experience in the house of Cornelius (10:17–48) suggest that to Peter the Torah was no longer binding in its injunctions against eating forbidden food, entering a gentile house, or admitting the uncircumcised to Christianity.

3. Peter and James spoke in favor of admitting Gentiles without circumcision (15:7–21), and James's opinion carried the Council of Jerusalem (15:22–29).

4. Peter and his companions accepted the Gentiles (11:17, 18).

However, Luke says explicitly that the charge against Stephen was false (6:11a, 13a). Moreover, so long as he dealt with the Torah, Stephen's defense seems to have been acceptable to the Jewish authorities. In fact, Stephen got into trouble only when he made the accusation (which Jesus also makes in K [Matt. 23:28]) that his opponents themselves violated the Torah (Acts 7:53).

Whatever Peter's experience meant to him at the time, note that (a) he had not previously violated these provisions of the Mosaic Law (Acts 10:14, 28; 11:8). (b) His act brought sharp censure from other Jewish Christians (11:1, 2). (c) Despite Peter's vision, the Council of Jerusalem kept a prohibition against certain foods (15:29; 21:25). (d) Acts does not say whether Peter repeated his preaching to Gentiles, but it implies that the rest of the Twelve did not do so (Acts 11:19; 21:20; cf. Gal. 2:7–9). This of course raises the question of Peter's traditional episcopate at Rome, a problem which must concern us at a later point.[1] If the tradition is correct, Peter must have had a more thoroughgoing conversion after the periods covered by Acts and Galatians.

Uncircumcised Gentiles had long been in the habit of attending synagogue services and of obeying so much of the Torah as they could without induction into Judaism. Such people were known among the Jews as "God-fearers." James's acceptance of

---

1. Below, pp. 151 ff. In any case, the tradition in the *Acts of Peter* which sends him permanently to Rome twelve years after the Crucifixion contradicts Gal. 2:1, 7–9.

gentile Christians seems to have been entirely on the analogy of these God-fearers:

> My judgment is, that we trouble not them that from among the Gentiles turn to God. . . . For Moses from generations of old hath in every city them that preach him, being read in the synagogues every sabbath [Acts 15:19, 21].

Nevertheless, the attitude of Peter and James was not shared by "brethren from Judea" who had visited Antioch (15:1), by Christian Pharisees (15:5), or by Jewish Christians generally (15:5; 16:3). Paul says, in fact, that, while some of the Twelve accepted his views privately (Gal. 2:2, 3, 9), most Jewish Christians did not accept them (Gal. 2:4). This accords exactly with the information at Acts 21:23: the Jewish Christian leaders tell Paul that they trust him but enjoin him to prove to the other Christian Jews that he keeps the Law.

Paul says that Peter was not firmly persuaded (Gal. 2:11 ff.) and that he continued to demand obedience to the Torah (Gal. 2:14b). Most Jewish Christian missioners preached to Jews only (Acts 11:19). Some Jews may have preached to Greeks (11:20), though there is strong textual evidence for reading "Hellenistic Jews" in the latter verse, while the preaching it describes is followed by no astonishment or perplexity such as we should expect if Gentiles were meant. As we have seen, it is elsewhere said that the Twelve confined their preaching to Jews.

In fact, Paul's own preaching was first confined to Jews and God-fearers (Acts 9:20; 13:16, 26). His failure with the Jews led him to turn to the Gentiles (13:46), and it was only then that he began to say (13:49) that Christianity supersedes the Law. The original apostles were far more successful with their compatriots than Paul was and made thousands of converts (2:41, 47; 4:4; 21:20). One inevitably wonders what might have been the history of Christianity had Paul been a success among his own people.

The truth seems to be that, while Paul obtained consent of a few Jerusalem leaders for his gentilizing activities, those leaders never gave more than halfhearted approval. Certainly Paul got no effective support from them. They did not win, probably they did not try to win, others of their community to his side.

And if, from their number, Peter did go the way of Paul, this explains the final, curt dismissal of Peter in Luke's Jewish Christian source: "He went to another place" (Acts 12:17).

Now Luke's own bias is pro-Gentile, and we cannot suppose that he has given the Judaizers a better case than they merited. Therefore we must take with utmost seriousness his evidence that Jewish Christians as a whole were staunch upholders of the Torah. They included priests and Pharisees among their number, and the latter continued after their conversion to be fervent adherents of the Law (Acts 6:7b; 15:5; cf. Matt. 13:52). The Jewish Christian leaders kept the ancient feasts (2:1 *passim*), appealed to the Torah (3:22-23), resorted to the Temple (2:46; 3:1 ff.; 5:12b, 21, 42), and reminded their hearers that persons "outside the Law" had put Jesus to death (2:23). "Thou seest, brother, how many myriads there are among the Jews of them that have believed; and they are all zealous for the Law" (21:20). They continued to be "zealous for the Law." Ireneus, and after him Eusebius and Theodoret, tell us that the Jewish Christians did not cease to "reject Paul, calling him an apostate from the Torah."[2]

Throughout the foregoing history one fact stands out. In Paul's long struggle with the Judaizers some of his sharpest problems revolved around his relation to the Twelve. To fortify his own position, he found that he must establish and maintain his own apostolic prerogative as being fully equal to theirs. This prerogative he defends again and again (Rom. 1:1; 11:13; I Cor. 1:1; 9:1-2; 15:8-9; II Cor. 1:1; 12:11-12; Gal. 1:1). But he goes further. In the heat of the Judaizing controversy he plays down his debt to the Twelve (Gal. 1:1, 11-12, 15-17, 19-21) and tells how they had progressively lost prestige in his eyes (Gal. 1:18—2:16 ff.). Years later he still spoke of the other apostles in terms of sarcasm, almost of scorn: "For if he that cometh preacheth another Jesus, whom we did not preach . . . or a different gospel, which ye did not accept, ye do well to bear with him. For I reckon that I am not a whit behind those preëminent apostles. But though I be rude in speech, yet am I not in knowledge" (II Cor. 11:4-6).

2. Ireneus *Haer.* i. 26. 2; Eusebius, *H.E.* iii. 27. 4; Theodoret *Haer. Fab.* i.

B. MARK DEPARTS FROM K IN ATTITUDE
TOWARD THE TWELVE

In the light of this, it is very significant that K took the part of the Twelve but that Mark did not. This appears first of all in a series of sayings which Mark lacks and which, in Matthew's K, are all addressed to the Twelve:

Matt. 5:13, 14. *Ye* are the salt of the earth. . . . *Ye* are the light of the world.

5:16. Let *your* light so shine before men, that they may see *your* good works. . . .

10:8. Heal the sick, raise the dead, cleanse the lepers, cast out demons. Freely *ye* received, freely give.[3]

13:51. Have *ye* understood all these things? They say unto him, Yea.

Compare this with Mark's insistence, discussed below, that the Twelve did *not* understand.

18:17–18. [After an aspersion against the Gentiles, Jesus continues,] What things soever *ye* shall bind on earth shall be bound in heaven; and what things soever *ye* shall loose on earth shall be loosed in heaven.

Similarly, Mark's omission of Matt. 10:41 may have been because it exalts the authority of the Twelve—or, perhaps, because it is obscure.

On two occasions M defends the Twelve against antagonism. Once (Matt. 28:11–15) it is against the charge by Jewish authorities that they had stolen the body of Jesus. Once (10:25*b*) it is against more general disfavor: "If they have called the master of the house Beelzebub, how much more them of his own household!"[4]

Besides rejecting passages like the foregoing, Mark is in parallels to Matthew constantly derogatory of the Twelve.

1. In Matthew the disciples show religious insight. In Mark they are pictured as without understanding.

Matt. 14:33. Disciples recognize Jesus as Son of God.	Mark 6:52. Disciples do not understand. Their hearts are hardened.

---

3. This also illustrates K's interest in wonder-working, on which see below, pp. 131 ff.

4. The last likewise illustrates K's concern over the charge that Jesus was a sorcerer. The sorcery charge is discussed below, pp. 132 ff., 144.

17:23. Disciples are "exceeding sorry" at Jesus' prediction of his death.

9:32. Disciples do not understand and are afraid to ask.

————

9:10. Disciples do not understand the meaning of the Resurrection.

2. In Mark the disciples are frequently crude and discourteous to Jesus; not so in Matthew.

8:25. Save, Lord; we perish.

4:38. Master, carest thou not that we perish?

————

5:31. And his disciples said unto him, Thou seest the multitude thronging thee, and sayest thou, Who touched me?[5]

18:1. Disciples ask Jesus, "Who is the greatest in the kingdom of heaven?"

9:33–34. Disciples argue which of themselves is greatest. When Jesus inquires what they are talking about, they refuse to answer.

With these compare Mark 3:21, where Jesus' "friends" say, "He is beside himself."

3. In Matthew, Jesus expresses confidence in the disciples. In Mark this confidence is placed in larger groups.

12:49. The *disciples* are Jesus' "mother and brothers."

3:34. *Those who sat about him* are his "mother and brothers."

13:10–11. To the *disciples* is given to know the mysteries of the kingdom.

4:10. Understanding of the kingdom is granted to *those who were about him* with the Twelve.

16:21. Jesus' prediction of his death is vouchsafed to the *disciples only*.

8:32. Jesus' prediction is given "openly" or "boldly" (*parrēsia*).

16:24. Jesus summons the *disciples* to take up the cross.

8:34. Jesus summons the *multitude* to take up the cross.

21:21. "If *ye* [disciples] shall say unto this mountain. . . ."

11:23. "*Whosoever* shall say unto this mountain. . . ."

24:3. Apocalyptic discourse is given to the *disciples privately* (*kat' idian*).

13:37. "What I say unto you I say unto *all*."

26:29. Jesus will drink the cup "with *you*" (disciples) in the kingdom.

14:25. Omits "with you."

5. Note how the context is complete without this verse.

With the foregoing may be compared one of the famous doublets that occurs in both these Gospels:

23:11. He that is greatest *among you* shall be *your* servant.	9:35. If *any man* would be first, he shall be last *of all*, and servant *of all*.
20:26, 27. . . . Whosoever would be first among you shall be *your* slave.	10:43, 44. . . . Whosoever would be first among you shall be slave *of all*.

Throughout these passages, as in others to be studied presently, Mark displays a universalism that is lacking in Matthew's K material. (It is not lacking in Matthew's Q.) It is hard to see how Mark's broader viewpoint can be called more primitive than Matthew's K at these points.

4. In Mark, Jesus himself is derogatory of the Twelve. In Matthew he is not.

——	3:17. James and John are nick-named "sons of thunder."
13:18. Hear ye then the parable of the sower.	4:13. Know ye not this parable? and how shall ye know all the parables?
17:17. "Faithless generation" is general.	9:19. "Faithless generation" is the disciples.
——	10:14. Jesus is indignant at the disciples for rejecting children.
26:23. He that dipped his hand with me in the dish, the same shall betray me.	14:20. It is *one of the twelve*, he that dippeth with me in the dish.
16:9–11a. Mild questions to the disciples.	8:17b–21. Do ye not yet perceive, neither understand? have ye your heart hardened? Having eyes, see ye not? and having ears, hear ye not? and do ye not remember? . . . Do ye not yet understand?

In the last passage note the resemblance of Mark's words to those at Mark 4:12 and at Mark 13:14-15 = Isa. 6:9-10. This is one of the places, omitted from the discussion in chapter vii, where Chapman saw signs of Markan abridgment.[6] The lesson on the leaven of the rabbis would have had little interest for gentile readers. By omitting it, however, and inserting this

6. Above, p. 52, n. 2.

sharp censure of the Twelve, Mark leaves the whole story dangling.[7]

Now Mark's constant depreciation of the Twelve has often been taken as a sign of primitivity on the supposition that an earlier modesty, on the apostles' part, was overruled by later writers when the apostles had achieved positions of authority and prestige. But is "modesty" a fit description of Mark's characterizations? Does not his attitude suggest, rather, a time when the Twelve had *lost* prestige in the eyes of, say, a Christian Gentile or a missionary to the Gentiles? For, whatever its origin, Mark's approach to these original apostles is in exact accord with Paul's own distressed view.

C. MARK DEPARTS FROM K IN ATTITUDE TOWARD PETER

Yet we cannot be sure that Paul was the immediate or only object of censure in K, or of defense by Mark, for there is a strange discrepancy between Mark and Matthew's K in their treatment of Peter. In both Matthew and Mark, Peter is singled out for attention. His prominence usually appears, however, at different points in the two Gospels and with singularly divergent emphases. In Mark it is Peter who, with his companions, finds Jesus praying (Mark 1:36 ff.); Peter calls attention to the withered tree (Mark 11:21); and he is named particularly by the angel at the Resurrection (Mark 16:7).

These references to Peter are absent from Matthew, and there we find another series altogether. When Peter's position in M is analyzed, it seems to be only partly one of honor. He had been appointed leader of the Christian community (Matt. 16:17 ff.) and had received the oracle on forgiveness (Matt. 18:21–22). Yet he is the only disciple besides Judas Iscariot who is singled out for rebuke. Not only does he fail to understand things of God (Matt. 16:23 = Mark 8:33) but he is a stumbling block to Messiah himself (Matt. 16:23 only). In the only other occurrence of *skandalon* (stumbling block) in K, it is applied to the

7. Perhaps to the foregoing passages should be added Mark 6:4: "A prophet is not without honour, save in his own country, *and among his own kin*, and in his own house." Matt. 13:57 lacks the italicized words, and this is one of the places where *ērxato* in Mark may show revision of his source (above, p. 57). James, the brother of the Lord, was head of the Jerusalem Church.

gentilizing of the gospel (Matt. 13:41; cf. I Cor. 1:23). In this connection there is a well-known variant reading at Matt. 17:25–26:

> Jesus spake first to him, saying, What thinkest thou, Simon? the kings of the earth, from whom do they receive toll or tribute? from their sons, or from strangers? And when he said, From strangers, Jesus said unto him, Therefore the sons are free. *Simon said, Yea. Jesus saith, Therefore give thou also unto them as a stranger.*

If authentic, this would be a reminder to Peter that he ought not to associate himself too closely with the Gentiles.

K's attitude toward Peter, as it appears in Matthew, is thus in striking contrast to its regard for the Twelve as a whole. Where the group receives only honor, Peter himself comes under criticism. Here is one more hint of Jewish Christian coolness toward this apostle and of the apparent wish that he had not departed from a pristine faith. A poignant allegory attaches, therefore, to K's story of the walking on the water (Matt. 14:28 ff.). Peter starts out all right, but later he fails and, "when he saw the wind, he was afraid and began to sink."

D. MARK DEPARTS FROM K IN ATTITUDE TOWARD THE LAW
AND RABBINIC TRADITION

Nor does K's rebuke to Peter stand in isolation. Independently of it, or of a like attitude toward Paul, K insisted (but Mark does not) that both the Torah and rabbinic tradition must be obeyed.

> Matt. 12:5. Have ye not read in the Torah . . . ?
>
> 5:17. Think not that I came to destroy the Torah or the prophets: I came not to destroy, but to fulfil.
>
> 5:19. Whosoever therefore shall break one of these least commandments, and shall teach men so, shall be called least in the kingdom of heaven: but whosoever shall do and teach them, he shall be called great in the kingdom of heaven.

How gratified an orthodox Jewish Christian might have been to quote this last against someone like Paul! It is in the light of such passages that we must understand K's revulsion against what is termed *anomia*. The full significance of this word is obscured by the customary renderings, "iniquity" or "evil-doing." It really means "lawlessness" or "violation of the Law."

7:23. And then will I profess unto them, I never knew you: depart from me, *ye that work violation of the Law.*

24:11–12. And many false prophets shall arise, and shall lead many astray. And because *violation of the Law* shall be multiplied, the love of many shall wax cold.

K's orientation toward the Torah is further bound up with its attitude toward the Jewish rabbis. This is by no means one of unrelieved hostility. They come under reproof, to be sure. Yet scribes themselves may belong to the Kingdom and thus bring forth things both new and old (Matt. 13:52). Indeed,

23:2–3. The Scribes and the Pharisees sit on Moses' seat: all things therefore whatsoever they bid you, these do and observe:

"but do not ye after their works; for they say, and do not," and that is the point. In K, Jesus' complaint against the Pharisees is that inwardly they themselves are full of "anomia" (Matt. 23:28). He commands his followers to "do more fully" than the rabbis (Matt. 5:20, *perisseusē . . . pleion*).

Once more, Mark not only omits all this but takes a completely different stand. Mark never once uses the word "law" (*nomos*). K said, "Pray that your flight be not on a sabbath" (Matt. 24:20), but Mark says, "The sabbath was made for man, and not man for the sabbath" (Mark 2:27). In K, Jesus summarized the Torah (Matt. 7:12; 22:37 ff.), and the words, "On these two commandments hang all the law and the prophets," kept the Torah's authority. In Mark 12:31 ff., however, love of God and of one's neighbor is "much more than" the Temple worship which the Torah enjoined; while "There is none other commandment greater than these" seems to depreciate other provisions in the Law. K's word, "To eat with unwashen hands defileth not the man" (Matt. 15:20), reflects the actual practice of the *am ha-aretz* ("people of the land") and specifically of Jesus' own companions; hence it is not gentilizing. Mark 7:19 reads, however, "This he said, making *all* meats clean," and this contradicts the Torah, the practice of Jesus' associates even after the Resurrection, and, indeed, the decision of the Council of Jerusalem (Acts 15:29). Yet Mark is in full accord with Paul's teaching (I Cor. 8; Col. 2:16) and with what was at least sometimes Peter's attitude (Acts 10:15-16, 48*b*; Gal. 2:12*a*).

E. MARK DEPARTS FROM K IN ATTITUDE TOWARD
MISSIONARY WORK AMONG GENTILES

K directly opposed taking Christianity to the Gentiles.

Matt. 7:6. Give not that which is holy unto the dogs, neither cast your pearls before the swine, lest haply they trample them under their feet, and turn and rend you.

10:5, 6. Go not into any way of the Gentiles, and enter not into any city of the Samaritans: but go rather to the lost sheep of the house of Israel.

One of the most important passages in this connection is the Parable of the Tares (Matt. 13:25–30) and especially its explanation (13:36–43). In the latter, "tares" are defined as violaters of the Law (*tous poiountas tēn anomian*), while "the good seed, these are the *sons of the kingdom*." "Sons of the kingdom" occurs only once elsewhere in the New Testament (Matt. 8:12), and there it refers explicitly to the Jews.[8] It is significant that Mark at this point has a completely different parable, about seed-growing "he knoweth not how" (Mark 4:26 ff.). Is this a sidewise reflection against the Judaizing mentality?

Similarly, the parable at Matt. 13:47 ff. seems to regret the necessity of gathering "all kinds" into the Kingdom. Mark, who is professedly abbreviating at this point (Mark 4:33–34), omits the whole of Matt. 13:44 ff. He deletes other passages which run down the Gentiles (e.g., Matt. 6:7, 8a; 18:17). He drops the statement that the multitudes "glorified the God of Israel" (Matt. 15:31b). He omits stories which would offend Romans, such as the dream of Pilate's wife (Matt. 27:19) and Pilate's hand-washing (Matt. 27:24, 25).

Yet Mark's gentile sympathies appear not only from these excisions. In the incident of the mother near Tyre and Sidon (Matt. 15:21 ff. = Mark 7:24 ff.) Mark not only lacks Jesus' words, "I was not sent but to the lost sheep of the house of Israel." It has other differences which completely alter the tone of the story:

8. That this identification is found in Q but redoubles its force. Q was pro-Gentile and probably would not have confined the term to Jews without strong justification. Paul likewise acknowledges that the Jews are the true sons, his gentile converts being so only by adoption.

Matthew	Mark
"a Canaanitish woman"	"The woman was a *Greek*."
She calls the Jews *masters*.	She calls the Jews *children*.
The daughter is healed through the mother's *faith*.	Healing is granted explicitly for the mother's *saying, that Gentiles should share in the gospel*.

Again, in Matt. 21:41 the Lord will "let out" his vineyard to another people; in Mark 12:9 he will "give" it. In Matt. 20:19 "the Gentiles" shall mock, scourge, and crucify Jesus; in Mark 10:34 "they" shall do these things, where the logical antecedent is the Jews who deliver him up. Matt. 15:29 locates the feeding of the four thousand "nigh unto the sea of Galilee"; Mark 7:31 places it in "the region of the Decapolis," a gentile area, and Mark 8:3 adds that "some of them have come from far (*apo makrothen*)." In the story of the Gerasene demoniac (Mark 5:1 ff.) Mark appends the information that, at Jesus' bidding, the man went to publish in Decapolis the work of the Lord Jesus on his behalf. And only Mark (11:17) completes the quotation from Isa. 56:7, "My house shall be called a house of prayer *for all the nations* (or *Gentiles, ethnesin*)."

Some harmonists likewise place in parallel Matt. 10:23, "Ye shall not have gone through *the cities of Israel*, till the Son of man be come," and Mark 13:10, "The gospel must first be preached unto *all the nations*." But the true parallel to the latter is probably Matt. 24:14, on which we comment elsewhere.[9]

It is not hard to see, now, why Mark omitted details of the Temptation, merely summarizing the story at 1:13. K, as we have concluded, lacked the Jerusalem Temple incident but had the other two.[10] In the Stones to Bread temptation, K's stand on the Torah would have offered Mark sufficient impediment. In K (but not Q, Luke 4:4) Jesus cites Deut. 8:3*b*, "By everything that proceedeth out of the mouth of the Lord [doth man live]." In its original context this clearly meant the Hebrew Law: "All the commandments which I command thee this day shall ye observe to do" (Deut. 8:1). Again, K's second temptation story lacks the universalism of Luke's Q: "all this authority," "to

9. Below, p. 179.
10. Above, pp. 61 ff.

whomsoever I will, I give it," and especially, "It shall all be thine." More significantly for Mark, K's story could have sounded like a positive rejection of any mission to Gentiles (or even as implying that Gentiles belong to Satan!):

> The devil . . . showeth him all the kingdoms of the world . . . and he said unto him, All these things will *I* give thee. . . . Then saith Jesus unto him, Get thee hence, Satan: for it is written, Thou shalt worship the Lord thy God, and him only shalt thou serve. Then the devil leaveth him.

That we do not so read it today is beside the point. The Judaizing issue is not alive for us. Moreover, we bring to these passages our heritage from all four canonical Gospels and from two thousand years of Christian tradition.

Finally, Mark (and Luke after him, but not Matthew) tells a story that sums up its whole attitude toward the carrying of the gospel to Gentiles:

> Mark 9:38. John said unto him, Master, we saw one casting out demons in thy name; and we forbade him, because he followed not us. 39 But Jesus said, Forbid him not: for there is no man who shall do a mighty work in my name, and be able quickly to speak evil of me. 40 For he that is not against us is for us.

In all these points where K and Mark differ, K plainly reflects the situation within Palestinian Jewish Christianity in the first century. It therefore follows that at other points, where there is not outside corroboration, still K is to be regarded as a reliable source of information about primitive Jewish Christianity. We here note just one such inference that is of supreme significance.

F. EFFECT OF THE CONTROVERSY ON PRIMITIVE APOCALYPTIC

As it appears in Matthew's K, the problem of gentile converts was a determining factor in Jewish Christian apocalyptic. New Testament apocalypticism follows a certain periodicity, becoming most intense at times like the Neronian and Domitianic persecutions and relaxing in between. Yet apocalyptic points of view appear nearly everywhere, from Paul, through Acts, to the Fourth Gospel. It may be, as E. W. Parsons suggests, that apocalypticism entered Christianity by way of John the Baptist.[11] In any case,

11. "The Significance of John the Baptist for the Beginnings of Christianity," in John T. McNeill, Matthew Spinka, and H. R. Willoughby (eds.),

in the words of McCown, "The fact that Jesus and the early Christians were of the apocalyptic faith, that they expected some kind of a divine intervention in the affairs of the world within a short time, will not be denied by anyone who has considered the evidence."[12]

Yet Jewish Christian apocalyptic, as seen in K, has an emphasis that is unique in the New Testament. Here we are told that the net of the Kingdom has, in this world, gathered in "all kinds" but that at the End the angels will separate "them" out and destroy them (Matt. 13:47-50). Violaters of the Law are weeds (Matt. 13:38, 41) which, so far from growing of themselves, have been sown by an "enemy" (13:28). They cannot be safely uprooted now, but at the End they will be collected and burned (Matt. 13:24-30, 36-43). In discourses addressed to the Twelve, Jesus' followers are told to beware of false prophets (7:15) who lead many astray (24:11) and whose violation of the Law causes love itself to weaken (24:12). However, the Lord had forewarned that false leaders would come (24:14), proclaiming false Messiahs[13] and working great signs and wonders. What if Law violaters (*hoi ergazomenoi tēn anomian*) do cast out demons and perform mighty works! Still the Lord will reject them on "that day" (7:22, 23). Yet he who is faithful will be saved. Preaching of the gospel to the Gentiles must needs be (24:14) but that preaching is itself the sign of the End.

Thus a strange and terrible significance attached to one other parable—of the Last Judgment. Throughout Jewish apocalyptic, sheep had been the traditional figure for Israel, and goats for the Gentiles. Yet:

Matt. 25:31. When the Son of man shall come in his glory, and all the angels with him, then shall he sit on the throne of his glory: 32 and before him shall be gathered all the nations: and he shall separate them

---

12. C. C. McCown, "The Eschatology of Jesus Reconsidered," *Journal of Religion*, XVI (1936), 39.

13. Matt. 24:5; 24:24 = Mark 13:22. This seems to mean individuals claiming falsely to be the Messiah. The second passage, however, could just as well mean false teachings about, or false loyalties to, Messiah. On either interpretation, such a saying as that of Paul at Gal. 2:20 might be repugnant to a Jewish Christian, especially since it was uttered during the heat of controversy.

one from another, as the shepherd separateth the *sheep* from the *goats;* 33 and he shall set the *sheep* on his *right* hand, but the *goats* on the *left.* 34 Then shall the King say unto them on his *right* hand, Come, ye blessed of my Father, inherit the kingdom prepared for you from the foundation of the world: . . . 41 Then shall he say also unto them on the *left* hand, Depart from me, ye cursed, into the eternal fire which is prepared for the devil and his angels: . . . 46 And these shall go away into eternal punishment: but the righteous into eternal life.

Let it be granted that the historic Church, and Matthew, and our Lord himself have set these sayings into the wider context of the full Christian faith. In the context of K's Jewishness, and of the Judaizing struggle, they express not simply opposition to Gentiles but agonized horror that the uncircumcised should have invested Messiah's Kingdom and the conviction that such an outcome surely presages the End.

Thus is answered the question, "Why was K so handled by the compiler of Mark?" The Torah presented the central problem for first-century Christianity. No controversy that ever rocked the Church was more portentous than this one. It has long been recognized that the struggle affected, yes, determined, nearly every New Testament epistle. What has not been so clear, up to now, is that the Judaizing controversy was crucial for the Gospels too.

In all the New Testament, only K espouses the Jewish Christian cause. We cannot say that even K was aimed at the controversy, for it contains too much besides. Certainly, however, K reflects it; and its choice of Jesus' sayings must have provided a prized arsenal for those on the Jewish Christian side. Mark has reworked the K material in the interest of Christians on the gentile side—and so has canonical Matthew, in its own way, as we shall see. But Matthew is the later and was put together after the decision of history had been given. That is doubtless why its compiler was less ruthless with K than the compiler of Mark was. For Mark, which came earlier, seems to have been composed while the controversy was still raging. Unlike Matthew, the compiler of Mark did not much concern himself with literary style. But in scores of passages he has changed or sharply excised from his source precisely in the manner of one devoted to the gentile side of the schism.

Bacon's argument, that Mark's Christology is Pauline, does not seem to have persuaded most New Testament scholars.[14] Yet, in revising whatever in K could be, and probably was, used against Paul, canonical Mark comes down heavily on the side of the apostle to the Gentiles.

14. B. W. Bacon, *The Gospel of Mark: Its Composition and Date* (New Haven: Yale University Press, 1925), pp. 221 ff.

XII

FURTHER NOTES ON THE CONTENT
OF MARK

TO COMPLETE our examination of Mark, we have to consider a few deletions from K which were not caused by K's
Jewishness. We must also look at the beginning and end of the
Second Gospel. None of these topics requires extended treatment, and all may be brought together at this point.

A. OTHER MARKAN EXCISIONS FROM K

The vast majority of Mark's deletions have already been considered. There remain a few whose omission is to be explained
not from gentile sympathies but from more pedestrian motives.
Some of these excisions appear to be due simply to the avoidance
of redundancies. Thus Matt. 18:4, "Whosoever humbleth himself like this child . . . ," is redundant after verse 3. Matt. 26:25,
if not redactorial, merely repeats the information of verse 23.

Similarly, the famous Matthean doublets are mostly absent
from Mark: Matt. 5:28-30 = 18:8-9 = Mark 9:43-47; Matt.
9:27-31 = 20:29-34 = Mark 10:46-52; Matt. 9:35b = 4:23 =
Mark 1:39 (but with Matt. 9:35 compare Mark 6:6; also note
how Mark 1:39 is more condensed than Matt. 4:23, and Mark
6:6b than Matt. 9:35); Matt. 13:49, 50 = 13:39b ff.; Matt.
24:30a = 30b = Mark 13:26; and possibly also Matt. 18:10 =
Matt. 19:13-14. Matt. 24:42, 44 and 25:13 are summarized in
Mark 13:33. However, Mark does share two sets of doublets
with Matthew (Matt. 20:26, 27 and 23:11 = Mark 10:43, 44
and 9:35; Matt. 3:2 and 4:17 = Mark 1:4 and 1:14, 15). This
suggests that doublets within the K portions of Matthew do reflect a genuine characteristic of K itself.

Again, some M passages are not really lacking in Mark. Matt.
4:24 is a succinct equivalent of Mark 3:7, 8, 10, 11. Possibly
also, Matt. 6:15 = Mark 11:26; this verse is absent from Neutral

texts of Mark but is found in Western, Caesarean, and other manuscripts and versions.

In a very few cases there seem to be no assignable reasons for Mark's omissions. In some of these we are dealing, no doubt, not with K material but with additions by the Matthean compiler:

Matt. 11:28-30, "Come unto me, all ye that labor. . . ." This might be from Q along with the preceding verse, though, if so, it is hard to see why Luke passed it by. More probably it represents an early Christian hymn that was inserted by the compiler of Matthew.

Matt. 16:27*b*, ". . . and then shall he render to every man according to his deeds," may be redactorial.

Matt. 17:6, 7, the disciples' reaction to the Voice at the Transfiguration. It could be redactorial, though with *ephobē-thēsan* (they were afraid) compare *ekphoboi egenonto* (they became afraid) in Mark 9:6.

Matt. 26:50*a*, "Friend, do that for which thou art come," may be redactorial.

Matt. 27:36, "They kept watch over him there," may be redactorial.

Matt. 27:62-66, the Watch at the Sepulchre. This story was treasured among Jewish Christians, and a variant of it was in the Gospel according to the Hebrews.[1] It is correlative with 28:11-15, and the latter would be of interest chiefly to Jewish Christians in Palestine.

However we dispose of the foregoing passages, the great bulk of M remains, a monument to Jewish Christianity and to the variance within the first-century church.

B. THE END OF MARK

The authentic text of Mark stops at 16:8 with an incomplete sentence, *ephobounto gar* . . . (for they feared . . .), and the last

---

1. Marginal note, Cod. 1424, at Matt. 27:65: *To Ioudaïkon· kai paredōken autois andras enoplous, hina kathezōntai kat' enantion tou spēlaiou kai tērōsin auton hēmeras kai nuktos* (The Jewish: And he delivered unto them armed men, that they should sit over against the tomb and guard it day and night). That these "Jewish" marginal readings are from the Gospel of the Hebrews is now generally accepted. Cf. Alfred Schmidtke, *Neue Fragmente und Untersuchungen zu den judenchristlichen Evangelien* (Leipzig: Hinrichs, 1890).

twelve verses of the Gospel have been added by a later hand. It looks as though an early copy of Mark got mutilated at this point, and its ending lost; and all subsequent copies were descended from that defective one.

Professor Goodspeed has argued that the author of Matthew had the original, full text of Mark's ending before him and that Mark's lost ending is preserved, substantially, in Matthew.[2] The chief points in Goodspeed's argument are that (*a*) Mark and Matthew are parallel to each other through Mark 16:8; that (*b*) Matt. 28:9 makes a better sequel to Mark 16:8 than it does to Matt. 28:8 itself; that (*c*) Mark 14:28 and 16:7 foretell a Resurrection appearance in Galilee, and these forecasts are fulfilled at Matt. 28:16 ff.; and that (*d*) the statement of Mark 13:10 is completed in the command of Matt. 28:19*a*.

Now obviously, if Matthew drew not from canonical Mark but from its parent K, these factors still hold good. They suggest that if not Mark then K, at least, had a Resurrection account resembling that in Matthew. For this thesis we are now able to submit additional evidence from the vocabulary of Matt. 28:9–20:

Matt. 28:9. And behold, Jesus met them, saying, All hail. And THEY CAME and TOOK HOLD OF his feet, and WORSHIPPED him. 10 THEN saith Jesus unto them, Fear not: GO, tell my brethren that they depart into Galilee, AND THERE shall they see me. 11 Now while they were going, BEHOLD, some of the guard came into the city, and told unto the chief priests all the things that were come to pass. 12 And WHEN THEY WERE ASSEMBLED with the ELDERS, and HAD TAKEN COUNSEL, they gave much MONEY unto the soldiers, 13 saying, Say ye, His disciples came by night, and STOLE him away while we slept. 14 And if this come to the GOVERNOR's ears, we will persuade him, and rid you of care. 15 So they took the MONEY, and did as they were taught: and this saying was spread abroad among the Jews, and continueth until this day. 16 But the eleven disciples went into Galilee, unto the mountain where Jesus had appointed them. 17 And when they saw him, THEY WORSHIPPED HIM; but some doubted.

18 And Jesus came to them and spake unto them, saying, All authority hath been given unto me in heaven and on earth. 19 Go ye therefore, and make disciples of all the nations, baptizing them into the name of the Father and of the Son and of the Holy Spirit:

2. E. J. Goodspeed, *New Solutions of New Testament Problems* (Chicago: University of Chicago Press, 1927), pp. 116 ff. Cf. also W. C. Allen, *A Critical and Exegetical Commentary on the Gospel According to S. Matthew* ("ICC" [New York: Scribner's, 1907]), pp. 302 ff.

20 teaching them to OBSERVE all things whatsoever I commanded you: and lo, I am with you always, even unto THE END of the world.

The expressions in small capitals are among the most typical of Matthew's usage throughout the K material. They occur 137 times in parallels to Mark and 69 times in M—almost exactly in the ratio of lengths of the two groups of material. *Krateō* (lay hold of) is a distinctively Markan word; while *hupagete* (go ye), *kakei* (and there), *presbuteros* (elder), and *sunagomai* (assemble) distinguish Matthew and Mark together. This looks like pretty strong confirmation of the Goodspeed thesis. The ending of K, at least, lies in Matthew.

However, K (and therefore Mark) probably lacked most of verses 18 and 19. The connection between 17 and 18 is a bit abrupt. The universalism of 18 and 19 hardly fits K's viewpoint. The theology is more fully developed than elsewhere in K and seems appropriate to a later period. And these verses have no distinctive K vocabulary at all. (In fact, "heaven and earth" sounds like Q!) It seems, therefore, that these lines have been inserted by the compiler of Matthew, in place of some connecting K phrase now lost.

But, now, what we have said shows only that the Matthean Resurrection narrative came from K. It proves nothing about canonical Mark, for K, not Mark, is what the Matthean author used. So the old question arises in new form: Was canonical Mark mutilated at this point, or did the author of Mark delete the whole story, just as he has done with so many other K passages? In favor of the latter possibility, note that in K the final revelation is vouchsafed to the original disciples (vss. 16 ff.); these original disciples are called Jesus' "brethren" (vs. 10); and they are the ones who have authority to teach (vs. 20). It is just such features as these that the Markan compiler has elsewhere constantly modified or excised. Finally, although *ephobounto gar* is certainly a strange sentence with which to end a book, it is not quite impossible. A sentence could end with *gar* at all events,[3] and the author of Mark was generally insensitive to requirements of Greek literary style.

3. Examples, from secular authors and from the LXX, have been collected by R. R. Ottley, *Journal of Theological Studies*, XXVII (1926), 40 ff.

Yet it is difficult to believe that the compiler of Mark would have eliminated all mention of the risen Christ. If Christianity proclaimed Messiah to the Jews, its appeal to Gentiles was precisely on the ground that it solved the problem of death. Canonical Mark needed the Resurrection story more, if possible, than K did. With no more revision than was practiced at numerous other points, the Markan editor could have continued his account of the Resurrection and even have indorsed the Christ mysticism of Paul (cf. vs. 20). For all the compiler's rough Greek, moreover, it still is hardly credible that he closed his book with *gar*.

From his reconstruction of Mark's ending, Goodspeed rightly omits Matt. 28:11-15. This is the sequel to Matt. 27:62-66 which Mark lacks. By the same token, however, we must suppose that Matt. 28:11 ff. did stand in K, for 27:62 ff. is hardly complete without it. Both passages exhibit a definite K style. Both would have been of chief interest to Jewish Christians, so that canonical Mark naturally leaves them out. We therefore think that Mark's story was substantially like Matt. 28:9, 10, 16, 17, 20, with some connecting phrase between the last two verses. As with other passages, the account may have been more discursive in K, and in Mark, than it is in Matthew. Almost certainly, the compiler of Mark revised elements in the K account that could be taken as anti-Pauline or anti-Gentile.

C. THE BEGINNING OF MARK

It used to be suggested that the mutilation of Mark came from wearing or tearing off the end of a papyrus roll. It is now known, however, that early Christians made comparatively little use of the roll and were in fact the first to introduce extensive use of the codex—sets of sheets folded and sewed down the middle like a modern copybook.[4] It is reasonable to suppose that Mark, like other New Testament books, was issued in the latter form. Yet if a codex lost its last leaf, it could hardly escape losing its first leaf too. Now, while our text of Mark ends in an incom-

---

4. See, e.g., C. C. McCown, "Codex and Roll in the New Testament," *Harvard Theological Review*, XXXIV (1941), 219 ff.

plete sentence, Mark also begins with an incomplete sentence! Did Mark lose both ends?

This is, of course, speculation, and what follows is put forward without the confidence that attaches to other parts of this study. Nevertheless, consider these three points.

1. If the beginning of Mark was lost, this would explain a passage whose proper construction has always puzzled commentators. The surviving text would have begun in the midst of a sentence, ". . . as it is written in Isaiah etc.," and this a later hand sealed up with a title, "The beginning of the gospel of Jesus Christ [the Son of God]."

2. What might have preceded our present Mark 1:1? On the analogy of Matthew, and equally of Luke, this could only have been some form of Infancy story. Now Mark does, in fact, give two hints that its compiler was acquainted with the Matthean Infancy narrative. Compare:

Matt. 2:22, 23. . . . of Galilee (*tēs Galilaias*) and came (*elthōn*) and dwelt in a city called *Nazareth*	Mark 1:9. And . . . came (*ēlthen*) from *Nazareth* of Galilee (*tēs Galilaias*)

More striking still, Mark 6:3, "Is not this the carpenter, the son of Mary?" is truer to Matthew's Infancy account than is Matt. 13:55 itself, "Is not this the carpenter's son? is not his mother called Mary?" If the Matthean author had had the canonical Markan form before him, it is hard to see why he should have changed it in this way. It would be much simpler to believe that Matt. 13:55 is the original reading, which Mark 6:3 revised in recollection of the Infancy story.

3. There is some evidence, furthermore, that an Infancy gospel on the lines of the Matthean one did stand in K. Matt. 1:18—2:23 contains 65 characteristically Matthean expressions, or about 2.1 to a verse. It has been said that this concentration is so high as to prove (*a*) that these verses are due to a special source or to the redactor; in fact, (*b*) that Matthean style generally must therefore have originated with the redactor.[5] But the 2.1 density actually puts the passage on a level with many other parts of the Gospel, for example:

5. Cf. B. W. Bacon, *Studies in Matthew* (New York: Henry Holt & Co., 1930), pp. 139 ff.

5:19–24	3.9	13:35–53	1.8
6:1–8	3.4	18:22–35	1.6
6:15–18	3.0	23:14–22	2.8

Furthermore, besides these "Matthean" expressions, Matt. 1:18–2:23 exhibits much of the vocabulary which Matthew elsewhere shares with Mark: *apolusai autēn* (to put her away [1:19]), *grammateis* (scribes [2:4]), *proēgen* (went before [2:9]), *lian, horiois* (exceeding, borders [2:16]), and *teleutēsantos* (was dead [2:19]). Also *methermēneuomenon* (being interpreted [1:23]) occurs nowhere else in Matthew and is listed by Hawkins as a typically Markan word.[6]

The genealogy (Matt. 1:1–17) contains, besides the frequent *gennaō* (beget), the expressions *Iēsous Christos* (1:1), *legomenos* with name (called, 1:16), and the article with a genitive (1:6). None of these occurs in M, but all distinguish Matthew's parallels to Mark. The style of both genealogy and Infancy is thus remarkably like that throughout Matthew's K.

Again, for K to have contained an Infancy story would accord completely with its Jewish Christian point of view. Eusebius says that many Jewish Christians of his time believed in the Virgin Birth.[7] Jerome found correspondences between Matthew's story and one appearing in the Gospel according to the Hebrews.[8] Marginal readings on Cod. Evang. 566 refer to "the Jewish" Gospel at Matt. 1:6, 20.[9]

These facts seem to justify the inference that Mathew's Infancy section was based on K. In that case, the story would have been known to the compiler of Mark. Still, to say that the latter actually used the story remains sheer guesswork.

One further point should be noted. If K began like Matthew, then the tradition of Jesus' supernatural birth was part of the primitive Jewish Christian message. Then it cannot have arisen later than whatever date we find for K itself.

6. John C. Hawkins, *Horae Synopticae: Contributions to the Study of the Synoptic Problem* (2d ed.; Oxford, 1909), p. 13.

7. *H.E.* iii. 27.

8. *Comm. in Matth.* at 2:5; *De Vir. Inl.* iii.

9. Cf. also the talmudic allusions to Jewish Christianity, discussed below, pp. 132 ff., 143–44. Of the talmudic references to Jesus, those recalling the New Testament all reflect a K-type tradition, while those on the Infancy all suggest Matthew.

XIII

THE EFFECT OF Q IN MATTHEW

THE development of canonical Mark now appears to have been more complicated than has been commonly supposed. Basing his Gospel on K, the Markan editor sometimes altered material from his source and occasionally added to it. By far the major part of his revision consisted, however, in leaving out K material to which proponents of the gentile mission might take exception.

Yet, if this process had its complexities, it still is simple in comparison with the history of Matthew. We have now to examine the content of Matthew. In this chapter we shall consider the effect upon this Gospel of the incorporation of Q.

A. THREE FAMOUS Q PROBLEMS

The results here achieved point toward solution of three famous Q problems. In the past it has often been said that Q lacks a distinctive vocabulary and style. Even so thoroughgoing an investigator as Hawkins came to the conclusion that

it might reasonably have been expected that words and expressions characteristic of [the Q] source could be found and noticed. . . . But it seems to me that such linguistic evidence is wanting here: with the exception of words which are required by the special subject matter, a renewed examination has failed to produce any expressions which I could definitely label as characteristic of Q.

He added that "this failure does not, of course, disprove the use of Q as a source."[1] By others, however, Q's alleged lack of a distinctive phraseology has at times been urged as an objection against the very existence of that document.

Now, whatever may be thought of the expressions given above in chapter viii, those discussed in chapter iii[2] do constitute

1. John C. Hawkins, *Horae Synopticae: Contributions to the Study of the Synoptic Problem* (2d ed.; Oxford, 1909), p. 113.
2. I.e., Table V of the Appendix.

a positive, distinctive Q vocabulary, for they occur more often in both Matthew's and Luke's Q than in the entire Second or Fourth Gospel. Moreover, these expressions are of more than merely linguistic interest. As will be seen presently, they combine with other factors in demonstrating that Q had at least two definite tendencies.

It has been further urged against Q that Matthew and Luke show little if any agreement about Q order, whereas in passages with Markan parallels they agree closely in order. Again, in some Q passages, Matthew and Luke are almost identical in both language and circumstance. In other passages the circumstances are similar but the language very different. In still others the circumstances are so different as to defy harmonization, yet there are impressive similarities of language.

But now we see why, in their non-Markan parallels, Luke and Matthew are at times so much alike and at other times so different. In the former cases both Gospels drew directly from Q. In the latter only Luke did so, Matthew's basis being K to which Q material was added. When, therefore, Q material appears under different circumstances in the two Gospels, the Matthean context is very likely to be from K; and the pristine Q context must be found, if anywhere, in Luke. It further follows that, when Q order varies as between Matthew and Luke, Luke's is more nearly the original order. This is evidently the case over all, and we saw it to be true also within individual passages.

B. LUKE PRESERVES MORE OF CONTENT OF Q

As a corollary to what has just been said, it follows that, although the style of Q appears less disturbed in Matthew than in Luke, Luke has preserved more of the content of Q. From the supposed Q material of the First Gospel there has been a net subtraction of about twenty-five verses.[3] In almost every instance, however, where Matthean material was transferred from Q to K there were excellent reasons for believing that Luke preserved a more nearly complete Q account and that Matthew simply excerpted from the latter in order to expand or modify a passage from K. Hence it appears probable that Q passages are

3. Above, p. 83.

imbedded in material peculiar to Luke to an extent far greater than is the case with Matthew. (Proof or disproof of this is, however, outside the province of this book.)

C. OVERLAPPING OF Q AND K

It appears certain that K and Q sometimes overlapped. Important instances are the Temptation narrative; Matt. 9:32–33 with 12:22–23; 9:34 with 12:24; and 13:31–32. But in the great majority of cases contacts between K and Q consist of passages (usually sayings of Jesus) that are superficially similar while actually different in content and purpose and which the compiler of Matthew has fused together.

This brings us to two features of Q that are interesting in themselves and which are of paramount importance for their effect in the making of the First Gospel.

D. ETHICAL INTEREST OF Q

Q has a predominantly ethical interest. This appears, first of all, in the words and phrases that characterize this document: good versus evil, bearing good and not evil fruit, avoiding anxiety, being blessed, being worthy, being at peace.

Besides such expressions, Q in Matthew sometimes gives a distinctly ethical turn to what was in K primarily eschatological. This is not to say that Q lacked eschatology. Its apocalyptic faith is plainly evident at such points as Matt. 19:28, 24:26 ff., and 24:37 ff., while *parousia* is one of its favorite words. Yet Q's intense preoccupation with ethics has, in fact, modified several Matthean expansions of eschatological passages in K. At Matt. 22:1 ff., as was seen, two K parables on the Judgment have been combined with a third from Q, and the resulting story teaches, in part, the need for worthiness.[4] At Matt. 25:14 ff. a K parable on watchfulness has been turned by Q additions into one on dependableness. And at Matt. 13:33 the only Q parable of the series is likewise the only one that is without a clear eschatological emphasis.

4. Above, pp. 65 ff.

E. GENTILE CHRISTIAN VIEWPOINT OF Q

Most important of all, addition of Q has modified K's Jewish Christian outlook, putting Matthew more in accord with the gentile Christian viewpoint. The effect has been subtle. Q is not altogether antinomian, as may be seen, for example, at Matt. 23:23. Q honors the Twelve (Matt. 19:28). Once or twice it quotes a saying of Jesus which seems to disparage Gentiles (Matt. 5:47; 6:32).

Nevertheless, consider that no good Jew would have entered a gentile home (cf. Acts 10:28a), yet, in the Q story of the centurion's slave, Jesus offers and actually sets out to do so (Luke 7:1 ff.); the original K story included no such offer (Matt. 8:5, 6, 13).[5] The Q additions at Matt. 3:7b ff. make John the Baptist deny, or at least depreciate, the value of Jewish descent:

Think not to say within yourselves, We have Abraham to our father: for I say unto you, that God is able of these stones to raise up children unto Abraham.

At 3:5b, Q reads, "Then went out unto him *all* the region round about Jordan," which seems to imply that others besides Jews partook of John's baptism. The Law and the Prophets "were until John" but have been superseded by the preaching of Christianity (Matt. 11:13 = Luke 16:16). Indeed, followers of Jesus are summoned to leave the faith of their fathers:

Matt. 10:35 I came to set a man at variance against his father . . . 36 and a man's foes shall be they of his own household. 37 He that loveth father or mother more than me is not worthy of me. . . .

Again, the carrying of the gospel to Gentiles is indorsed by appeal, first, to the story of Jonah and the Ninevites (Matt. 12:41) and, then, to the story of the "queen of the south" (12:42). It may be that gentile converts are figured in the sheep that "went astray" and was recovered (18:12 ff.). In any case, it is roundly declared that the Kingdom will be taken from Israel and given to others (21:43). It has even been suggested, regarding the latter verse, that readers would have taken "a more fruitful nation" to mean Rome![6] If the original K parables at 22:1–

5. Cf. above, pp. 63 ff.

6. John Chapman, *Matthew, Mark and Luke* (London: Longmans, 1937), p. 16.

14 were on the Judgment, at least one of them was directed also to experiences of early Jewish Christians. Combined with Q, however, they become a single parable on the admission of "worthy" Gentiles. Finally, of the condemnations of Palestinian cities (Matt. 10:15; 11:20–24; 23:37–38), every single one is taken from Q.

To the foregoing features must be added most impressive indications from Q vocabulary. With the exception of "Beelzebul" there is not a distinctively Jewish word in our lists of typical Q expressions. Yet both the Matthean and the Matthew-Mark lists abound in Jewish expressions, and these are again frequent throughout Matthew's K but infrequent in Q:[7]

	M	Parallels to Mark	Q
Matthean expressions:			
lawlessness, altar, oath, fulfill, Scripture, chief priests, Sadducees, through the prophet(s)	25	16	4
Matthew-Mark expressions:			
Gehenna, sabbath, Sanhedrin, scribe, elder, to fast	22	26	11
Total	47	42	15

Here the standard solutions to the Synoptic Problem come face to face with two inescapable questions.

1. When Papias spoke of the Matthean *logia*, what was he talking about?[8] It has been customary, in some quarters, to equate these *logia* with Q and to find here the reason why the name of Matthew was attached to the First Gospel. But Papias described a "Hebrew" (i.e., Aramaic) Jewish book, while other Fathers wrote of a complete Gospel, in Aramaic, produced among Jews and for Jews. Q simply does not fit any of this. Indeed, its use in our First Gospel has had precisely the opposite effect of making Gentile what once had been Jewish. If, then,

7. The following summary adheres to the previously made lists as they stand. With the reassignments of various passages, in chaps. viii and ix above, the difference between Q and K is actually greater than here indicated.

8. "Matthew drew up the *logia* in the Hebrew tongue, and each one interpreted (*or* translated) them as he was able" (Eusebius *H.E.* iii. 39). The passage is discussed more fully below, pp. 153 ff.

Papias' and the other patristic descriptions have any meaning at all, we shall have to look elsewhere than to Q for the *logia* of the apostle Matthew.

Not all proponents of the Two-Document hypothesis equate Q with the Matthean *logia*. That hypothesis has, however, a still more serious weakness.

2. The contrast between K (or M), on the one hand, and Q and Mark, on the other, produces a situation which under the Two- and Four-Document theories can only be called bizarre. From these we should have to suppose that the compiler of Matthew took the pro-gentile Gospel of Mark, gave not simply a Syrian but a pro-Jewish Palestinian cast to passage after passage in it, combined the result with the pro-gentile Q which he did not similarly modify, cemented these together with strongly pro-Jewish materials of his own, and did all this, in Greek, for a gentile or at best a Hellenistic community and long after Christian ascendancy had passed from Jew to Gentile!

Is this credible?

XIV

MATTHEW AND THE AGE OF DOMITIAN

A. DIFFICULTY WITH STANDARD TWO-DOCUMENT THEORY

THE standard Two- and Four-Document theories require us to picture a rather zigzag process in the making of canonical Matthew. The K hypothesis seems much simpler, for it says that, just as Jewish Christianity *preceded* gentile Christianity, so the Jewish Christian K was the predecessor of the gentilizing Gospels of Mark and Matthew.

The difficulty which confronts the more familiar theories would be less devastating if we could suppose that the Judaizing controversy continued, or flared up again, toward the close of the first century. Then it might be said that the canonical Matthean editor Judaized his materials because he himself was a protagonist for the Jewish Christian cause. (It would still be hard to see why he used Q as he did.)

Now, from certain words of Ignatius some scholars have concluded that there was, indeed, a resuscitation of the Judaizing issue around the turn of the century.[1] The relevant passages in Ignatius are as follows:[2]

Magn. viii. 1. Be not led astray by strange doctrines or by old fables which are profitless. For if we are living until now according to Judaism, we confess that we have not received grace.

Magn. x. 3. It is monstrous to talk of Jesus Christ and to practise Judaism. For Christianity did not base its faith on Judaism, but Judaism on Christianity, and every tongue believing on God was brought together in it.

Philad. vi. 1. If anyone interpret Judaism to you, do not listen to him; for it is better to hear Christianity from the circumcised than Judaism from the uncircumcised.

1. E.g., B. S. Easton, *Christ in the Gospels* (New York: Scribner's, 1930), pp. 24, 25 n.

2. Following the translations of Kirsopp Lake in the "Loeb Classical Library."

Does Ignatius refer to a Judaizing controversy, like the one we have hitherto discussed in connection with Paul and Mark? This hardly seems possible.

1. Ignatius does not say that the issue is whether Christians shall be circumcised and obey the Torah. So far from echoing the anti-Judaizing arguments of Paul, Ignatius implies, in the last quoted passage, that at least part of the trouble originated in circles of the uncircumcised. And the same passage evinces considerable tolerance toward circumcised Christians.

2. If Ignatius is unclear about the origin or nature of the Jewish trouble, he is abundantly clear on another point, viz., the strength and prevalence of Docetism. Indeed, the above passages all fall within contexts in which Docetism is refuted at length. It could well be, therefore, that the Jewish danger arose among Christian Docetists; or even that Jewish gnosticism was itself the danger. In either case, Ignatius' words are a far cry from the Judaizing controversy of the New Testament.

3. Yet is there not a simpler, more natural explanation? In all three of the above passages the opponent named by Ignatius is not Jewish Christianity but, explicitly, Judaism. Now Judaism and Christianity carried on rival missionary activities throughout the Greco-Roman world. While both sought to convert pagans, each also made inroads on the other. Certainly *Magn.* viii. 1 reads as though it reflected such a rivalry. And following *Magn.* x. 3, Ignatius' case against "Judaism" is comprised in the facts of our Lord's life, death, and Resurrection:

> Now I say this, beloved . . . because I wish to warn you . . . to be convinced of the birth and passion and resurrection which took place at the time of the procuratorship of Pontius Pilate; for these things were truly and certainly done by Jesus Christ [*Magn.* xi].

But these facts were not disputed by Judaizing Christians! These facts were the refutation against (*a*) Docetists who denied the physical reality of the historic Jesus and (*b*) orthodox Jews who, so all Christians said, failed to apprehend the fulfilment of their own Covenant in Jesus the Messiah. The situation which Ignatius describes seems to have been the all-too-familiar one of pagans and half-converted Christians toying with competing

cults. His words do not at all reveal the type of struggle that en-
gulfed Paul and which is so vividly reflected in K and Mark.

Therefore the difficulty with the Two- and Four-Document
hypotheses, and the superior simplicity of the K alternative, remain. Now, however, let us plunge more deeply into the problem
of the Matthean redaction. From four directions there come
distinct but mutually supplementary indications of this compiler's motivations.

B. THE SYNTHESIS OF Q AND K

We have seen how K was, for the Matthean compiler, the
basic document, to which he added Q material here and there.
At times this has given an ethical cast to what in K had been
chiefly eschatological. Generally it has given a pro-gentile cast to
what in K had been strongly pro-Jewish. This is much the more
important effect: It is more extensive throughout the Gospel,
and it has been the largest single factor in making this Gospel not
just accepted but nearly the most prized of all throughout the
gentile Church.

One further point needs emphasis. While Matthew combines
K and Q materials, the compiler has made, in comparison with
the other evangelists, few changes in matters of detail. The evidence for this has appeared again and again. Indeed, it is this fact
which has made analysis of the Gospel's language and structure
a fairly simple and straightforward study. Now the compiler's
willingness to place Jewish and gentile materials side by side, in
something like their pristine state, can mean but one thing. It
points to a time when the Judaizing controversy had subsided,
when Jew and Gentile could be tolerated within the same Christian community on equal or nearly equal footing, and when the
compiler could hope to bring about a unification of what had
once been violently contrasting positions.

C. MIRACLE IN THE FIRST GOSPEL

The attitude toward wonder stories, exhibited in canonical
Matthew, has long been regarded as evidence of lateness and
editorial revision. This conclusion is in many respects entirely

valid. Nevertheless, preoccupation with the miraculous is not always and necessarily a sign of late derivation. Early Jewish Christians had it too.

1. Many of Matthew's miracles came, as we have seen, from K. These seem to have included portions of both the Nativity and the Resurrection narratives, besides many healings, and at least part of the story about a coin in a fish's mouth. (On the last, however, see point 5 following.)

2. In Acts, miracles of a high order are associated with the activities of the Church in Palestine (Acts 5:1-12, 16, 17-24; 6:13, 26, 29-30; 9:17, 18, 36-41; 10:9-16; 12:5-11 ff.). Indeed, Jewish Christians are said to have believed that wonder-working was primary evidence for the authority of Jesus (2:22; 3:12, 13, 16; 10:38, 39), of the apostles (2:43; 3:6; 4:29*b*, 30; 5:12*a*, 14-16, 19-20; 9:35, 42), and of other Christian leaders (6:8; 8:6). The wonders thus described include spirit levitations, angelic visitations producing physical effects, and the like.

3. Among non-Christian Jews of the first century, Christianity was thought of as particularly, one might almost say essentially, a religion of wonder-working. Although the famous passage in Josephus is suspect, it is worth quoting at this point:

Ant. xviii. iii. 3. Now there was about this time Jesus, a wise hero (*anēr*) if it be proper to call him a hero, *for he was a doer of wonderful works*, a teacher of such as receive the truth with pleasure.

More significant are some passages in the Talmud that tell of Jesus and the Christians. While the Talmud does not offer much reliable information about Jesus, it does show what Jews and Jewish Christians thought of him at an early period. Throughout these passages Jesus' messianic claims are never mentioned, and there is no suggestion that they (or any other personal claim) were a reason for his execution. But the talmudic writers have much to say about his miraculous powers. The following are from the earlier Tannaitic period:

b. Sanh. 43*a.* On the eve of Passover they hanged Jesus the Nazorean (*ha-Notzri*). And the crier went before him forty days, saying, Jesus the Nazorean goeth forth to be stoned *because he hath practised magic* and deceived and led astray Israel.

b. Sanh. 107*b*. Jesus the Nazorean practised magic, and deceived and led astray Israel.[3]

Similar powers are allowed to the followers of Jesus. Here the rabbis seem to have been less concerned to disprove Christian abilities than to show that they had them too:

b. Sanh. 25*d*. R. Jehoshuah ben Hananiah said, I can take cucumbers and melons and make them into kids and goats, and they really are made into kids and goats. R. Jannai said, I was walking in a certain street of Sepphoris and I saw a certain Min [i.e., heretic, a term commonly reserved for Christians] take a bird and he cast it up and it fell down and was made into a calf. . . . R. Lazar said . . . Let us not say not that this Min [did these things] but that he called to his [familiar spirit] and he stole a calf from the herd and brought it to him.

Other talmudic references are on a higher plane:

j. A. Zar. 40*d*, 41*a*. The case of R. El'azar ben Damah whom a serpent bit. There came in Jacob, a man of Chephar Sama, to cure him in the name of Jeshua' ben Pandera. . . . He said, We will speak to thee in the name of Jeshu ben Pandera.[4]

j. Shabb. 14*d*. The grandson had something stuck in his throat. There came a man and whispered to him in the name of Jeshu Pandera and he recovered.

b. A. Zar. 27*b*. A man shall have no dealings with the Minim nor be cured by them even for the sake of an hour of life.

The matter is well summarized by Klausner, who says that the talmudic authorities

tried to transform the merits which later in the Gospels were held up for admiration . . . into drawbacks and even grave faults. They never doubted that he worked miracles: they merely looked upon them . . . as acts of sorcery; while his birth by the Holy Spirit they transformed into an illegitimate birth. Furthermore, it is not in the earlier passages from the *Talmud*, but at the very end of the *Tannaitic* era, some two hundred years after the Crucifixion, that we find a *Tanna* . . . accusing Jesus of "making himself God." The early *Tannaim* knew nothing whatever of this. They only knew that his disciples used to heal the sick in his name; and they used to prohibit this method of healing even when there was danger of the illness proving fatal.[5]

3. Cf. also *b. Shabb.* 104*b*: "And did not Ben Stada bring magic spells from Egypt?" The identification of Ben Stada with Jesus is uncertain.

4. The origin of the name *Ben* (son of) *Pandera* for Jesus is obscure. Some think it an aspersion against Jesus' birth, Pandera being the name of a Roman soldier. Others regard it as a distortion of *parthenos*, "virgin."

5. Joseph Klausner, *Jesus of Nazareth: His Life, Times and Teaching* (New York: Macmillan Co., 1929), p. 47. Quoted by permission of the publishers.

Klausner's contention that early Jewish Christians had a low
Christology is hardly consonant with his admission that they
taught the Virgin Birth. Surely that would be one of the highest
ways in which a church could explain to itself the meaning of its
Lord. Nevertheless, it is plain that early Jewish opposition to
Christianity was based not so much on its teachings about Jesus'
person as on a quality which the rabbis called magic. It is as
though they said, "By Beelzebul, the prince of demons, he casteth
out demons." As is commented in K, "If they have called the
master of the house Beelzebul, how much more they of his own
household!"

In all these respects Matthew's attitude toward miracle evidently reflects the most primitive Palestinian Christian attitude.
Nevertheless, this cannot be a complete explanation for all the
phenomena in this Gospel.

4. While interest in wonder stories appears to have been especially strong among Jewish Christians, somewhat analogous attitudes were to be found in gentile Christian circles too. Miracles
are attributed to Paul (Acts 13:11-12; 14:3, 8 ff.; 16:18;
19:11 ff.; 20:9-12), who himself recognizes wonder-workers as
legitimate functionaries in the Church (I Cor. 12:9, 10, 28 ff.).
And signs and wonders continued to be related of the gentile
Church until the time of Constantine.

Therefore, when Matthew and Mark differ in their treatment
of wonder stories, this does not so clearly portray a difference
between Jewish and gentile Christians as do other differences between these Gospels. On the contrary, the heightening of the
miraculous in Matthew definitely places this Gospel at a further
remove than Mark from the original accounts of these events:

Matt. 4:23. And Jesus went about . . . healing *all* manner of disease and *all* manner of sickness among the people.	Mark 1:39. And he went . . . throughout all Galilee, preaching and casting out demons.
8:16. And he cast out the spirits with a word, and healed *all* that were sick.	1:34. And he healed *many* that were sick with divers diseases, and cast out *many* demons.
8:28 ff. [Jesus heals *two* demoniacs.][6]	5:1 ff. [Jesus heals *one* demoniac.]

6. This is not so clear an example of heightening, or of affection for the
number two, as the other instances here given. The compiler may simply have
been misled by the "we" in the demoniac's reply.

12:15. And he healed them *all*.	3:10. For he had healed *many*.
14:21. About five thousand men, besides women and children.	6:44. Five thousand men.
15:38. Four thousand men, besides women and children.	8:9. About four thousand.
19:2. He *healed* them.	10:1. He *taught* them.
20:29 ff. [Jesus heals *two* blind men.]	10:56 ff. [Jesus heals *one* blind man.]

Mark also lacks the healing of two blind men who call Jesus "Son of David" (Matt. 9:27 ff.), but Mark may have regarded this as a doublet of Matt. 20:29 ff. = Mark 10:46 ff.

5. There is in Matthew a whole series of wonder stories that are different in character from those which Mark relates. At the death of Jesus, besides the rending of the Temple veil and the appearance of "saints," there are an earthquake, rending rocks, bursting tombs, and walking corpses (Matt. 27:51 ff.). Mark has only the torn veil (Mark 15:38). At the Resurrection there is another earthquake, and an angel descends whose appearance is like lightning, and who frightens the guard into a coma (but not the women! [Matt. 28:2 ff.]). Again, while Matthew appears to have taken its Nativity story from K, it is not at all certain that K had all the elements such as angelic visitations, a miraculous star, or a visit by astrologers—though some of these would have been congenial to it.

A pretty clear case of Matthean revision appears in the story of Peter and the tribute payment. Mark has traces of this incident, so that at least part of it must have come from K.[7] However, the part about the coin in the fish's mouth evinces redaction, for, (*a*) as it stands, this is incomplete: Matthew does not actually say that the miracle was performed; (*b*) insertion of the miracle sidesteps the original, anti-gentile point of the story (particularly if the reading of MS 713 should be authentic).

6. For all its concern with miracles, primitive Jewish Christianity did not go to such extremes as appeared in later literature. From points 1, 2, and 3 above there is almost no evidence of curiosity, among early Jewish Christians, over details of the Nativity and the Resurrection or of interest in pointless wonders like those sometimes found in Matthew. The latter suggest, in-

7. Cf. above, pp. 54 and 108.

stead, a period resembling that of the later apocryphal Gospels of the Hebrews, the Ebionites, the Egyptians, or Thomas.

The truth seems to be that Matthew combines viewpoints on miracle that were partly early and partly late, although both tended to extremes. Here, again, the Gospel offers a kind of synthesis or adaptation of primitive notions to a later era.

D. REDACTORIAL PASSAGES IN MATTHEW

In preceding pages these verses have been suggested as probably due to the compiler of Matthew himself: Matt. 3:14*b*; 5:5, 31, 45, 48; 6:26; 8:1, 19*a*; 9:32*a*; 11:1, 20, 28–30; 12:12; 14:14*b*; 16:27*b*; 17:6, 7; 20:9–13; 22:11–13; 25:35–40, 42–45;[8] 26:50*a*; 27:36; 28:18, 19—thirty-eight verses, or almost exactly the equivalent of an average Matthean chapter. In two or three cases these may be vestiges of K passages now lost. For the most part, however, they exhibit a series of striking characteristics which set them in marked contrast with the rest of the Gospel:

1. The majority of these passages lack any distinctive marks of either K or Q vocabulary. The K-like *tote* occurs once each in 11:20 and 16:27*b*; *deute* (come) once in 11:28; *probaton* (sheep) in 12:12; *ekeithen* (thence) in 11:1. The Q-like *ouranos kai gē* (heaven and earth) occurs in 28:18. In a few cases the style points both ways (5:45, 48; 6:26; 22:11–12; 25:35 ff.).

2. *Diapherō* (make a difference) occurs twice in these verses and only once elsewhere in the Gospel. *Praüs* (meek) occurs twice here and only twice elsewhere in the New Testament, one of the latter being in an Old Testament quotation at Matt. 21:5. The vocative *hetaire* (friend) occurs three times in these verses and nowhere else in the New Testament. Thus these passages carry positive hints of a distinctive redactorial style which has not touched the source material itself.

3. A single, dominant theme runs through most of these passages, and it differs from the rest of the Gospel. It is consolation for the weak and oppressed. Two of the verses, of course, simply set the stage for Q sayings (5:31; 11:20), one subordinates John the Baptist to Christ (3:14*b*), and one passage expresses the fuller theology of the close of the first century (28:18–19). Pre-

8. Cf. above, pp. 113–14.

dominantly, however, Matthew's editorial additions speak to the hungry, the naked, the sick, and those in prison (25:35 ff.), to the weary and heavily burdened (11:28 ff.), and to those who have borne the burden and heat of the day (20:9-13). God is impartial, and his judgment must be accepted (5:45; 20:8 ff.). Christ was meek (11:29), and we too must be meek (5:5). Yet there is comfort. God, who cares for the beasts, will care much more for his children (6:26; 12:12a). He will punish those who neglect others' need (25:35 ff.). Those who turn to the meek Christ will find rest for their souls (11:28 ff.), and their own submission will bring rich reward (5:5).

This is indeed a different note from that struck in either K or Q when standing by itself. To appreciate its full significance we must consider, finally, the apocalypticism of the First Gospel.

E. APOCALYPTICISM OF THE FIRST GOSPEL

It has been a universal law of Christian history that apocalypticism develops in times of stress and anguish and subsides in times of peace. That law needs no underscoring for observers who have lived through the early decades of the twentieth century. Now most of Matthew's apocalyptic passages stood in K also. In K they reflected, at least in part, the horror that early Jewish Christians felt over the admission of the uncircumcised to Messiah's Kingdom. That Mark kept part of this material, though he changed its intent, accords with the evidence that Mark was produced close to the time of the Neronian persecutions. In Luke, and later in the Fourth Gospel, the relaxing of apocalyptic tension corresponds to the periods of comparative quiet in which these Gospels appeared.

Yet in Matthew there is more apocalypticism than in any of the others—more, probably, than in the original K, since to K's apocalyptic has been added that of Q. This increase points to circumstances of still greater distress than is reflected in those other materials. Indeed, it is not unreasonable to suppose that this distress was the occasion which led the redactor to try to synthesize the gentile and Jewish Christian points of view. When the Church is beset from without, it is time for unity within.

So it must again be recalled that Matthean apocalyptic carries a different lesson from that either of K or of Mark. K and Mark both taught (though for different reasons) that the End was at hand and that this necessitated watchfulness on the Christians' part.[9] Canonical Matthew does not ignore the lesson of watchfulness, but it follows Q in placing far greater emphasis on constancy and faithfulness in the face of trouble. This is not far removed from the compiler's call for meekness and acceptance of the Divine Will.

F. SUMMARY

Here, then, are the positive indications which the First Gospel gives, of the circumstances in which it appeared, and of the redactor's motives: (*a*) It reveals a period when the miraculous element in Jesus' life was becoming increasingly a subject of speculation; hence it cannot long have preceded the composition of the earlier apocryphal Gospels. (*b*) Jewish and gentile Christians were no longer battling but could at least tolerate one another. (*c*) Danger beset the Church, and it was a danger more extreme than anything known at the time Mark was published. (*d*) There were intense weariness and suffering and persecution of Christians. (*f*) The redactor feared defection within the Christian ranks. Therefore, (*g*) Christians must be urged to be faithful and to present a united front to the outside world.

To meet these compulsions of his age, the compiler of Matthew brought together the messages of Christian Jew and Gentile. He fused them into a Gospel of comfort but, above all, of a God who is sovereign, who will judge men according to their treatment of one another, and whose soon coming, through his Christ, required that Christians be loyal to their trust.

There seems to be one age that fits all this supremely. It was the age of the first broadside persecution of the Church. Though spreading widely, that persecution was focused on Asia Minor and northern Syria. In the same age another writing, the Book of Revelation, reflected the very same circumstances and taught the same lesson of constancy as does canonical Matthew. It was the age of Domitian.

9. Cf. above, pp. 67–68, 112 ff., 126–27.

Part IV

K AND THE SYNOPTIC SOLUTION

XV

WHAT WAS THE K DOCUMENT?

IN PRECEDING pages stress has been laid on three major weaknesses in previous solutions to the Synoptic Problem. (*a*) They fail to account adequately for the peculiar materials of Matthew. (*b*) They require us to believe that the compiler of Matthew dealt with his materials in a strange, a grossly inconsistent way. (*c*) They are incompatible with a mass of evidence, adduced above, from the language, structure, and content of Mark and Matthew. The K hypothesis is consistent with this evidence, it does not picture an absurd behavior on the part of the Matthean compiler, and it does explain the M material.

There are two further questions that seem to be incompletely answered by former theories. We shall discuss the questions first and then try to suggest what bearing the K hypothesis has on them.

A. CRITICAL VERSUS PATRISTIC EVIDENCE
ON MATTHEW

How is it that critical evidence regarding the origin of Matthew flatly contradicts the testimony of the Early Fathers? The critical evidence seems overwhelming. That Mark is in some sense the middle term between Matthew and Luke is proved by three facts.[1] (*a*) About 90 per cent of the content of Mark reappears in Matthew and about 55 per cent of it in Luke. (*b*) In passages common to all three Gospels, Matthew and Luke rarely agree against Mark in their wording, yet the majority of Mark's words appear also in Matthew or Luke or both. (*c*) The order of events in Mark is generally like that in both Luke and Matthew, and, when one of these disagrees with Mark, the other is usually with him.

Now these three points, taken by themselves, could be made

[1]. See also below, pp. 159 ff.

to fit the theory that Mark used Matthew and Luke used both of them. Roman Catholic scholars have been quick to point this out.[2] But (d) Mark's Greek is usually more colloquial and his style less polished than canonical Matthew's. It is hardly conceivable that, with the Matthean exemplar before him, Mark would in so many places have used a degenerate style. (e) Why should Mark have omitted so much, not just that is pro-Jewish in Matthew, but that is pro-Gentile (Q) as well? The latter would have fitted Mark's purpose admirably. (f) In many parallels, Matthew seems decidedly secondary in comparison with Mark. (g) Since, according to tradition, Mark depended on Peter's preaching, why should he, or Peter, have used Matthew at all? (This question must be asked, also, about Mark's and Peter's use of K. But in the latter case there is a simple, logical answer.) Finally, (h) on internal grounds the best date for canonical Mark seems to be in the seventh decade, that for canonical Matthew in the tenth decade, of the first century.

Most of this is elementary to New Testament students. Yet it has seemed to lead to conclusions at widest variance from the tradition of the Church. That tradition, moreover, is of high respectability and extends back into the second century:

PAPIAS: Matthew drew up (*sunetaxato*) the logia in the Hebrew tongue. But each one translated (or interpreted, *hērmēneuse*) them as he was able (Eusebius *H.E.* iii. 39).

IRENEUS: Matthew published a written Gospel among the Hebrews in their own tongue, while Peter and Paul were preaching the gospel in Rome and founding the church (Eusebius *H.E.* v. 8; Ireneus *Adv. Haer.* iii. 1).

EUSEBIUS: Matthew, having first preached to the Hebrews, when he was about to go to others, transmitted in writing in his native tongue the Gospel according to himself and thus supplied by his writing the lack of his own presence to those from whom he was sent; but Mark and Luke had already [i.e., before publication of the Gospel of John] published the Gospels according to them (*H.E.* iii. 24. 6, 7).

TERTULLIAN: Of the apostles, John and Matthew instil the faith into us; and of apostolic men, Luke and Mark renew it (*Adv. Marc.* iv. 2).

ORIGEN: As I have received from tradition concerning the Four Gospels which alone are admitted without controversy in the universal Church of God which is under the heavens: first, namely, was written the Gospel

2. See, e.g., J. M. Vosté, *De Synopticorum mutua relatione et dependentia* (Rome: Collegio Angelico, 1928); cf. John Chapman, *Matthew, Mark and Luke* (London: Longmans, 1937).

according to Matthew, formerly a publican, then an apostle of Jesus Christ, and he issued it in Hebrew for the Jews converted to the faith (Eusebius *H.E.* vi. 25).

AUGUSTINE: Of these four, Matthew alone wrote in Hebrew, the others in Greek. . . . Mark, it appears, followed [Matthew], being a kind of lackey and abbreviator thereof (*De Cons. Ev.* i).

Similarly EPIPHANIUS, who appears, however, to confuse Matthew with the Gospel according to the Hebrews: [The Jewish Christians] have the Gospel according to Matthew quite complete (*plērestaton*) in Hebrew (*Haer.* xxix. 9. 41).

Now, of these, only Origen and Augustine actually say that Matthew preceded Mark (though Tertullian implies it). Yet the priority of Matthew and its original composition in "Hebrew" (i.e., Aramaic) are deeply imbedded in Christian tradition. Roman Catholic scholars are forbidden to find otherwise.[3] Among non-Romans it is usual to say that later Fathers all took their cue from Ireneus and that Ireneus was misinformed. But is it really satisfactory to make Ireneus solely responsible for so widespread and insistent a tradition?

B. "MATTHEANISM" IN THE NEAR EAST

This brings us to the further question. If the compiler of Matthew wrote in Greek, long after the destruction of Jerusalem (and if he depended on canonical Mark which was written, presumably, at Rome), then how is it that, in early Christianity of the Near East, the Matthean influence predominated over all other Gospel traditions? The evidence that this was so comes from many directions.

1. The Talmud, chiefly in its earlier strata, tells us (*a*) that there was a genealogical roll of Jesus which contained a record of his birth outside of normal wedlock (*Yeb.* iv. 3. 49*a*)[4] (cf. Matthew, chap. 1); (*b*) that Jesus had been in Egypt (*Shabb.*

---

3. Decisions of the Pontifical Biblical Commission, June 19, 1911, and June 26, 1912. Complete English texts of these and related decisions are given conveniently in John Chapman, *The Four Gospels* (New York: Sheed & Ward, 1944), pp. 75 ff.

4. That most of the talmudic passages here mentioned do refer to Jesus seems evident (Joseph Klausner, *Jesus of Nazareth: His Life, Times and Teaching* [New York: Macmillan Co., 1929], pp. 18 ff.). Cf. R. T. Herford, *Christianity in Talmud and Midrash* (London: Williams & Norgate, 1903); Morris Goldstein, *Jesus in the Jewish Tradition* (New York: Macmillan Co., 1950).

104*b; Sanh.* 67*a*)[5] (cf. Matt. 2:13–21); (*c*) that Jesus was a sorcerer (*Sanh.* 43*a*; 107*b*) (this Jewish charge is echoed more frequently in Matthew [9:34; 10:25; 12:24 ff.] than in either Mark [3:22 ff.] or Luke [11:15 ff.]); (*d*) that Jesus had five disciples, the first of whom was named Mattai (*Sanh.* 43*a*), which seems clearly to mean Matthew; and (*e*) that about A.D. 73 a dishonest Christian judge used a Gospel which, he said, superseded the Torah. His book contained the saying, "I am not come to take away from the Law of Moses, neither to add to the Law of Moses am I come," while the woman whose case the judge tried quoted the words, "Let your light shine as a lamp" (*Shabb.* 116*a, b*) (cf. Matt. 5:16, 17).

2. The Mandeans are, as we have seen,[6] a Mesopotamian religious sect who trace their origin to John the Baptist. Their story of Jesus' Baptism resembles that in Matthew far more closely than it does any other Christian tradition.

3. Early Jewish Christians used two Gospels which, in various ways, show Matthean influence. The Gospel according to the Hebrews contained passages reminiscent of the Matthean genealogy, Infancy, Peter and the tribute money, and the watch at the sepulcher. In each case the story differs from the canonical one. Moreover, surviving fragments of the Gospel include much apocryphal matter and much from sources that underlay Luke, while they reflect neither the apocalypticism nor any of the peculiar sayings of Matthew. Plainly, therefore, this was no mere recension of the First Gospel. Yet the superficial resemblance was such that several patristic writers mistook it for the original Aramaic Matthew.[7]

The Gospel of the Ebionites, a work very inferior to that according to the Hebrews, singled Matthew out for special attention at the calling of the Twelve (Epiphanius *Haer.* xxx. 13. 2).

4. Pantaenus, we are told by Eusebius, "was appointed as a

---

5. The allusions to Jesus are more doubtful here than in the other passages cited.

6. Above, pp. 95 and 97.

7. See Pierson Parker, "A Proto-Lukan Basis for the Gospel According to the Hebrews," *Journal of Biblical Literature*, LIX (1940), 471 ff.

herald for the gospel of Christ to the heathen in the east, and was sent as far as India," by which it is commonly thought that he meant Arabia. Eusebius continues, "The tradition is that he found there that among some of those there who had known Christ, the Gospel according to Matthew had preceded his coming" (*H.E.* v. 10).

5. Ignatius of Antioch made his Gospel citations almost exclusively from Matthew, which to him was "the" Gospel.

6. The *Didache*, which was produced in Syria or Palestine not later than A.D. 100, has numerous reflections of Matthew.[8]

These six pieces of evidence are for the most part unrelated. They are by no means all equally dependable. Yet all are unanimous on one point: The distinctively Matthean tradition was, from remotest times, dominant throughout Near Eastern Christianity. Now, if canonical Matthew was produced in Antioch, this will account, at least in part, for its popularity in Syria. But it does not explain the wide currency of Matthean ideas wherever we find Christian Jews. At least one of the above sources, the Talmud, includes materials earlier than the destruction of Jerusalem and therefore earlier than the date of Matthew itself.

Furthermore, mere geographical proximity is not enough to explain why a late Greek Gospel should have been so acceptable to Jewish Christians. Their fathers had known Jesus personally. They, with the other Palestinian Jews, had been through the wreck of Jerusalem, with all the ensuing revulsion against gentile ways. That they should, from the beginning at least until the time of Jerome, find Matthean ideas so congenial can mean only one thing: Matthew enshrined a tradition that was already indigenous to Jewish Christianity. That this was indeed the case, and that Matthew's special materials reflect not just Jewish attitudes but a highly primitive, Palestinian tradition, has been one outcome of the discussion in preceding pages.

Now the anterior Jewish Christian Gospel, on which Matthew and Mark were severally based, we have hitherto labeled simply as K. But what was K? Specifically, was it a proto-Mark, or a proto-Matthew, or something else? In trying to answer this, we

---

8. A convenient listing is given in B. H. Streeter, *The Four Gospels* (2d ed.; London: Macmillan & Co., 1930), pp. 508 ff.

shall see the bearing of the K hypothesis on the two problems just raised—the meaning of the patristic evidence and the spread of "Mattheanism" in the Near East.

C. THE DATE OF K

Quite apart from the Judaizing controversy, numerous signs indicate that K must be dated well before A.D. 70. James, "the brother of the Lord," was head of the Jerusalem church until his martyrdom about A.D. 63.[9] According to Eusebius, who got his information from Hegesippus, no other bishop was appointed there until about 70 (*H.E.* iii. 11). From then until the capture of the city by Hadrian in 135, after the Bar-Kochba rebellion, a succession of Jewish Christian bishops presided over the Jerusalem church. This church came to an end, however, when Hadrian's edict forbade any circumcised person to approach the city. Thereafter, the Christian church of Jerusalem was Greek, as were most of the church institutions in Palestine soon afterward. Small Jewish Christian communities probably formed themselves here and there throughout Palestine, but, so far as we can tell, they had no common center or organized life. Political convulsions and persecutions must have harassed the Jewish church from 62 onward for half a century or more.

1. Now K assumes that its readers are in a Palestinian religious situation, where Pharisaism is dominant. Of course, both rabbinic religion and Jewish Christianity continued after the destruction of Jerusalem. Nevertheless, a date before 70, even before 62, is easier, since after that time the Jewish Christian community was mostly scattered or under duress.

2. A still clearer case for a date before 70 comes from K's assumption that the Temple is standing and that readers are familiar with the Temple and resort to it for worship (Matt. 5:23, 33 ff.; 12:7–8; 23:16 ff.; 26:3; 27:6, 62). To these must be added Matt. 27:7, 8:

And they took counsel, and bought . . . the potter's field, to bury strangers in. Wherefore that field hath been called, The field of blood, *unto this day* (*heōs tēs sēmeron*).

9. Eusebius *H.E.* ii. 23; Josephus *Antiquities* xx. ix.

This is another example of how the Matthean compiler left his sources unaltered in matters of detail. For it to make good sense, however, normal Judean life must have been still undisturbed at the time it was first written.

3. Evidence of a different sort comes from K's attitude toward John the Baptist. K both recognizes and seems to accept a close connection between his movement and the movement of Jesus. One or two exceptions to this might be proposed, such as John's preaching about the baptism of the Spirit (Matt. 3:11; Mark 1:7-8) or his words, "I have need to be baptized of thee" (Matt. 3:14b). But the latter is probably due, as we have seen, to the redactor; while the former actually says only what Jewish Christianity regularly proclaimed, viz., that Christian baptism by the Spirit is supplemental to John's water baptism.[10] K's friendly approach to John's movement certainly favors a date before the rise of sharp rivalries between the two groups.

4. We are able to reach a somewhat narrower dating when, to K's connection with the Judaizing controversy, we add the fact that it was produced before canonical Mark. The controversy reached its height not earlier than seventeen years after Paul's conversion (Gal. 1:18; 2:1), or around A.D. 48. No one knows how long it remained at high pitch, though it must have abated after 70. Now K may have been directly aimed at some individual on the gentile side (cf. Matt. 5:19; 7:22-23; 13:28; 24:11-12). At all events, the compiler of Mark evidently felt that K lent support to an attack, whether on Paul or on some other gentilizing leader. In that case, Mark itself must have appeared before or not long after the death of the man it was defending. Then K must be even earlier. Furthermore, if the K passages which Mark cut out were not intentionally marshaled for the controversy, they must have been put together before it arose. In that case, the date will be earlier still.

All these considerations point to a period not only before the

---

10. Still it is strange that, in Acts, only Paul is said to have attributed such a saying to John (cf. above, p. 99). It seems probable that the quotation was current among early Jewish Christians; that they regarded it not as depreciating John but only as indorsing the baptism of the Spirit (cf. Acts 1:5); and that later the gentile church used it in its rivalry with the Baptist's sect.

destruction of Jerusalem but considerably before the deaths of Peter and Paul. A date within the sixth decade, say, around 55, seems likely.

D. THE LANGUAGE OF K

Earlier in this study we saw how Mark's use of *kai* (and) and *de* (but) at points where Matthew has *tote* (then) implies some kind of Aramaic literary phenomenon behind these two Gospels.[11] Since then, however, it has been emphasized that Mark and Matthew resemble each other in their Greek. So close are they, in this respect, that it seems impossible to suppose that each of them translated K separately. As K came to the compilers of our two Gospels, it must have been in the same, or nearly the same, Greek form.

There are two possibilities, either of which will explain these facts:

1. K was composed in Greek, but by a Jew to whom Greek was a second and not too familiar language. Anyone who has tried to write in a foreign tongue knows how hard it is to avoid unidiomatic constructions. If the author of K wrote in Greek while thinking in Aramaic, his idiom would almost certainly be poor here and there. The compilers of Matthew and Mark, revising independently of each other, would not always polish at the same places. The Markan editor, being less concerned for literary style, made fewer such improvements, but Matthew kept *tote* and a few other rough or roundabout passages.

2. K was composed in Aramaic, but an early, rough translation was made into Greek. This came to the hands of the Markan and Matthean compilers, and they severally revised it.

The latter is the more likely. K was written, evidently, by and for Christian Jews in Palestine, perhaps half a generation before Jerusalem was destroyed. True, some of the Palestinian converts were Greek-speaking Jews, and no doubt many of these had their homes in Palestine (cf. Acts 6:1; 9:29; 11:20). Indeed, Alexandrian Jews had a synagogue in Jerusalem. Yet it is plain from Acts that the Hellenistic adherents were a subordinate group. The enormous majority of the Palestinian converts were native-

11. Above, pp. 38–39.

born, Aramaic-speaking Jews. The most reasonable supposition is that their Gospel was produced in their own tongue.

A possible objection to this appears in a talmudic story, previously mentioned, about a Jewish Christian judge and his Gospel.[12] The story makes a play on words, the Gospel being called an *evan-gilyon*, which in Aramaic means "a worthless thing of a book" or "a book of idolatry." This has been held to imply that the only Gospel known to the Jews was a Greek *euaggelion*. However, (*a*) this story was written, probably, toward the close of the century, and the event it describes seems to have taken place around A.D. 73.[13] Hence, even if the inference were correct, it would tell us little about conditions at the time K was written. (*b*) The inference is uncertain. The Talmud contains many Greek words taken over into Aramaic—there is another, *philosoph*, in this very passage. Four hundred years' contact with Hellenic culture was bound to affect Aramaic usage, for the same thing happens to all languages. If a Jewish Christian called his book an *evangelion*, this proves nothing as to the language of the book itself.

E. WAS K A PROTO-MARK?

Let us suppose, then, that K was written about A.D. 55 and probably in Aramaic. There follows the question, "Was K a proto-Mark?" This is by no means an unattractive suggestion. Indeed, in the earlier stages of this investigation the writer believed that that was just what K was. Consider these features in Eusebius' quotation from Papias:[14]

1. It is said that Mark wrote down "whatever he remembered" (*hosa emnēmoneusen*) and was careful "to leave out nothing that he heard" (*tou mēden hōn ēkousen paralipein*). To this twice-repeated description it is difficult to fit canonical Mark, for the latter leaves out a great deal that a follower of Peter surely must have heard.

2. The content of Peter's preaching is described as "the *logia*

12. See above, p. 144, and attendant references.

13. Cf. E. B. Nicholson, *The Gospel According to the Hebrews* (London, 1879), p. 146 n.

14. Cf. pp. 142 and 152 and attendant references.

made by the Lord" (*tōn kuriakōn poioumenos logiōn* [or *logōn*]), and Mark's Gospel, it is said, comprised "what was *spoken* or done by Christ" (*to hupo tou Christou ē lechthenta ē prachthenta*). Once more, if *logia* means discourses, we have a twofold description which poorly fits canonical Mark and which would much better describe a book having the substance of Mark plus M.

3. If Mark got his material from Peter, why should Mark simply have abridged a non-Petrine source? At first blush, it would seem easier to suppose that K was the Peter-Mark Gospel, which some later hand abridged.

4. Peter himself is mentioned more frequently in K than in canonical Mark.

5. If K is anti-Pauline, this might fit the theory very nicely. Peter and Paul quarreled (Gal. 2:11 ff.), and Mark and Paul also became estranged (Acts 13:13; 15:37-39). Though there was a later reconciliation, Mark had more than enough time, after he forsook Paul and returned to Jerusalem, to produce the K Gospel. (This would, of course, set the date of K back several years.)

These look like imposing arguments for the theory that what Papias described was not canonical Mark but its source and therefore that K was itself the original Markan Gospel. Yet they are outweighed by most important considerations on the other side. These considerations are partly negative, showing that John Mark could not have written K; and partly positive, suggesting a more plausible alternative.

F. K CANNOT HAVE BEEN A PROTO-MARK

1. The foregoing arguments would place the writing of the original Mark in Jerusalem, whereas universal tradition places it in Rome and after Peter's conversion to the gentile side. (Also Mark's fondness for Latin words like *centurio* and *grabattus* fit a Roman better than a Palestinian milieu.)

2. While K is not explicitly against Paul, it does oppose explicitly, and with apparent anxiety, the admission of uncircumcised Gentiles to the Christian fold. Yet John Mark himself was thoroughly committed to the gentile mission. He went with Paul

and Barnabas to Antioch (Acts 12:25) thence to Salamis (Acts 13:5) and to Perga in Pamphylia (Acts 13:13). Though he quarreled with Paul—or was it only Barnabas who quarreled?— Mark at once set out with Barnabas on another mission to Gentiles (Acts 15:39). Mark and Paul made up their differences, and about A.D. 61–63 the two were together in Rome (Philemon 24; Col. 4:10). There is nothing in John Mark's career to suggest that he would compose so Judaizing a Gospel as K, while there is a great deal that might have prepared him to compose canonical Mark itself.

3. Too much weight ought not to be placed on a single interpretation of Papias' word *logia*. The word had many uses. In Rom. 3:2, for example, it means the whole Old Testament, or at least the whole Pentateuch. In I Clement, chapter 53, it describes Exod. 22:7–11 and Deut. 9:11–14. Ireneus once used it to refer to the miracle of the raising of Jaïrus' daughter (*Adv. Haer.* i. 8). *Logia* is not so determinate but that it could be used in speaking of the contents of an entire Gospel such as canonical Mark.

4. Actually, however, we cannot tell how much of the passage in Eusebius is a quotation from the Elder. This may cover only the first sentence, "Mark, having become Peter's interpreter, wrote down accurately, though not in order, whatever he recalled (*emnēmoneusen*) of the things said or done by Christ," and the rest may be elaboration by Papias or even comment by Eusebius himself.

5. Furthermore, what is the real meaning of *emnēmoneusen*, and who is the subject? The subject may be not Mark but Peter; and the word could mean "mentioned," "reminded," or "taught from memory." In that case, we have a set of possibilities quite different from those ordinarily associated with the passage. For Papias may have been saying only that Mark wrote the gospel story as Peter recalled it. Then, instead of implying that Peter's preaching was the ultimate ground of Mark's Gospel, the passage could very well mean that this Gospel is Peter's reinterpretation of a tradition that originated elsewhere.

Did K make its way to Rome, and there undergo abridgment and recasting at the instigation of Peter? Had we only the sentence from Papias, just quoted, to go on, such a reconstruction of the history would of course seem strained. But there is other evidence.

6. Notice what Eusebius adds immediately after this very sentence from Papias:

> For neither did he (Mark) hear the Lord, nor did he follow him; but afterwards, as I said, he followed Peter, who *adapted his instructions to the needs* (*pros tas chreias epoieito tas didaskalias*) but *had no design of giving the Lord's* logia *in order* (*ouch hōsper suntaxin tōn kuriakōn poioumenos logiōn*). So then Mark did not sin (*hēmarte*) when he thus wrote down some things (*enia*) as he (Mark? Peter?) related them from memory (*apemnēmoneusen*).

Now nobody defends what nobody attacks. If it was necessary to acquit Mark of "sin" or error, this means that in some quarters Mark was felt to have given an incomplete and disconnected account—just as, we have seen, Mark did. The Elder (or Papias, or Eusebius) tells why. Peter himself had provided, not a complete gospel story, but disconnected explanations to fit his current needs. Similarly, Origen said that Mark "put his Gospel together as Peter *explained* it to him."[15] Clearly, both the Origen and the Papias passages fit the theory that canonical Mark represents Peter's reinterpretation of an existing written tradition.

7. If Peter became a missionary to Gentiles, then it becomes abundantly clear why he should inspire a revision of the K Gospel. Not only did K oppose the gentile mission. It singled Peter out for blame in connection with that enterprise.[16] Recognizing his eminence, it nonetheless pictured him as falling away from a prior strength. Peter, alone with Judas the traitor, is individually rebuked by the Lord. He is a "stumbling-block"—a word which K elsewhere applies only to the carrying of the gospel to Gentiles. Indeed, there was much in K that Peter would feel impelled to "recollect," "explain," "make to fit his needs," and handle anew in the light of his own matured understanding of his Lord's intent.

Thus two factors are in tension with each other. On the one hand, tradition has it that Mark was composed at Rome under

15. Eusebius *H.E.* vi. 25.

16. Above, pp. 107 ff.

the motivation of Peter's recollections and explanations. On the other hand, this Gospel, whose compiler was plainly familiar with Palestine, was yet a gentilizing extract from a Judaizing original. For these factors to come into synthesis, we must suppose that, after his variance with Paul, Peter came round to something like Paul's position and that he went to Rome. Then K's attitude toward him becomes entirely understandable. And the picture that results is of this Jewish Christian Gospel originating in Palestine, being carried to the Roman capital, and there causing no little embarrassment to Peter; and of Mark abridging and reworking it, on the basis of what Peter said, until it came into line with the faith of Peter and the gentile Church. If this is in some respects an unfamiliar reconstruction, yet something like it surely happened, for it appears to be the only account that squares with all the facts. In particular, therefore, the points which might have led to calling K a proto-Mark are to be explained by this other and, we think, superior description of the Gospel's history.

One more question intervenes before we can deal finally with that which forms the title of this chapter. This is a problem which ought unhesitatingly to be faced and regardless of what attitude is taken to the thesis of this or any other study.

G. WHAT DID PAPIAS MEAN BY THE "LOGIA" OF MATTHEW?

Plainly Papias' words do not fit canonical Matthew, for this was composed in Greek, at a fairly late date, and probably for gentile Syrian Christians at Antioch. Equally clearly, the Q document fails to accord with Papias' description.

It has sometimes been suggested that the *logia* were a collection of Old Testament prophecies, drawn up for the Church by the apostle Matthew, and that their frequent use in the First Gospel caused Matthew's name to be attached to the whole book. Among the many meanings of *logia* this one is possible. However, (*a*) while *testimonia* are more prominent in Matthew than elsewhere, those peculiar to this Gospel comprise only nine citations, of scarcely thirteen verses. (*b*) The First Gospel omits most of the testimonia that are used elsewhere in the New Testament.[17] Hence, if the apostle Matthew was a chief collector of these prophecies, it is not clear why his name should have been associated particularly with this one book. (*c*) In Eusebius' context, Papias is not discussing *testimonia*. He is discussing Gospels.

Thus Papias' description does not correspond to any of the documents with which it has customarily been identified. Either, therefore, we must accept the shoulder-shrugging conclusion that Papias' words have no discoverable meaning, or we must search for their import somewhere else. Since, then, *logia* could mean an entire book, the way is open for suggesting K as proto-Matthew.

H. K AS PROTO-MATTHEW

The reader is referred to the patristic descriptions of the Gospel of Matthew, assembled earlier in this chapter.[18] The various Fathers, there quoted, say of Matthew that:

1. It was a complete Gospel (Ireneus, Origen, Eusebius, Augustine, Epiphanius).

2. It preceded the other Gospels (Origen, Augustine, Tertullian).

3. It was written in "Hebrew," that is, in Aramaic (Papias, Ireneus, Eusebius, Origen, Epiphanius).

4. It was written among the Jewish Christians (Ireneus, Eusebius).

5. It was written for the Jewish Christians (Eusebius, Origen).

6. It was written while Peter and Paul were carrying on a mission to Gentiles (Ireneus).

7. It was variously interpreted or variously translated (*hērmēneuse*; Papias).

8. Canonical Mark is an abridgment from it (Augustine), and Mark is in some respects disconnected and incomplete (Papias).

Let it be granted that not all the Fathers are equally dependable; that sometimes they guessed, and at other times merely repeated what Ireneus had said, though Ireneus could have been

17. E.g., at Mark 1:1; Luke 4:18–19; John 2:17; 12:38, 40; 18:24; Acts 1:20; 2:25 ff., 34; 3:22, 25; 4:25–26; 8:32–33; 13:33, 34, 35.

18. Pp. 142–43 and 152.

responsible for at most four of the above eight points. These allowances are not sufficient to explain the phenomenon that is now before us. For these eight statements about Matthew name precisely the features which, on internal grounds, we have found to be the most outstanding characteristics of the K document. Can coincidence, of the most extreme and surprising sort, be called upon to explain this correspondence?

Consider further that if K was the original Gospel of Matthew, then we have the solution to both the problems named at the beginning of this chapter. We can see why the peculiar features of Matthew were popular in the Near East and especially among Jewish Christians. We can see why the Talmud, so far as it reflects the gospel story at all, reflects it in its Matthean form. We can see why later Jewish Christian Gospels had a Matthean skeleton. We can see why the name of Matthew was associated with such Gospels and with the canonical Gospel too. All these events will have come about naturally, indeed inevitably, if K was both the original Gospel of Matthew and the original Gospel of the Jewish Christian Church.

Finally, and in some respects most importantly of all, K is a document, the only document, which fits both the tradition of the early Fathers and the critical postulates of the Synoptic Problem.

It requires little imagination now to complete the history of the making of Mark and Matthew. The K Gospel was written in Palestine, probably in Aramaic, and, with considerable likelihood, by the apostle Matthew. It appeared in the face of the Judaizing controversy, at a time when not only Paul but Peter had gone over to the gentile side. It made its way to Rome, possibly in Aramaic, more likely in a Greek translation. There, under Peter's influence, it was abridged and its content revised by John Mark, himself an active missionary to the Gentiles. Meanwhile it was preserved and prized by the Jewish Christian community in Palestine. It was made the basis for later Jewish Christian expansions, the most notable of which was the Gospel according to the Hebrews. Before that, but long after the Judaizing controversy had ceased to be of moment, this original Gospel was combined with the Antiochean sayings source Q to make the present Gospel of Matthew.

XVI

SOME NOTES ON LUKE

THE investigation of Q, earlier in this study, led to the conclusion that Luke dealt with Q in a manner very different
from that of canonical Matthew. Unlike the latter, Luke has apparently put Q on a level with his other sources, has adhered
more closely to its structure, and has kept more of its content. At
the same time he has been freer than the redactor of Matthew in
adapting the Q style and vocabulary to those of his other sources
and of his Gospel as a whole. These inferences are not altogether
new. In varying degrees they have been reached by some stellar
figures in the history of Synoptic criticism.[1]

In connection with the present study, two further conclusions
can be formed about Luke.

A. MARK-LUKE VOCABULARY NOT COMPARABLE TO
MATTHEW-MARK VOCABULARY

The Mark-Luke vocabulary is different, in both extent and
significance, from the Matthew-Mark vocabulary.

1. A search of the concordances reveals 37 expressions that
occur at least three times in Mark; and in Mark, and in Matthew's
parallels to Mark, as often as in Luke-John-Acts combined:

1. Bernhard Weiss, *Evangelium des Lukas* (Göttingen, 1901); *Die Quellen
des Lukasevangeliums* (Stuttgart, 1907); *Die Quellen der synoptischen Über-
lieferung* (Leipzig, 1908); B. S. Easton, "Linguistic Evidence for the Lucan
Source L," *Journal of Biblical Literature*, XXIX, 139 ff.; and "The Special
Source of the Third Gospel," *ibid.*, XXX, 78 ff.; *The Gospel According to St.
Luke* (New York: Scribner's, 1926); B. H. Streeter, *The Four Gospels* (2d
ed.; London: Macmillan & Co., 1930). These studies have been particularly
valuable in establishing the independent existence of Luke's special source L.
Cf. also C. C. McCown, "The Temptation of Jesus Eschatologically and So-
cially Interpreted," *Biblical World*, LIII (1919), 402 ff.; Henry J. Cadbury,
The Style and Literary Method of Luke, Part II: *The Treatment of Sources
in the Gospel* (Cambridge: Harvard University Press, 1920); *The Making of
Luke-Acts.*

aganakteō (be displeased), *apoluō gunaika* (put away one's wife), *blasphēmia* (blasphemy), *geenna* (Gehenna), *grēgoreō* (be watchful), *daimonizomai* (be possessed of demons), *deute* (come ye), *epitimaō . . . hina* (command . . . that), *euaggelion* (gospel), *Zebedaios* (Zebedee), *thelō* (wish) and finite vb., *katheudō* (sleep), *kakōs* (miserably), *kalon estin/ēn* (it were better), *kat' idian* (by one's self), *kērussō* (preach) used of the gospel, *krateō* (seize), *lian* (exceedingly), *noeō* (think), *xērainō* (dry up), *hopou an/ean* (wherever), *horia* (borders), *opsia* (evening), *paragō* (bring/lead), *paralutikos* (paralytic), *to peran* (the other side), *peritithēmi* (place around), *planaō* (lead astray), *potērion* (cup) used metaphorically, *proagō* (go before), *pur* (fire) metaph., *hriza* (root), *skandalizō* (offend) ac., *skandalizomai* (be offended) without *en* (in/at), *speirō* (sow), *splagchnizomai* (be moved with compassion), *hupagete* (go your way).

An exactly similar count of Mark-Luke expressions (3 in Mark; in Mark, and in Luke's parallels to Mark, as often as in Matthew-John-Acts combined) yields only 5 items: *archiereis kai grammateis* (chief priests and scribes), *gunaika lambanō/echō* (take/have a wife), *epitassō* (put under orders), *epitimaō* (command) without *hina* (that), and *makrothen* (from afar).

2. There is a more general definition for eliciting the common vocabulary of two out of four books. It was used by Hawkins in comparing Luke-Acts with Matthew-Mark.[2] A style is common to A and B if it appears in each of them a chosen minimum number of times and if it occurs in A and B together at least four times as often as in C and D together.

Applying this definition first to Matthew-Mark, it is found that the following occur at least three times in Matthew and three in Mark and in these together at least four times as often as in Luke and John together:

aganakteō, apoluō gunaika, blasphēmia, geenna, grēgoreō, daimonizomai, epitimaō . . . hina, euaggelion, eutheōs/euthus (straightway), *Zebedaios, katheudō, kakei* (and there), *kalon estin/ēn, kat' idian, kērussō (to euaggelion), krateō, lian, noeō, xērainō, hopou an/ean, horia, opsia, paralutikos, to peran, peritithēmi, planaō, proagō, pur* metaph., *skandalizomai* without *en, skandalizō* ac., *sunagomai* (assemble), *teleutaō* (die/come to an end), *hupagete, hōste* (just as).

This second definition yields, for Matthew-Mark, almost the same group of expressions as the first one: 34 items as compared

2. John C. Hawkins, *Horae Synopticae: Contributions to the Study of the Synoptic Problem* (2d ed.; Oxford, 1909), pp. 27 ff.

with 37, those not translated being identical in the two lists.[3]

But now, when we use the second definition to elicit a Mark-Luke vocabulary, all the following appear three times in Mark, three in Luke, and four times as often in Mark plus Luke as in Matthew plus John:

anestēn (arose) 2d aor. mid. intrans., *hapas* (all together), *archiereis kai grammateis*, *basileia tou Theou* (kingdom of God), *gunaika lambanō/echō, ei tis* (if anyone), *eisporeuomai* (enter), *existēmi* (astonish), *epitassō, epitimaō* without *hina, ērxato/ērxanto* (he/they began), *Hērōdes* (Herod) the tetrarch, *Iakōbos* (James) son of Zebedee, *Iōanēs* (John) son of Zebedee, *kai autos* (and he himself), *kōluō* (hinder), *makrothen, paratithēmi* (set before), *pneuma akatharton* (unclean spirit), *chēra* (widow).

Instead of 5 items, as under the first definition, we now have 20—more than half as many as in the Matthew-Mark list.

The fundamental difference between the two definitions just used is that the first excludes items occurring frequently in Acts but that the second does not. When we discard from the distinctive Matthew-Mark vocabulary expressions found extensively in Acts, the list is hardly affected at all. When we make the same exclusion from the Mark-Luke list, the list is reduced to quite negligible proportions.

A similar effect appears when we count expressions that are found only in the two Gospels and only in these plus Acts:

	Matthew-Mark	Mark-Luke
Number of expressions found only in these two books	75	35
Number of expressions found only in these two and Acts	18	21

In the latter case there is a slight excess in favor of Mark-Luke.

Thus any supposedly distinctive Mark-Luke vocabulary reappears extensively in Acts too. This must mean one of two things. Either (*a*) the apparent Mark-Luke usage was simply an acceptable usage for narrative writing generally, in which case it loses much of its significance for the comparison of Luke with Mark; or (*b*) to the extent that he shares a peculiar usage with Mark, Luke has permitted this to affect nearly all his other writ-

3. This confirms the validity of the first list, as used in chaps. viii and ix to show part of the distinctive K vocabulary.

ing. We had already inferred from the study of Q that Luke, unlike canonical Matthew, fused together the vocabularies of his several sources. Yet to find that he has extended this to Acts is somewhat surprising. Perhaps, therefore, the first alternative is preferable.

In any case, both of the really distinctive Matthew-Mark lists are far larger than the corresponding Mark-Luke lists. This confirms the conclusion reached previously in chapter iv:[4] The relationship between Mark and Luke is not comparable with that between Matthew and Mark.

B. LUKE USED CANONICAL MARK BUT NOT K

A feature of the Synoptic Problem that has become almost hackneyed has to do with the agreements of Matthew and Luke against Mark in passages common to all three. These Matthew-Luke "contacts," as they are called, are by no means inconsiderable. (*a*) Matthew and Luke frequently agree against Mark in the phrasing of common passages. (*b*) Both Matthew and Luke insert over two hundred and fifty verses of Q material. To be sure, they usually use this material differently. Sometimes, however, there is an astonishing likeness of treatment. For example, both insert the same Q phrase at the same point in the preaching of the Baptist (Matt. 3:11-12 = Luke 3:16-17). (*c*) Matthew and Luke both contain genealogies and Infancy gospels. Here again, despite enormous differences, there are some remarkable coincidences in wording:

Cf. Matt. 1:1	with Luke 3:31, 34
Matt. 1:18*a*, 20	with Luke 1:27
Matt. 1:18*b*	with Luke 1:35
Matt. 1:21	with Luke 2:7*a*, 21
Matt. 2:1	with Luke 1:5

(*d*) The following passages, found in canonical Mark, are absent from both Matthew and Luke: Mark 1:1, 2*b*; 3:19*b*-21; 4:26-29, 34*b*; 6:31; 7:2-4, 32-37; 8:22-26; 9:21-25, 48, 49; 10:24, 38*b*, 39*b*; 11:11, 16; 12:32*b*-34, 37*b*; 14:51, 52, 59—about forty verses, or more than an average Markan chapter. These Matthew-Luke "omissions" run to entire sentences or more and

4. Above, pp. 36-37.

few of them can be ascribed to condensation or to improvements in the style of the source.

With identification of the K document as the source of Mark, it would be attractive to explain all these Matthew-Luke contacts by supposing that Luke too used K, perhaps to the exclusion of canonical Mark itself. The insertions of some supposedly Q material at the same points in Luke and Matthew would then be because it was not actually from Q but from K. Their common "omissions" would simply be material that neither of these evangelists ever saw, because it was added by the final Markan redactor.

An alternative suggestion, somewhat analogous to the foregoing, has often been made by both Roman and Protestant scholars. It is that Luke used both Mark and canonical Matthew.[5] This too would account for most of the above phenomena, though it would less readily explain the common "omissions."

Attractive as each of these suggestions may be, however, they encounter obstacles so weighty that it seems impossible to accept either of them.

1. There is the well-known difficulty that Matthew and Luke never agree against Mark's order. Luke, and especially Matthew, vary from Mark's arrangement at numerous points. But only at Mark 3:10 and 9:50 do they displace the same Markan order, and in neither case do they agree in the manner of displacement.

2. Matthew and Mark share an extensive K vocabulary which Luke does not have; and Mark and Luke share a less extensive vocabulary which Matthew and K lack. Both these facts indicate that canonical Mark is the only connecting link between Luke and the K portions of Matthew. This consideration is especially forceful, since Luke was disposed to allow the style of one source to affect his editing of other sources. Had Luke had either K or Matthew before him, therefore, their usage would almost certainly have influenced his writing in the same way; indeed, we should have had far more difficulty in isolating a distinctive Matthew-Mark usage at all.

3. Although much of Matthew's K material is Jewish Chris-

---

5. So M. S. Enslin, *Christian Beginnings* (New York: Harper & Bros., 1938), pp. 431 ff. For two Roman Catholic references see above, p. 142, n. 2.

tian, still there is much that Luke surely could have used if he had known it. L, which Luke did use, is likewise somewhat Jewish Christian. If Luke had wished to avoid an excess of such material, still there were parts of K, or of Matthew, that ought to have appealed to him (e.g., Matt. 4:24; 5:16; 11:28–30; 12:12, 36, 37; 13:44, 45; 17:7; 18:4, 10, 19, 20; 21:14; 23:9; 25:1–13).

4. Consider, finally, the sixteen instances of Markan abridgment and condensation which were discussed in chapter vii. All

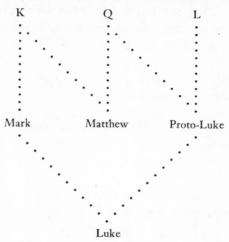

these fall opposite M material in Matthew. It is plain, as we saw, that Mark's breaks in continuity embarrassed Luke, for he constantly omits or radically alters Mark's transitional phrasing. Surely, therefore, he would have filled at least some of these breaks from the K or Matthew exemplar, had he had it before him. Yet he fills just one or two from L and leaves the others empty. Even without the previous considerations, this is enough to show (*a*) that Luke's source was Mark and not K and (*b*) that Luke did not afterward use either K or Matthew to correct his extracts from Mark.[6]

Therefore, to account for the Matthew-Luke contacts in passages having Markan parallels, we are thrown back on more familiar explanations: common improvements in style, Matthew

6. And, since Luke did not use Matthew, this further confirms the independent existence of the Q document.

of K, Luke of K's daughter Mark; occasional overlappings of Q with K (and hence with Mark);[7] and textual corruption of Matthew or Luke or both.

Thus, in regard to Luke, the K solution is in full accord with findings that previously led to the Two- and Four-Document hypotheses. Indeed, those findings are somewhat strengthened.

It will be noticed, furthermore, that the discussion of this chapter completes the establishment of the diagram given at the end of chapter i. It is not within the scope of this book to discuss the L source or to prove or disprove the existence of a proto-Luke. A fuller diagram, embracing both of these, would be as shown above.

7. Occasional overlapping of Q and K is altogether to be expected. For a fuller discussion see pp. 125 and 167.

XVII

K AND THE SYNOPTIC SOLUTION

IT IS now time to draw together some of the principal results of this study and to consider their relationship to the wider field of criticism of the Synoptic Gospels. The central thesis has been this: There was an original Jewish Christian Gospel, here labeled "K," which consisted roughly of the canonical Markan material plus the materials peculiar to canonical Matthew. Canonical Mark is an abridgment from K. Canonical Matthew is a combination of K with the independent sayings source Q.

It has further been concluded (a) that the Markan abridgment had a polemical purpose, having been made on behalf of the gentile side in the Judaizing controversy; (b) that canonical Matthew was put together long after that controversy had waned and when it was possible to place Jewish and gentile gospel materials side by side; (c) that Luke did not use K but used our present Mark and, of course, Q; and (d) that Luke preserves the content and order of Q better than Matthew does but that Matthew better keeps Q's characteristic language. In addition, there are grounds for supposing (e) that K was originally written in Aramaic and even (f) that K was the original Gospel of Matthew. In important respects, however, the last two items are not essential to the hypothesis. That K existed is independent of whether Matthew or Mark or someone else wrote it, or in what tongue.

A. SUMMARY OF GROUNDS FOR K HYPOTHESIS

There are four kinds of evidence for the conclusions just outlined.

1. *Evidence from language.*—M and Q are similar in length and content, whereas the Markan material is different in both respects. Yet, despite these facts, (a) the peculiar vocabulary of Matthew's special materials pervades its parallels to Mark too,

but it does not pervade Matthew's Q, and Q has its own distinctive style; (*b*) the vocabulary of Matthew's parallels to Mark pervades its M material also, but it does not pervade Q; and (*c*) the distinctive Matthew-Mark vocabulary pervades M but not Q. In all three of these cases the linguistic relation of M to the Markan material, and their distinctness from Q, is much too thoroughgoing to be attributed to the Matthean redactor. In fact, (*d*) the distinctive vocabulary of the redactor is different from that of any of the above materials.

2. *Evidence from structure.*—(*a*) When Matthew's Markan material is removed, the M remainder is often badly disconnected and lacking in structure. M looks, in fact, exactly like the parings that would be left after a process of excision.

b) When the Q material is removed, the M remainder is, on the contrary, nearly always smooth-flowing and well connected. (It often carries, however, a different import from that of the completed Gospel.)

c) Canonical Mark carries many internal indications that it was excerpted from a longer document. These signs fall consistently opposite material that is peculiar to Matthew. Mark's gaps obviously troubled Luke, yet Luke did not know how to fill them.

d) Matthew's treatment of Q becomes most clearly intelligible on the assumption that M and the Markan material were in prior unity. In the First Gospel Q appears everywhere as supplementary material, which often modifies the cast of the fundamental document.

e) By the same token, we have the explanation for the discrepancies between Matthew's and Luke's use of Q. Q is used more extensively in Luke, and is more nearly on equal footing with other sources, than it is in Matthew.

3. *Evidence from content.*—(*a*) While Mark's signs of omission fall regularly opposite M material in Matthew, the M material at those points is itself strongly anti-Gentile. Furthermore, when Matthew and Mark differ in passages retained by both, the Markan variants are strongly and consistently pro-Gentile. Thus we are able to assign a reason for Mark's revision, and this strengthens the case for the revision having occurred.

b) Under the standard Two- and Four-Document hypotheses, the M material must have been added to Mark and Q to form canonical Matthew. This would mean that, whereas the most primitive Christianity was Jewish, its most primitive Gospels were Gentile. More serious, it would imply that this Jewish Christian material was published only after it had lost much of its relevance and that it was combined with the pro-Gentile materials in a very inconsistent way. If, however, the M and Markan material were originally one, then what the Matthean redactor did was to change his basic Jewish source, by additions from Q, in the direction of gentile Christianity. This process is far easier to understand, for it parallels the history of primitive Christianity itself.

4. *Evidence from tradition.*—(*a*) Gospel materials, of an exclusively Matthean type, were widespread through the Near East, and in Jewish Christianity, at an early period. Probably, therefore, they represent an early and indigenous Jewish Christian tradition. The latter is just what, on internal grounds, we have decided that the K Gospel contained.

b) Patristic descriptions of Matthew, and no less of Mark, seem to fit the K hypothesis better than they do other hypotheses.

B. AREAS OF THE SYNOPTIC SOLUTION NOT AFFECTED BY THIS HYPOTHESIS

In many areas the general solution to the Synoptic Problem is not affected by the K hypothesis. Nearly every solution to the Synoptic Problem hitherto offered has had in the end to postulate some kind of source for canonical Mark. In identifying that source, therefore, as roughly M plus Mark, we simply make definitive what has long been a necessary assumption in Synoptic criticism.

1. Mark is still a middle term between Matthew and Luke.
2. The relative datings of the canonical Gospels are not affected. Of course, as regards the interdependence of these books, it would now make no difference whether canonical Mark was produced before or after canonical Matthew. However, we have seen important reasons for dating Mark early in the seventh decade, canonical Matthew late in the tenth decade, of the first

century. These datings are close to those reached by nearly all competent students of these Gospels.

3. Internal features which had previously seemed to show the priority of Mark now point far more certainly to the priority of Mark's parent K. Furthermore, the same reasons which led Mark to excise parts of K led many times to modifying what was retained. Nevertheless, Mark is often (and, in matters not affected by the Judaizing controversy, usually) closer to the K source than Matthew is. Mark's Greek is usually rougher. In parallel passages Mark is generally the more discursive. Matthew's miracles are generally more marvelous than Mark's—and shortening and heightening commonly attend the development of wonder stories as these pass from person to person. So far as these features hold good, they are clear signs of evolution from a less to a more sophisticated point of view.

In all these areas the new hypothesis is completely in accord with those that have gone before. Furthermore, as New Testament students will have recognized, some individual features of the K hypothesis have been anticipated by other writers in the Synoptic field. It is important to see the resemblances of the new theory, particularly to two or three earlier ones with which it is most closely allied. It is no less necessary to indicate wherein the K theory is distinctive and where it offers what appears to be a more adequate synthesis of the data.

C. COMPARISON WITH EARLIER THEORIES

In the following summaries of earlier hypotheses, italics indicate *areas of significant difference from the K solution*.

1. B. S. Easton recognized that Mark has frequently abridged.[1] He said, significantly enough, that Matt. 10:17, 18 (but not Luke 12:11–12) is more primitive than Mark 13:9, 10 and that chapter 10 of Matthew as a whole is often more primitive than chapters 6 or 10 of Mark. He called special attention to the obscurity of Mark 3:13, as showing that Mark had major portions of the Sermon on the Mount before him. Easton agreed that these differences between Mark and Matthew cannot be ex-

1. *Christ in the Gospels* (New York: Scribner's, 1930), pp. 18 ff.

plained simply by supposing that the Matthean compiler added material to his Markan contexts.

He took all this to mean, however, that *Mark abridged the Sayings Source.* He concluded, as is perforce necessary if Mark did that, that *M and Q are from one document;* and he believed that *M plus Q = (roughly) the Matthean Logia described by Papias.* It is not necessary here to restate the grounds on which, in preceding chapters, the unity of M and Q has been rejected. It may be useful, however, to indicate why, in this writer's opinion, Mark cannot have used Q.

a) There is no reason why Mark's source should not sometimes have overlapped Q. On the contrary, it would be astonishing if two primitive books about our Lord did not occasionally cover the same ground. There have been, moreover, strong indications that K and Q did sometimes overlap. That is quite enough to explain all the observable contacts between Mark and the Q material of Matthew or Luke.

b) If Mark used Q at all, it is not easy to see why he used so little of it—and at such casual, out-of-the-way points. This is especially difficult, since many parts of Q would have served Mark's pro-gentile purposes exceptionally well.

c) Of Mark's many internal gaps, almost none is filled in Luke, while virtually all are filled in Matthew, with M material. Since M and Q are from different sources, this consideration is enough by itself to show that the compiler of Mark did not have Q before him.

Many scholars have suggested that Mark might have used Q. Many others have defined the sayings source so as to include varying amounts of M. Hence in reviewing Easton's position we have, in effect, compared the K hypothesis with a host of others that reach one or both of those conclusions.

2. F. C. Baur saw reflections of a Jewish-gentile controversy in such passages as Matt. 7:22, 23.[2] He recognized that *anomia* originally meant not just iniquity but violation of the Law. He

2. Baur's views are summarized in Vol. I of his *Geschichte der christlichen Kirche* (1863), trans. *Church History of the First Three Centuries* (3d ed.; London and Edinburgh, 1878). Cf. also *Paulus* (1845); *Kritische Untersuchungen über die kanonischen Evangelien* (1847); *Das Markusevangelium nach seinem Ursprung und Charakter* (1851).

regarded Mark as derived from *canonical* Matthew *and canonical Luke*. He said that *Mark was docetic in tendency* and that it omitted pro-Jewish materials *of canonical Matthew, in order to play down the controversy*. Baur thought *all the canonical Gospels subapostolic*,[3] yet he thought both *canonical* Matthew and *canonical Luke* were *aimed directly at the controversy and took opposite sides. Peter was an unyielding protagonist for the Jewish Christians*, so that *the Jewish-gentile struggle was equivalent to and subsumed under a struggle between Peter and Paul*. Finally, on the basis of the Clementine Homilies and Recognitions, Baur concluded that *the controversy continued, in substantially its original form, into the third century* and that *the difference between Marcionites and Ebionites was an extension of the struggle between Paul and the first-century Judaizers*.

There is space only to summarize the objections to the italicized parts of Baur's theory. (*a*) Baur had to reject as unhistorical a large mass of early Christian writing (e.g., Acts and I Clement) which conflicted with his theory. (*b*) In particular, he had to discount the many passages in Matthew itself which show the canonical Gospel to be sympathetic to the gentile cause. (*c*) It is unsound to equate the contentions of first-century Paulinism with those of third-century gnosticism. (*d*) It is no less unsound to equate so closely the faith of Jesus' first followers with the Ebionism of the Clementine writings. These reflect not just the developed Jewish Christianity of, say, the Gospel according to the Hebrews but the extremer (vegetarian and possibly Essene) form to be seen in the Gospel of the Ebionites.[4] (*e*) How could these Jewish Christian groups, scattered and decentralized after A.D. 70, and living chiefly in Transjordania, have exerted the effective pressure on the gentile Church which Baur's theory demanded? (*f*) True, the Clementine Homilies reflect a form of Jewish Christianity of the late second century, and the Homilies, though not the earlier Recognitions, made covert attacks on Paul under the name of Simon Magus. This is not surprising, for, as is

---

3. Of all the New Testament books, Baur allowed only Romans, I and II Corinthians, Galatians, and Revelation to the apostolic period.

4. Epiphanius, *Haer.* xxx. 3 ff.

plain from Ireneus and Eusebius,[5] Jewish Christians long retained their antagonism to Paul. This, however, is a long way from saying that the *struggle* continued through all that period. On the contrary, the fact that these attacks were veiled suggests that anti-Paulinism would, at the close of the second century, have had short shrift from any influential party in the Church at large or, indeed, from anyone outside Ebionite circles.

3. The K hypothesis comes closer, at some points, to solutions which take seriously the patristic tradition of an early, complete Aramaic Gospel. Among the latter, we consider first the normal position of Roman Catholic scholarship.

On June 19, 1911, the Pontifical Biblical Commission issued a decision which set the bounds within which members of that communion might reach conclusions about the Synoptic Gospels.[6] This decision rejects the Two-Document hypothesis and *denies the existence of Q.* It affirms that *the First Gospel* was written in Aramaic, in Palestine, by the apostle Matthew; and that *canonical Matthew* preceded the other Gospels. It holds that *the Greek Matthew is virtually identical with the Aramaic Gospel.* Roman Catholic students may not conclude otherwise.

It will suffice to notice two solutions along these lines. J. M. Vosté, O.P., agrees that the apostle Matthew wrote his Gospel in Aramaic. Mark used both this and Peter's preaching. *The Greek Matthew is substantially identical with the Aramaic,* and yet *it made use of canonical Mark!* Luke used Mark, but *Luke also used Matthew.* Chapman's solution differs from Vosté's in holding that *Mark used the canonical, Greek Matthew,* which he modified on the basis of Peter's preaching. Luke's *first* draft was based on canonical Mark; but *our present Luke was based not on Mark but on this first draft together with the Greek Matthew.*

These Roman Catholic answers are strikingly like that proposed and defended with great skill by the Protestant scholar Theodor Zahn.[7] For Zahn, also, canonical Mark is based on the

---

5. Ireneus *Haer.* i. 26. 2; Eusebius *H.E.* iii. 27. 4.

6. For references to the Roman Catholic works here discussed see above pp. 142–43.

7. *Introduction to the New Testament* (1897).

original Aramaic Matthew. *Canonical Matthew is a translation* of the original, yet *canonical Matthew also used canonical Mark.*

Nearly all writers who have taken positions like these have had to say that canonical Mark drew from *Aramaic* Matthew and that the Greek Matthew, supposedly *a close reproduction of the latter*, somehow *depended on Mark too.* But why should such a Matthean translator, who would have known Greek better than Mark did, use Mark at all, since we are usually told that he did not employ Mark in order to change Matthew but only to *translate* it? This seems like a strange kind of jugglery. One suspects that it could never have been suggested but for the strong desire to square patristic tradition with the acknowledged priority of the Markan material.

Recourses like the above are easily avoided if we assume simply that both canonical editors had K in substantially the same form and that canonical Mark kept many of K's primitive features.

4. Others have sought to justify the patristic tradition in various ways. We note only a few whose solutions touch the K hypothesis at significant points.[8]

Pfleiderer held that there was a primitive Aramaic gospel source. This was first used by Mark. Then *Luke used both Mark and this Aramaic original.* The latter continued in favor among Jewish Christians and was the basis of their apocryphal Gospels, notably the Gospel according to the Hebrews. Mark and Luke both represented gentile Christianity. So Matthew was written in order to combine the gentile tradition *which Mark and Luke represent* with the Jewish Christian tradition. *The existence of Q is not recognized. All the Q and Markan materials are supposed to have lain before Mark in the Aramaic original and before Matthew and Luke in a Greek translation of it.* The evidence need not be reviewed which leads to decisive rejection of the positions here italicized. Pfleiderer's position is at one with the K hypothesis, however, in recognizing the existence of a primitive Gospel be-

8. Summaries of the following three positions are given in James Moffatt, *Introduction to the New Testament* (3d ed.; New York: Charles Scribner's Sons, 1918), pp. 182–83.

hind Mark and in asserting the paramount importance of that early document.

C. E. Scott-Moncrief held to the theory of an original Gospel *used independently by all three Synoptists. It was written by John Mark,* and the present Mark is a revision of it.

B. Bonkamp recognized the existence of an original Aramaic Gospel on which, he said, both Matthew *and Luke* depended. Canonical Mark is a *compilation* differing from the original Gospel.

Out of the vast literature on the Synoptic Problem the above hypotheses have been selected because each has one or more points of contact with prominent features of the K hypothesis. Yet it is plain that, in each case, the differences are almost greater than the resemblances. With nearly all these theories except Easton's and Baur's (and except Scott-Moncrief's in part) the similarity to the K theory lies in positing some kind of Aramaic source behind Mark and the other Gospels of the New Testament. As we have pointed out, however, the Aramaic composition of K, while likely, is not fundamental to the K hypothesis. Unlike most of the above theories (but like Easton and most recent scholars), the K hypothesis maintains the independent use of Q by Matthew and Luke; and it underscores the fact that canonical Mark is the only link between Luke and the non-Q parts of Matthew. Finally, the present hypothesis is unique in the way it conceives the nature of the primitive Gospel and the uses that were made of it in producing Matthew and Mark.

D. ADVANTAGES OF THE NEW SOLUTION

Besides corresponding to an enormous mass of evidence, the K solution offers some not inconsiderable advantages.

1. The existence of Q is established, and that document becomes more homogeneous than it has appeared under some previous reconstructions.

2. The new solution is simple. Apart from editorial revisions (which were made, of course, by all the canonical evangelists), we have to deal with just three sources, all of them written: K, the original Gospel from which Mark was drawn; Q, which was merged with K to form our First Gospel; and L, which,

with Q and canonical Mark, entered into the composition of Luke.

3. The "lost" ending of Mark is recovered.

4. The peculiar materials of Matthew are seen to furnish uniquely important information about the earliest forms of Jewish Christianity.

5. The ancient, painful discord between Jewish and gentile Christians is seen to have been crucially determinative in the making not only of the Epistles but of the Gospels too.

For the New Testament scholar, gains like these are enough. But scholars are few, and Christians are many. Among the great body of Christians the K solution will, if it finds scholarly acceptance, carry a more precious import. K must have been, not just an important Jewish Christian document, but very nearly the first Gospel of Christianity itself. Yet it is in this earliest Gospel, written amid what had been our Lord's own environs and probably in his own tongue, that we find first told the stories of an Empty Tomb and, it seems, of a Virgin Mother. It is here, finally, that he, whom his first followers knew to be the Lord's Messiah, said to those first followers, "Where two or three are gathered together in my name, there am I in their midst," and, "Lo, I am with you alway, even unto the end of the world."

Part V

THE RECONSTRUCTION OF K

XVIII

ON THE RECONSTRUCTION OF K

O UR final chapter will offer a restoration of the text of the
K Gospel. Most of the principles underlying the reconstruction are evident from what has already been said, but a few
need fuller discussion.

A. ORDER OF EVENTS IN K

Regarding the structure of K, the chief remaining problems
arise out of differences in the arrangement of our first two Gospels. Some of these are trivial, and their solution will be evident
from inspection of the restored text itself. At fourteen points,
however, the differences are of major importance.

The order in Matthew is evidently due, in many cases, to a
liking for topical and numerical schemes. Now, topical arrangements and the stressing of mystic numbers often characterized
Jewish religious writing. Their presence in Matthew has sometimes been explained by supposing that the compiler was a converted Jew. But, even if this were so, K too was Jewish. On
a priori grounds, then, there is no reason for preferring the compiler rather than K itself as the source of the Matthean arrangements. Each difference of order between Matthew and Mark
needs to be considered on its merits.

When this is done, it is found that Mark's order does sometimes appear more primitive than Matthew's, but not always.
Both compilers have done some redistributing of their material,
just as both have revised along other lines as well. In fact, of
these fourteen major differences, eleven fall at points where, on
quite independent grounds, we had already decided that Mark
revised!

1. Matt. 3 : 1, 2, 3 vs. Mark 1 : 3, 4. Matthew puts the Old Testament quotation after the event to which it is related. This is superior from a literary standpoint and so may indicate revision.

Note, however, that Matt. 3:1 refers to a preceding context which Mark now lacks. We cannot be sure whether this lack represents an omission by Mark or a later mutilation of his Gospel.[1] If the former, then Mark has done the changing in order to cover his omission.

2. Matt. 3:4, 5, 6 vs. Mark 1:5, 6. Mark puts the personal description of John the Baptist between the descriptions of the crowds and of what is said to them. This certainly seems more crude and therefore more primitive.

3. Matt. 4:13 relates the settling in Capernaum to a testimonium and places it before the calling of Simon, James, and John. Mark 1:21 relates it to a recognition of Jesus by demons and puts it after that call. Mark's order is historically more probable, but superior historicity could be due to redaction. The Matthean testimonium probably came from K, and Mark may have deliberately substituted 1:23 for it.[2] Mark's arrangement may well be secondary.

4. Matt. 7:28-29; Mark 1:22. In Mark this precedes a passage that Matthew lacks, and in Matthew it follows a discourse that Mark lacks. K did have part of the Sermon on the Mount and probably did not have the Markan story. Hence Matthew's arrangement is more likely to be that of K.

5. Matt. 8:2-4, 14-16 vs. Mark 1:29-34, 40-44. The arrangements are, respectively:

Matt. 8:2-4	Healing of leper	Mark 1:29-34	Peter's mother-in-law
8:5-13	Centurion's child	1:35-39	Peter and others find Jesus
8:14-16	Peter's mother-in-law	1:40-44	Healing of leper

Mark 1:29 follows awkwardly after verse 28, and its position seems to have been necessitated by the insertion of 1:23-27 at this point. Mark 1:40 would have been a better sequel either to 1:26 (as in Matthew) or to 1:20 than to 1:39. Note that Mark has numerous other insertions hereabouts: 1:34*b* (apparently a substitute for Matt. 8:17); 1:35-38; 1:45. Now the story of the

1. See above, pp. 120 ff.

2. Above, pp. 93-94.

centurion's child was in K (Matt. 8:5, 6, 13) and probably also the testimonium at Matt. 8:17. The latter is, moreover, a natural and thoroughly Jewish Christian conclusion to the three healings in Matthew. It appears that Mark has done the disarranging, which was caused chiefly by his insertions of new matter.

6. Matt. 8:26*a*, *b* vs. Mark 4:39, 40. Note the awkward transition from Mark 4:40 to 41. Luke must have felt this, for he omits Jesus' first question. Yet to place 40 before 39 would be more awkward still. Hence Mark's present arrangement is probably original, with the Matthean passage a definite editorial improvement.

7. The three incidents of the palsied man (Matt. 9:2-8 = Mark 2:3-12), the call of Matthew and the dinner (Matt. 9:9-13 = Mark 2:14-17), and the question about fasting (Matt. 9:14-17 = Mark 2:18-22) are placed in Matthew between the healing of the Gadarene demoniacs and the raising of Jairus' daughter. Mark puts them between the healing of the leper and the plucking of grain. In Mark this group follows immediately upon the group (Mark 1:29-44) where it is plain that Mark has done considerable revising.

Moreover, it is Matthew which, in the first of these stories, seems to preserve the more primitive lesson by saying that mankind has authority to forgive sins:

> Matt. 9:4, 6, 8. And Jesus . . . said, . . . The son of man hath authority on earth to forgive sins . . . And . . . the multitudes . . . glorified God, who had given such authority unto men.

On both these counts the presumption would seem to favor the Matthean arrangement.

8. The above setting in Matthew raises, however, the further problem of where K put the calling of the Twelve. Matthew has the list of the Twelve just before the mission of the Twelve (Matt. 10:2-4). Mark has omitted much of the latter from K and gives the list at the point (Mark 3:13 = Matt. 5:1) where Jesus goes up into the mountain. Mark then omits most of the subsequent discourse. If the list is awkwardly placed in Matthew, its position in Mark is bad for a different reason: there it is not followed by any assignment of duties or other appropriate sequel.

(What Mark does add is that Jesus' "friends" thought him to be beside himself.)

Yet while the present Markan position is clumsy, a similar arrangement in K would have been very suitable, since there it would have been followed by those portions of the Sermon on the Mount that are directed particularly to the Twelve. Since, moreover, Matt. 10:1 actually assumes that the choosing of the Twelve had come earlier, and since Matt. 5:1 summarizes Mark 3:13-19a, we are justified in supposing that, in K, the list of the Twelve originally stood at the latter point.

If that is so, however, then the call of Matthew (Matt. 9:9-13) must have preceded the Sermon on the Mount, for Matthew's name is included in the roster. Either, then, K placed Matt. 9:9-13 earlier, or it placed the Sermon later. Now there is no good way to put the Sermon later: K introduced the Sermon with the list of the Twelve, and the latter is presupposed at Matt. 10:1. Therefore we must suppose that, in K, the call of Matthew was put earlier than it appears in our First Gospel. Yet this in turn involves all three of the incidents, Matt. 9:1-8, 9-13, 14-17 = Mark 2:1-12, 13-17, 18-22. These are in the same order in both canonical Gospels, so that to move one of them seems to require moving the others also.

Where, then, may we suppose that K placed the whole of Matt. 9:1-17 = Mark 2:3-22? In Mark the three incidents follow Mark 1:40-45 = Matt. 8:1-4, and the latter is not early enough for our purposes. But just before that in Mark is Mark 1:39 = Matt. 4:23-24; and it turns out that, by placing Matt. 9:1-17 immediately after 4:24, we get an arrangement which fits every requirement of the problem: (a) it puts the call of Matthew before the designation of the Twelve; (b) it puts both of these at an early point, which is what Matt. 10:1 assumes; (c) it gives point to the fact that, in K, the Sermon on the Mount was addressed to the Twelve particularly; (d) it makes the Sermon's discussions of the Torah far more pertinent, since they are now preceded (as they are not in canonical Matthew) by incidents involving interpretation of the Law; and (e) it automatically puts K's story of the Gadarene demoniac just before the raising of Jairus' daughter, and that is the actual arrangement in Mark itself.

We therefore conclude that both canonical Gospels have displaced Matt. 9:1–17 = Mark 2:3–22 (item 7 above) but that only Matthew has displaced the list of the Twelve (item 8). The poor setting of the latter in Mark is not due to displacement but to Mark's having omitted subsequent matter from his source.

9. Matt. 10:17–20, (23) = Mark 13:9–12, (13). Mark puts this in the apocalyptic discourse. Matthew has it in the mission charge where, especially with 10:41, 42, it is related directly to the authority of the Twelve. This fits K's bias. Within the passage the order is the same in both Gospels except that Matthew appends 10:23 on going through the cities of Israel, while Mark inserts 13:10 on the gospel to the nations. The latter Matthew does have in the apocalyptic discourse, and there it falls in naturally, whereas in Mark it is an interruption. The facts that Matthew's arrangement fits K's viewpoint and that Mark 13:10 interrupts the passage as it stands in Mark, yet is at about the same point that Matthew puts it, suggest that Matt. 10:17 ff. has kept the K order.

10. Matt. 10:41, 42 vs. Mark 9:37b, 41. In Matthew these verses follow a long Q insertion and precede a transitional passage, 11:1. Note, however, that, if the Q insertion is removed, Matt. 10:41 follows readily on 10:17–23. Mark 9:37b and 41, respectively, introduce and conclude the story about John's question, and the latter is one of the most palpable of Mark's additions to his source. Plainly, therefore, the Markan verses cannot be in their original K position. Matthew's is far more likely to be the K order.

11. Matt. 13:12 is a general and frequently quoted saying of Jesus, which could fit many incidents. Here, however, it interrupts the close connection between 13:11 and 13. Mark 4:25 places the saying just before a parable, 4:26–29, which is peculiar to Mark and which may have been directed against the Judaizers.[3] It looks as though both Gospels have displaced the saying.

12. Matt. 15:3–6, 7–9 vs. Mark 7:6–7, 8–13. Here Matthew flows more smoothly, but Mark seems more natural and hence more primitive.

13. Matt. 15:29b, 31 vs. Mark 7:37; 8:1. Immediately before

3. Cf. above, p. 110.

this, Mark has a story peculiar to itself (7:32–35) which may very well have come from K. However, (*a*) Mark 7:36*b* is an obvious editorial comment, and possibly 7:36*a* is also. (*b*) This is at the feeding of the four thousand, which Matthew sets against a Jewish background but Mark against a gentile one. On both counts, Mark seems to have revised, and this puts some weight on the side of the Matthean arrangement.

14. Matt. 17:12, 13 vs. Mark 9:12*b*, 13. The Markan passages would themselves read better if reversed. Such roughness might be regarded as a sign of primitivity were it not that we already had reason to think that Mark revised this passage: This is where Matthew explicitly identifies John the Baptist as Elijah *redivivus* but Mark does not.[4] Hence the Markan order is more probably due to revision.

This analysis of Matthean versus Markan order has been done primarily in order to reconstruct K itself, but it likewise bears on the K hypothesis as a whole. Of the fourteen differences of arrangement in the two Gospels, both seem to have disarranged at least twice (7, 11), Matthew four other times (2, 6, 8, 12), Mark six (4, 5, 9, 10, 13, 14), while two (1, 3) are uncertain. Mark's dislocations seem to have been caused chiefly by omission of material from K. It is anything but clear that Mark is always more primitive than Matthew. The differences in order furnish one more area in which both Gospels have independently worked over a common source.

B. OTHER STRUCTURAL PROBLEMS

Matt. 2:1–12. It has been concluded that K probably opened with a genealogy and an Infancy section. It is highly doubtful, however, that it had the story of the magi. The chief interest of the story is Gentile, and its supernaturalism is of a type more appropriate to a later period. It will be omitted from the restoration.

Matt. 7:16 is probably from K, as we have seen,[5] but it is not certain just where it stood in the original. It will be kept in its

4. Cf. above, p. 95.
5. Above, p. 72.

present relative position only because there is no more obvious place for it.

Matt. 8:18 = Mark 4:35. The changes of order, proposed above, automatically put the following incident in the evening, just as Mark says it was.

Matt. 8:19a. It is uncertain whether this is a vestige of a lost K story or just the redactor's introduction to the following Q passage. It will be omitted from the restored text.

Matt. 11:1; Mark 6:12, 13, 30. The Markan verses make the smoother connection between the Mission Charge and the next K story on the plucking of grain. We cannot follow Mark, however, in placing the death of John the Baptist here. That would partly contradict Matt. 11:12, 14 which is K. More decisively, Mark has done much rearranging hereabouts.

Matt. 11:12,14 is buried in the midst of a Q context. It will be transferred to the nearest point in K where it makes a tolerable connection, viz., before Matt. 10:41. The connection would be smoother, but more startling, if it preceded 10:16b, or 10:23b!

Matt. 14:1, 2; Mark 6:14, 15. Mark 6:15 is thoroughly in the spirit of K. The Matthean compiler may have omitted it because of Matt. 16:14.

Matt. 14:14 = Mark 6:34. For Mark's "He began to teach them many things" K perhaps had a discourse which both canonical Gospels have left out. The best we can do now is to follow Mark.

Matt. 22:11–13 is omitted from the reconstruction. It might, however, be part of a K parable now lost.

Matt. 24:30. The words, "And then shall all the tribes of the earth mourn," recall Rev. 1:7 and may be redactorial. They will be kept in brackets.

C. PARTICULAR REFERENCES TO THE OLD TESTAMENT

Matt. 1:1–11. The Matthean genealogy omits the names of Ahaziah, Joash, Amaziah, and Jehoiakim (cf. I Chron. 3:10 ff.). The haplography would have been as easy for the author of K as for any later translator or copyist. Besides, the presence of these names would destroy the numerical symmetry of the list, whereas the stress on such symmetry (vs. 17) is characteristically Jewish. K probably resembled Matthew here.

Matt. 4:4 *et al.* In both Matthew and Mark, as we have seen,[6] Old Testament quotations on the lips of Jesus are closer to the LXX than are those used elsewhere. This is uniformly true of all the K material and so probably reflects the true character of the primitive translation. An Aramaic original would have followed the Hebrew more closely.

Matt. 21:7 = Mark 11:7. Matthew's "ass *and colt*" is due presumably to misinterpretation of the parallelism at Zech. 9:9. It is hard to say whether the mistake first occurred in canonical Matthew or was due to K's own love for the fulfilment of prophecies. The reconstruction will follow Mark, but with some doubt.

Matt. 27:35 = Mark 15:24. It seems strange that K should have missed the testimonium at Ps. 22:18 (cf. John 19:24), but there is no evidence that it had it.

D. TREATMENT OF SEMITIC TERMS

1. Mark often gives an expression both in its Semitic form and in Greek translation:

Mark 5:41. *Talitha cumi,* which is, being interpreted, Damsel, I say unto thee, arise.
7:11. *Corban,* that is to say, Given [to God].
7:34 *Ephphatha,* that is, Be opened.
9:43. . . . into *Gehenna,* into the unquenchable fire.
10:46. *Bartimaeus,* the son of Timaeus.
14:36. *Abba,* Father.
15:34. *Eloi, Eloi, lama sabachthani?* which is, being interpreted, My God, my God, why hast thou forsaken me?

Matthew does this only twice:

Matt. 1:23. *Immanuel,* which is, being interpreted, God with us.
27:46. *Eli, Eli, lama sabachthani?,* that is, My God, my God, why hast thou forsaken me?

Elsewhere Matthew gives either the Semitic term alone (5:22*a, c;* 16:17; 27:6) or the Greek alone (5:22*b;* 15:5; 18:8; 26:39).

Now, if Mark stood by itself, we might suppose that it depended directly on Aramaic K: At various points it clarified this

6. Above, pp. 90 ff.

for gentile readers, while at 5:41 and 7:34 the Aramaic was kept because of reverence for the exact words of healing. If Matthew stood alone, we might again suppose that it used the Aramaic K and that K itself had translated from Hebrew into Aramaic at 1:23 and 27:46. But when Matthew so often gives one or the other, and Mark so often gives both, it looks as though K, as it came to the canonical authors, did often have both the Semitic and the Greek forms. This again implies that K, as they knew it, was in a rough Greek rendering. An Aramaic original would have offered translations only at points like Matt. 1:23 and 27:46 where it used the Hebrew.

2. However, Mark does not translate *rabbi* (9:5; 14:45) or *rabboni* (10:51). Neither does Matthew usually (23:7, 8; 26:49), though twice it substitutes "Lord" (Matt. 17:4 = Mark 9:5; Matt. 20:33 = Mark 10:51). Doubtless "rabbi" was a sufficiently familiar term in the gentile world. When Jesus is called *Kurios* (Lord) or *Didaskalos* (Master/Teacher) in Matthew's K, these must often represent "Rabbi" in the original.

3. For Peter, James, etc., an Aramaic original would have had Cephas (*Kepha*), Jacob, etc. In an English restoration little would be gained by changing these famous names to their Semitic forms. The Greek forms will be kept.

E. PROBLEMS ABOUT PARTICULAR MIRACLES

Mark 5:1-20 = Matt. 8:28-34. For the "two" demoniacs of canonical Matthew the simplest explanation seems to be that the compiler thought them implied by the plurality of demons. It is difficult, however, to say how much of the Markan form of the story is really primitive and how much represents later elaboration. Any reconstruction can be regarded only as approximate.

Matt. 9:27 ff. Perhaps K told of one blind man, and the Matthean redactor changed it under his penchant for the number two. In the other instances (8:28 ff.; 21:2, 7), however, it is easy to conjecture a misunderstanding. Here there is little evidence to go on. The passage might be equivalent to Mark 8:22-26, but the latter reads far more like an allegory of Peter's Confession which immediately follows:

Mark 8:23–26	Mark 8:27–30
And he took hold of the blind man by the hand and brought him out of the village; and when he had spit on his eyes, and laid his hands upon him, he asked him,	And Jesus went forth, and his disciples, into the villages of Caesarea Philippi: and in the way he asked his disciples, saying unto them,
Seest thou aught? And he looked up, and said, I see men; for I behold them as trees, walking.	Who do men say that I am? And they told him, saying, John the Baptist: and others, Elijah but others, One of the prophets. And he asked them, But who say ye that I am?
Then again he laid his hands upon his eyes; and he looked stedfastly,	Peter answereth and saith unto him, Thou art the Christ.
and was restored, and saw all things clearly. And he sent him away to his home, saying, Do not even enter into the village.	And he charged them that they should tell no man of him.

The resemblances between these Markan passages can hardly be accidental. Since Mark's treatment of the disciples, and particularly of Peter, is nearly always different from K's, it is unlikely that Mark 8:22–26 is from K. Hence Matt. 9:27 ff. must be followed in the reconstruction, even with the "two."

Mark 7:32–37, on the healing of a deaf and dumb man, might be considered equivalent to Matt. 12:22, 23 on a blind and dumb man. From its location, however, the Markan passage is more likely to correspond to Matt. 15:30, 31. The latter likewise speaks of the blind and of the wonder of the people. The Matthean compiler will have followed his own bent in substituting many healings for the one of K and Mark.

Mark 9:14 ff. = Matt. 17:14 ff. Here, as with the Gadarene demoniac, it is hard to tell how much of Mark's story of the epileptic boy is primitive and how much represents later, Petrine reminiscence. Mark seems to have done *some* revising here.[7] Fur-

7. See above, pp. 95 and 180.

thermore, the Matthean form follows more closely the K pattern as seen in Matt. 8:5, 6, 13 and 15:21-28 (= Mark 7:24-30). So it seems better to follow Matthew in this story.

Mark 11:12-14, 20-24; Matt. 21:18-22. By allowing a whole day for the tree to wither, Mark's miracle seems slightly less heightened than that in Matthew. Mark's form was produced, however, by his rearrangement of incidents hereabouts.[8] Therefore in this instance the Matthean form does not involve a deliberate heightening.

F. MISCELLANEOUS CHOICES OF READING

1. In ancient, and particularly Semitic, storytelling direct quotation was easier and more natural than indirect. When Matthew and Mark differ in this respect, direct quotation is usually to be preferred.[9]

2. In forecasts of the Resurrection, expressions like "after three days" would have been difficult for early Christians, and they would readily change them to "the third day." A change in the contrary direction was extremely unlikely. The reading "three days" is always to be preferred.

3. Since Mark is disposed to explain, and sometimes modify, K's notes on geography and social customs, those in Matthew are generally preferable. But at Matt. 15:39 = Mark 8:10, "Magdalutha" seems to be the best name to account for both Mark's "Dalmanutha" and Matthew's "Magadan."

4. Mark 2:18 = Matt. 9:14. Mark's "they come" with an indefinite subject seems to be the original reading. The Matthean compiler evidently misunderstood the verb as referring to John's disciples. Similar misunderstandings elsewhere (e.g., at Matt. 9:29; 21:5) have produced more serious transformations of the K text. On the other hand, Mark's "and the Pharisees" seems to have been drawn back from the people's question.

Mark 9:41 = Matt. 10:42. "In the name that ye are Messiah's"

---

8. Cf. above, p. 179.

9. Where the two Gospels differ, a rough count shows Matthew giving direct quotation, Mark indirect, 14 times; while the reverse (Mark direct, Matthew indirect) occurs 10 times.

is literal. Matthew's smoother "in the name of a disciple" is a definite editorial improvement.

Mark 11:9, 10 = Matt. 21:9. The Markan form of the chant carries the more primitive eschatology, yet Matthew's "Son of David" is certainly in K's manner. It is likely that each Gospel has kept aspects of the K passage which the other has omitted.

Mark 15:9 = Matt. 27:17. The Markan form of Pilate's question seems to have been drawn back from 15:26. The Matthean form would suit Jewish sensibilities better and is like that preserved later in the Gospel according to the Hebrews.[10]

Mark 16:1, 2; Matt. 28:1. The puzzling words in Matthew seem to come from telescoping two distinct time notes in the source:

Matthew	Mark
Now late on the sabbath day	And when the sabbath was past Mary Magdalene, and Mary the mother of James, and Salome, bought spices, that they might come and anoint him.
as it began to dawn toward the first day of the week, came Mary Magdalene and the other Mary to see the sepulchre.	And very early on the first day of the week, they come to the tomb.

If K read "late on the sabbath day" (i.e., in the evening of the sabbath) it would be just like Mark to clarify it for gentile readers. Otherwise the Matthean compiler's revisions, throughout Matt. 28:1–5, make it much preferable to depend on Mark for the opening lines of the Resurrection story.

G. GENERAL PRINCIPLES

In the restored K text use is made, as hitherto, of both the Revised Versions of 1881 and 1901. Departures from these are sometimes necessary in order to bring out the full Jewishness of terms like *anomia, skandalizomai,* etc.

As between Matthew and Mark in parallel passages, the more Jewish Christian account is preferred to the less Jewish Christian, but the less miraculous to the more miraculous. The rougher language is preferred to the smoother *unless* the roughness seems

10. Jerome, *Comm. in Matth.* 27:16.

to have arisen from omission, rearrangement, or other revision. The longer or more redundant passage is ordinarily to be preferred, though here again caution is necessary. Mark's elaborations are often plainly due to gentile concerns and sometimes may have come from later, Petrine recollections. Similarly, Matthean expansions may sometimes have been inspired by the situation in the Church toward the close of the century.

These considerations make a choice difficult at times, and finality is not claimed for every reading here adopted. For the most part, however, the following is believed to be a dependable restoration of the K text, as this pulsates through canonical Mark and Matthew.

XIX

THE TEXT OF K[1]

Matt. 1:1. The book of the generation of Jesus the Messiah, the son of David, the son of Abraham. Abraham begat Isaac; and Isaac begat Jacob; and Jacob begat Judah and his brethren; and Judah begat Perez and Zerah of Tamar; and Perez begat Hezron; and Hezron begat Ram; and Ram begat Amminadab; and Amminadab begat Nahshon; and Nahshon begat Salmon; and Salmon begat Boaz of Rahab; and Boaz begat Obed of Ruth; and Obed begat Jesse; and Jesse begat David the king. And David begat Solomon of her that had been the wife of Uriah; and Solomon begat Rehoboam; and Rehoboam begat Abijah; and Abijah begat Asa; and Asa begat Jehoshaphat; and Jehoshaphat begat Joram; and Joram begat Uzziah; and Uzziah begat Jotham; and Jotham begat Ahaz; and Ahaz begat Hezekiah; and Hezekiah begat Manasseh; and Manasseh begat Amon; and Amon begat Josiah; and Josiah begat Jechoniah and his brethren, at the time of the removal to Babylon. And after the removal to Babylon, Jechoniah begat Shealtiel; and Shealtiel begat Zerubbabel; and Zerubbabel begat Abiud; and Abiud begat Eliakim; and Eliakim begat Azor; and Azor begat Sadoc; and Sadoc begat Achim; and Achim begat Eliud; and Eliud begat Eleazar; and Eleazar begat Matthan; and Matthan begat Jacob; and Jacob begat Joseph the husband of Mary, of whom was born Jesus who is called Messiah. So all the generations from Abraham unto David are fourteen generations; and from David unto the removal to Babylon fourteen generations; and from the removal to Babylon unto the Messiah fourteen generations.

Matt. 1:18. Now the generation of the Messiah was on this wise. When his mother Mary had been betrothed to Joseph, before they came together she was found with child of the Holy Spirit.

---

1. References at the head of each section show where the corresponding passage begins in Matthew or Mark.

And Joseph her husband, being a righteous man, and not willing
to make her a public example, was minded to put her away priv-
ily. But when he thought on these things, behold, an angel of the
Lord appeared unto him in a dream, saying, Joseph, thou son of
David, fear not to take unto thee Mary thy wife: for that which
is begotten in her is of the Holy Spirit. And she shall bring forth
a son; and thou shalt call his name Jesus; for it is he that shall
save his people from their sins. Now all this is come to pass, that
it might be fulfilled which was spoken by the Lord through the
prophet, saying,

> Behold, the maiden shall be with child,
>   and shall bring forth a son,
> And they shall call his name Immanuel;

which is, being interpreted, God with us. And Joseph arose from
his sleep, and did as the angel of the Lord commanded him, and
took unto him his wife; and knew her not till she had brought
forth a son: and he called his name Jesus.

Matt. 2:13. And an angel of the Lord appeareth to Joseph in a
dream, saying, Arise and take the young child and his mother,
and flee into Egypt, and be thou there until I tell thee: for Herod
will seek the young child to destroy him. And he arose and took
the young child and his mother by night, and departed into
Egypt; and was there until the death of Herod: that it might be
fulfilled which was spoken by the Lord through the prophet,
saying,

> Out of Egypt did I call my son.

But when Herod was dead, behold, an angel of the Lord appeareth in a dream to Joseph in Egypt, saying, Arise and take the
young child and his mother, and go into the land of Israel: for
they are dead that sought the young child's life. And he arose
and took the young child and his mother, and came into the land
of Israel. But when he heard that Archelaus was reigning over
Judaea in the room of his father Herod, he was afraid to go
thither; and being warned in a dream, he withdrew into the parts
of Galilee, and came and dwelt in a city called Nazareth; that it
might be fulfilled which was spoken through the prophets, that
he should be called a Nazorean.

Matt. 3:1; Mark 1:2. And in those days cometh John the Baptist, preaching in the wilderness of Judaea, saying, Repent ye; for the kingdom of heaven is at hand. For this is he that was spoken of through Isaiah the prophet, saying,

> The voice of one crying in the wilderness,
> Make ye ready the way of the Lord,
> Make his paths straight.

And there went out unto him all the country of Judaea, and all they of Jerusalem; and they were baptized of him in the river Jordan, confessing their sins. And John was clothed with camel's hair, and had a leathern girdle about his loins, and did eat locusts and wild honey. And he preached, saying, There cometh after me he that is mightier than I, the latchet of whose shoes I am not sufficient to stoop down and unloose. I baptized you with water; but he shall baptize you with the Holy Spirit.

Matt. 3:13; Mark 1:9. Then cometh Jesus from Galilee to the Jordan unto John, in order to be baptized of him. But John would have hindered him, saying, Comest thou to me? But Jesus answering said unto him, Suffer it now: for thus it becometh us to fulfil all righteousness. Then he suffereth him. And Jesus, when he was baptized, went up straightway from the water: and he saw the heavens rent asunder, and the Spirit as a dove descending upon him: and a voice came out of the heavens, saying,

> Thou art my Son,
> my Beloved in whom I am well pleased.

Matt. 4:1; Mark 1:12. Then the Spirit driveth him forth into the wilderness to be tempted of the Tempter. And he fasted forty days and forty nights, and he was with the wild beasts. And the Tempter came and said unto him, If thou art the Son of God, command that these stones become bread. But he answered and said, It is written,

> Man doth not live by bread alone,
> But by every word that proceedeth out of
> the mouth of God [doth man live].

Again he taketh him unto an exceeding high mountain, and sheweth him all the kingdoms of the world, and the glory of them; and he said unto him, All these things will I give thee, if thou wilt fall down and worship me. Then saith Jesus unto him, Get thee hence, Satan: for it is written,

>Thou shalt worship the Lord thy God,
>and him only shalt thou serve.

Then he leaveth him; and behold, angels came and ministered unto him.

Matt. 4:12; Mark 1:14. Now when he heard that John was delivered up, he withdrew into Galilee; and [leaving Nazareth] he came and dwelt in Capernaum, which is by the sea, in the borders of Zebulun and Naphtali: that it might be fulfilled which was spoken through Isaiah the prophet, saying,

>The land of Zebulun and the land of Naphtali,
>The way of the sea, beyond Jordan,
>Galilee of the nations,
>The people which sat in darkness
>Saw a great light,
>And to them which sat in the region and shadow
>   of death,
>To them did light spring up.

From that time began Jesus to preach, and to say, Repent ye; for the kingdom of heaven is at hand.

Matt. 4:18; Mark 1:16. And passing along by the sea of Galilee, he saw two brethren, Simon who is called Peter, and Andrew his brother, casting a net into the sea; for they were fishers. And he saith unto them, Come ye after me, and I will make you to become fishers of men. And straightway they left the nets, and followed him. And going on from thence he saw other two brethren, James the son of Zebedee, and John his brother, in the boat with Zebedee their father, mending their nets; and straightway he called them: and they left their father in the boat [with the hired servants] and went after him.

Matt. 4:23; Mark 1:39. And he went about in all Galilee, teaching in their synagogues, and preaching [the gospel of the kingdom] and casting out demons. And the report of him went forth into all Syria: and they brought unto him all that were sick, holden with divers diseases and torments, demoniacs, and epileptic, and palsied; and he healed them.

Matt. 9:2; Mark 2:3. And they come, bringing unto him a man sick of the palsy, borne of four. And Jesus seeing their faith saith unto the sick of the palsy, Child, be of good cheer; thy sins are forgiven. But there were certain of the scribes [sitting there, and] reasoning in their hearts, Why doth this man thus speak? he blasphemeth. And straightway Jesus, perceiving in his spirit that they so reasoned within themselves, saith unto them, Why reason ye these things in your hearts? Whether is easier, to say to the sick of the palsy, Thy sins are forgiven; or to say, Arise, and take up thy bed, and walk? But that ye may know that the son of man hath authority on earth to forgive sins (then saith he to the sick of the palsy), Arise, and take up thy bed, and go unto thy house. And he arose, and straightway took up the bed, and went forth before them all. But when the multitudes saw it, they were afraid, and glorified God, which had given such authority unto men.

Matt. 9:9; Mark 2:13. [And he went forth again by the sea side; and all the multitude resorted unto him, and he taught them.] And as he passed by from thence, he saw a man, called Matthew, sitting at the place of toll: and he saith unto him, Follow me. And he arose, and followed him. And it came to pass, that he was sitting at meat in his house, and many publicans and sinners sat down with Jesus and his disciples. [For there were many, and they followed him.] And the scribes of the Pharisees, when they saw that he was eating with the sinners and publicans, said unto his disciples, He eateth with publicans and sinners. And when he heard it, he saith unto them, They that are whole have no need of a physician, but they that are sick. But go ye and learn what this meaneth,

I desire mercy, and not sacrifice:

for I came not to call the righteous, but sinners.

Matt. 9:14; Mark 2:18. And John's disciples were fasting: and they come and say unto him, Why do John's disciples and the disciples of the Pharisees fast, but thy disciples fast not? And

Jesus said unto them, Can the sons of the bride-chamber fast, while the bridegroom is with them? [As long as they have the bridegroom with them, they cannot fast.] But the days will come, when the bridegroom shall be taken away from them, and then will they fast in that day. No man seweth a piece of un-dressed cloth on an old garment: else that which should fill it up taketh from the garment, and a worse rent is made. And no man putteth new wine into old wine-skins: else the wine will burst the skins, and the wine perisheth, and the skins: but they put new wine into fresh wine-skins [and both are preserved].

Matt. 4:25; Mark 3:7. And there followed him great multi-tudes from Galilee and Decapolis and Jerusalem and Judaea and beyond Jordan.

Matt. 5:1, 10:2; Mark 3:13. And seeing the multitudes, he goeth up into the mountain, and calleth unto him whom he himself would: and they went unto him. And he appointed twelve, that they might be with him, and that he might send them forth to preach [and to have authority to cast out demons]: the first, Simon, who is called Peter, and Andrew his brother; James the son of Zebedee, and John his brother; Philip, and Bartholomew; Thomas, and Matthew the publican; James the son of Alpheus, and Thaddaeus; Simon the Cananaean, and Judas Iscariot, who also betrayed him.

Matt. 5:2. And he opened his mouth and taught them, saying, Ye are the salt of the earth: but if the salt have lost its saltness, wherewith shall it be salted? it is thenceforth good for nothing, but to be cast out and trodden under foot of men. Ye are the light of the world: a city set on a hill cannot be hid. Even so let your light shine before men, that they may see your good works, and glorify your Father which is in heaven. Think not that I came to destroy the Law or the Prophets: I came not to destroy, but to fulfil. Whosoever therefore shall break one of these least commandments, and shall teach men so, shall be called least in the kingdom of heaven: but whosoever shall do and teach them, he shall be called great in the kingdom of heaven. For I say unto you, that except your righteousness shall exceed the righteous-ness of the scribes and Pharisees, ye shall in no wise enter into the kingdom of heaven.

Matt. 5:21. Ye have heard that it was said to them of old time, Thou shalt not kill; and whosoever shall kill shall be in danger of the judgment: but I say unto you, that every one who is angry with his brother shall be in danger of the judgment; and whosoever shall say to his brother, Raca, shall be in danger of the Sanhedrin; and whosoever shall say, Moreh, shall be in danger of Gehenna. If therefore thou art offering thy gift at the altar, and there rememberest that thy brother hath aught against thee, leave there thy gift before the altar, and go thy way, first be reconciled to thy brother, and then come and offer thy gift. Ye have heard that it was said, Thou shalt not commit adultery; but I say unto you, that every one that looketh on a woman to lust after her hath committed adultery with her already in his heart. And if thy right eye causeth thee to stumble, pluck it out, and cast it from thee: for it is profitable for thee that one of thy members should perish, and not thy whole body be cast into Gehenna. And if thy right hand causeth thee to stumble, cut it off, and cast it from thee: for it is profitable for thee that one of thy members should perish, and not thy whole body go into Gehenna. Again, ye have heard that it was said to them of old time, Thou shalt not forswear thyself, but shalt perform unto the Lord thine oaths: but I say unto you, Swear not at all; neither by the heaven, for it is the throne of God; nor by the earth, for it is the footstool of his feet; nor by Jerusalem, for it is the city of the great King. Neither shalt thou swear by thy head, for thou canst not make one hair white or black. Ye have heard that it was said, An eye for an eye, and a tooth for a tooth: but I say unto you, Resist not him that is evil: but whosoever smiteth thee on thy right cheek, turn to him the other also. And whosoever shall impress thee to go one mile, go with him two. Ye have heard that it was said, Thou shalt love thy neighbor, and hate thine enemy: but I say unto you, Love your enemies [that ye may be sons of your Father who is in heaven].

Matt. 6:1. Take heed that ye do not your righteousness before men, to be seen of them: else ye have no reward with your Father who is in heaven. When therefore thou doest alms, sound not a trumpet before thee, as the hypocrites do in the synagogues and in the streets, that they may have glory of men. Verily I

say unto you, They have received their reward. But when thou
doest alms, let not thy left hand know what thy right hand
doeth: that thine alms may be in secret: and thy Father who
seeth in secret shall recompense thee. And when ye pray, ye shall
not be as the hypocrites: for they love to stand and pray in the
synagogues and in the corners of the streets, that they may be
seen of men. Verily I say unto you, They have received their
reward. But thou, when thou prayest, enter into thine inner
chamber, and having shut thy door, pray to thy Father who is in
secret, and thy Father who seeth in secret shall recompense thee.
And in praying, use not vain repetitions, as the Gentiles do: for
they think that they shall be heard for their much speaking. Be
not therefore like unto them: for your Father knoweth what
things ye have need of, before ye ask him. And whensoever ye
stand praying, forgive, if ye have aught against any one; that
your Father also who is in heaven may forgive you your trespasses. Moreover when ye fast, be not, as the hypocrites, of a sad
countenance: for they disfigure their faces, that they may be
seen of men to fast. Verily I say unto you, They have received
their reward. But thou, when thou fastest, anoint thy head, and
wash thy face; that thou be not seen of men to fast, but of thy
Father who is in secret: and thy Father, who seeth in secret, shall
recompense thee.

Matt. 6:19; 7:6. Lay not up for yourselves treasures upon the
earth, where moth and rust consume, and where thieves break
through and steal. Give not that which is holy unto the dogs,
neither cast your pearls before the swine, lest haply they trample
them under their feet, and turn and rend you. Beware of false
prophets, who come to you in sheep's clothing, but inwardly
are ravening wolves. By their fruits ye shall know them. [Do
men gather grapes of thorns, or figs or thistles?] Many will say
to me in that day, Lord, Lord, did we not prophesy by thy
name, and by thy name cast out demons, and by thy name do
many mighty works? And then will I profess unto them, I never
knew you; depart from me, ye that work lawlessness.

Matt. 7:28. And it came to pass, when Jesus ended these words,
they were astonished at his teaching. [And when he was come
down from the mountain, great multitudes followed him.] For

he taught them as one having authority, and not as their scribes.

Matt. 8:2; Mark 1:40. And there came to him a leper and worshipped him, saying, If thou wilt, thou canst make me clean. And he stretched forth his hand, and touched him, and saith unto him, I will; be thou made clean. And straightway the leprosy departed from him, and he was made clean. And he strictly charged him, and straightway sent him out, and saith unto him, See thou say nothing to any man: but go thy way, show thyself to the priest, and offer the gift that Moses commanded, for a testimony unto them.

Matt. 8:5. And when he was entered into Capernaum, there came unto him a centurion, beseeching him, and saying, Lord, my child lieth in the house sick of the palsy, grievously tormented. And Jesus said unto the centurion, Go thy way; as thou hast believed, so be it unto thee. And the child was healed in that hour.

Matt. 8:14; Mark 1:29. And when Jesus was come into the house of Simon and Andrew, he saw Simon's wife's mother lying sick of a fever. And he came and took her by the hand, and raised her up; and the fever left her, and she arose, and ministered unto them. And when even was come,[2] they brought unto him all that were sick, and them that were possessed with demons. And he healed many that were sick with divers diseases, and cast out many demons: that it might be fulfilled which was spoken through Isaiah the prophet, saying,

> Himself took our infirmities,
> and bare our diseases.

Matt. 8:18; Mark 4:35. And on that day he said unto [his disciples], Let us go over unto the other side. And leaving the multitude, they take him with them, [even as he was,] in the boat. And other boats were with him. And there ariseth a great storm of wind, and the waves beat into the boat, insomuch that the boat was now filling. And he himself was asleep. And they came to him, and awake him, and say unto him, Save, [Rabbi,] we perish. And he arose, and rebuked the wind, and said unto

---

2. Note that in K, as here restored, the preceding healings have not violated the Sabbath. Contrast Mark 1:21–34.

the sea, Peace, be still. And the wind ceased, and there was a great calm. And he saith unto them, Why are ye fearful, O ye of little faith? And the men marvelled, saying, What manner of man is this, that even the winds and the sea obey him?

Matt. 8:28; Mark 5:1. And they came to the other side, into the country of the Gadarenes. And when he was come out of the boat, straightway there met him out of the tombs a man with an unclean spirit, who had his dwelling in the tombs: and no man could any more bind him, no, not with a chain; because that he had been often bound with fetters and chains, and the chains had been rent asunder by him, and the fetters broken in pieces: and no man had strength to tame him. And always, night and day, in the tombs and in the mountains, he was crying out, and cutting himself with stones. And when he saw Jesus from afar, he ran and worshipped him; and crying out with a loud voice, he saith, What have we to do with thee, thou Son of God? I adjure thee by God, torment me not. And he asked him, What is thy name? And he saith unto him, My name is Legion; for we are many. And he besought him much that he would not send them away out of the country. Now there was afar off from them a herd of many swine feeding. And they besought him, saying, If thou cast us out, send us away into the herd of swine. And he said unto them, Go. And the unclean spirits came out, and went into the swine: and the whole herd rushed down the steep into the sea, and they were drowned in the sea. And they that fed them fled, and went away into the city, and told everything, and what was befallen to the demoniac. And they came to see what it was that had come to pass. And they come to Jesus, and behold the demoniac sitting, clothed and in his right mind, even him that had the legion: and they were afraid. And when they saw him, they besought him that he would depart from their borders. And he entered into a boat, and crossed over, and came into his own city.

Matt. 9:18; Mark 5:22. And there cometh one ruler, Jaïrus by name, and worshipped him, saying, My little daughter is at the point of death: I pray thee, that thou come and lay thy hands on her, that she may be saved, and live. And Jesus arose, and followed him, and so did his disciples. And a woman, which had an issue of blood twelve years, and had suffered many things of many physicians, and had spent all that she had, and was nothing bettered, but rather grew worse, having heard the things concerning Jesus, came in the crowd behind, and touched his garment. For she said, If I touch but his garments, I shall be made whole. And straightway Jesus, perceiving in himself that the power from him had gone forth, turned him about in the crowd, and said, Who touched my garments? And he looked round about to see her that had done this thing. But the woman fearing and trembling, knowing what had been done to her, came and fell down before him, and told him all the truth. And he said unto her, Daughter, thy faith hath saved thee; go in peace, and be whole of thy scourge. And the woman was made whole from that hour. And they come from the ruler of the synagogue's house, saying, Thy daughter is dead: why troublest thou the Master any further? But Jesus, overhearing the word spoken, saith unto the ruler, Fear not, only believe. And they come to the ruler's house, and he saw the flute-players, and the crowd making a tumult. And when he was entered in, he saith unto them, Why make ye a tumult, and weep? the child is not dead, but sleepeth. And they laughed him to scorn. But he, having put them all forth, taketh the father of the child and her mother and them that were with him, and goeth in where the child was. And taking the child by the hand, he saith unto her, [Talitha cumi; which is, being interpreted,] Damsel, I say unto thee, Arise. And straightway the damsel arose, and walked; for she was twelve years old. And they were amazed straightway with a great amazement. And the fame hereof went forth into all that land.

Matt. 9:27. And as Jesus passed by from thence, two blind men followed him, crying out, and saying, Have mercy on us, thou son of David. And when he was come into the house, the blind men came to him: and Jesus saith unto them, Believe ye that I am able to do this? They say unto him, Yea, Lord. Then touched he their eyes, saying, According to your faith be it done unto you. And their eyes were opened. And Jesus strictly charged them, saying, See that no man know it. But they went forth, and spread abroad his fame in all that land.

Matt. 9:35; Mark 6:6b. And Jesus went about all the cities and the villages, teaching in their synagogues, and preaching the gospel of the kingdom [and healing all manner of disease and all manner of sickness]. But when he saw the multitudes, he was moved with compassion for them, because they were distressed and scattered, as sheep not having a shepherd. And he called unto him his twelve disciples, and gave them authority over unclean spirits, to cast them out. These twelve Jesus sent forth, and charged them, saying, Go not into any way of the Gentiles, and enter not into any city of the Samaritans: but go rather to the lost sheep of the house of Israel. Cleanse the lepers, cast out demons: freely ye received, freely give. Get you no gold, nor silver, nor brass in your purses; no wallet for your journey, neither two coats, nor shoes, nor staff. And he said unto them, Wheresoever ye enter into a house, there abide till ye depart thence. And whatsoever place shall not receive you, and they hear you not, as ye go forth thence, shake off the dust that is under your feet [for a testimony unto them].

Matt. 10:16b; Mark 13:9. Be ye wise as serpents, and harmless as doves. But beware of men: for they will deliver you up to the Sanhedrin, and in their synagogues they will scourge you; yea and before governors and kings shall ye be brought for my sake, for a testimony to them [and to the Gentiles]. But when they deliver you up, be not anxious how or what ye shall speak: for it shall be given you in that hour what ye shall speak. For it is not ye that speak, but the Spirit of your Father that speaketh in you. And brother shall deliver up brother to death, and the father his child: and children shall rise up against parents, and cause them to be put to death. And ye shall be hated of all men for my name's sake: but he that endureth to the end, the same shall be saved. For verily I say unto you, Ye shall not have gone through the cities of Israel, till the son of man be come. And from the days of John the Baptist until now the kingdom of heaven suffereth violence, and men of violence take it by force. And if ye are willing to receive it, this is Elijah, that is to come. He that receiveth a prophet in the name of a prophet shall receive a prophet's reward; and he that receiveth a righteous man in the name of a righteous man shall receive a righteous man's reward. For whosoever shall give you a cup of water to drink, in the name that ye are Messiah's, verily I say unto you, he shall in no wise lose his reward. And they went out, and preached that men should repent. And they cast out many demons, and anointed with oil many that were sick, and healed them.

Mark 6:30. And they gather themselves together unto Jesus; and they told him all things, whatsoever they had done, and whatsoever they had taught.

Matt. 12:1; Mark 2:23. And it came to pass, that he was going on the sabbath day through the grainfields; and his disciples began, as they went, to pluck the ears. But the Pharisees, when they saw it, said unto him, Behold, thy disciples do that which it is not lawful to do upon the sabbath. But he said unto them, Have ye not read what David did, when he was hungry, and they that were with him; how he entered into the house of God, and ate the showbread, which it was not lawful for him to eat, neither for them that were with him, but only for the priests? Or have ye not read in the Law, that on the sabbath day the priests in the temple profane the sabbath, and are guiltless? But I say unto you, that a greater thing than the temple is here. But if ye had known what this meaneth,

I desire mercy, and not sacrifice,

ye would not have condemned the guiltless. For the son of man is lord even of the sabbath.

Matt. 12:9; Mark 3:1. And he departed thence, and entered again into the synagogue; and there was a man there who had his hand withered. And they asked him, saying, Is it lawful to heal on the sabbath day? that they might accuse him. And he said unto them, [What man shall there be of you, that shall have one sheep, and if this fall into a pit on the sabbath day, will he not lay hold on it and lift it out? Wherefore] it is lawful to do good on the sabbath day. And when he had looked round about on them with anger, being grieved at the hardening of their heart, he saith unto the man, Stretch forth thy hand. And he stretched it forth; and his hand was restored. And the Pharisees went out, and straightway with the Herodians took counsel against him, how they might destroy him.

Matt. 12:15; Mark 3:9. And Jesus perceiving it withdrew from thence: and a great multitude followed him; and he healed many, and charged them that they should not make him known: that it might be fulfilled which was spoken through Isaiah the prophet, saying,

> Behold, my servant whom I have chosen;
> My beloved in whom my soul is well pleased:
> I will put my spirit upon him,
> And he shall declare judgment to the Gentiles.
> He shall not strive, nor cry aloud;
> Neither shall any one hear his voice in the streets.
> A bruised reed shall he not break,
> And smoking flax shall he quench,
> Till he send forth judgment unto victory.
> And in his name shall the Gentiles hope.

Matt. 12:22; Mark 3:22. Then was brought unto him one possessed with a demon, blind and dumb: and he healed him, insomuch that the dumb man spake and saw. And the multitudes were amazed, and said, Is this the son of David? And the scribes who came down from Jerusalem said, He hath Beelzebub, and, By the prince of the demons casteth he out the demons. And he called them unto him, and said unto them, How can Satan cast out Satan? And if a kingdom be divided against itself, that kingdom cannot stand. And if a house be divided against itself, that house will not be able to stand. And if Satan hath risen up against himself, and is divided, he cannot stand, but hath an end. But no one can enter into the house of the strong one, and spoil his goods, except he first bind the strong one; and then he will spoil his house. Verily I say unto you, All their sins shall be forgiven unto the sons of men, and their blasphemies wherewith soever they shall blaspheme: but whosoever shall blaspheme against the Holy Spirit hath never forgiveness, but is guilty of an eternal sin. And I say unto you, that every idle word that men shall speak, they shall give account thereof in the day of judgment. For by thy words thou shalt be justified, and by thy words thou shalt be condemned: [because they said, He hath an unclean spirit.]

Matt. 12:46; Mark 3:31. And there come his mother and his brethren; and standing without, they sent unto him, calling him.

And a multitude was sitting about him. And they say unto him, Behold, thy mother and thy brethren without seek for thee. And he answereth them, and saith, Who is my mother? and who are my brethren? And he stretched forth his hand towards his disciples, and said, Behold, my mother and my brethren! For whosoever shall do the will of my Father who is in heaven, the same is my brother, and sister, and mother.

Matt. 13:1; Mark 4:1. On that day went Jesus out of the house, and sat by the sea side. And there is gathered unto him a very great multitude, so that he entered into a boat, and sat in the sea; and all the multitude were by the sea on the land. And he spake to them many things in parables, saying, Hearken: Behold, the sower went forth to sow: and it came to pass, as he sowed, some seed fell by the way side, and the birds came and devoured it. And other fell on the rocky ground, where it had not much earth; and straightway it sprang up, because it had no deepness of earth: and when the sun was risen, it was scorched; and because it had no root, it withered away. And other fell among the thorns, and the thorns grew up, and choked it, and it yielded no fruit. And others fell into the good ground, and yielded fruit, growing up and increasing; and brought forth, thirtyfold, and sixtyfold, and a hundredfold. And he said, Who hath ears to hear, let him hear. And when he was alone, the disciples came, and said unto him, Why speakest thou unto them in parables? And he answered and said unto them, Unto you it is given to know the mysteries of the kingdom of heaven, but to them it is not given. For whosoever hath, to him shall be given, and he shall have abundance: but whosoever hath not, from him shall be taken away even that which he hath. Therefore speak I to them in parables; because seeing they see not, and hearing they hear not, neither do they understand. And unto them is fulfilled the prophecy of Isaiah, which saith,

> By hearing ye shall hear, and shall in no wise understand;
> And seeing ye shall see, and shall in no wise perceive:
> For this people's heart is waxed gross,
> And their ears are dull of hearing,
> And their eyes they have closed;

Lest haply they should perceive with their eyes,
And hear with their ears,
And understand with their heart,
And should turn again,
And I should heal them.

Hear then ye the parable of the sower. When any one heareth the word of the kingdom, and understandeth it not, then cometh the evil one, and snatcheth away that which hath been sown in his heart. This is he that was sown by the way side. And he that was sown upon the rocky places, this is he that heareth the word, and straightway with joy receiveth it; yet hath he not root in himself, but endureth for a while; and when tribulation or persecution ariseth because of the word, straightway he stumbleth. And he that was sown among the thorns, this is he that heareth the word; and the care of the age, and the deceitfulness of riches, choke the word, and he becometh unfruitful. And he that was sown upon the good ground, this is he that heareth the word, and understandeth it; who verily beareth fruit, and bringeth forth, some thirtyfold, some sixty, some a hundred. And he said unto them, Is the lamp brought to be put under the bushel, or under the bed, and not to be put on the stand? For there is nothing hid, save that it should be manifested; neither was anything made secret, but that it should come to light. [If any man hath ears to hear, let him hear.] And he said unto them, Take heed what ye hear: with what measure ye mete it shall be measured unto you: and more shall be given unto you.

Matt. 13:24; Mark 4:30. Another parable set he before them, saying, The kingdom of heaven is likened unto a man that sowed good seed in his field: but while men slept, his enemy came and sowed tares also among the wheat, and went away. But when the blade sprang up and brought forth fruit, then appeared the tares also. And the slaves of the householder came and said unto him, Sir, didst thou not sow good seed in thy field? whence then hath it tares? And he said unto them, A man, an enemy, hath done this. And the slaves say unto him, Wilt thou then that we go and gather them up? But he saith, Nay; lest haply while ye gather up the tares, ye root up the wheat with them. Let both

grow together until the harvest: and in the time of the harvest
I will say to the reapers, Gather up first the tares and bind them
in bundles to burn them; but gather the wheat into my barn.
Another parable set he before them, saying, How shall we liken
the kingdom of God? or in what parable shall we set it forth?
It is like a grain of mustard seed, which, when it is sown upon
the earth, though it be less than all the seeds that are upon the
earth, yet when it is sown, groweth up, and becometh greater
than all the herbs, and putteth out great branches; so that the
birds of the heaven can lodge under the shadow thereof.

Matt. 13:34; Mark 4:33. All these things spake Jesus in parables unto the multitudes; and without a parable spake he nothing
unto them: that it might be fulfilled which was spoken through
the prophet, saying,

> I will open my mouth in parables;
> I will utter things hidden from
> the foundation of the world.

Then he left the multitudes, and went into the house: and his
disciples came unto him, saying, Explain unto us the parable of
the tares of the field. And he answered and said, He that soweth
the good seed is the son of man; and the field is the world; and
the good seed, these are the sons of the kingdom; and the tares
are the sons of the evil one; and the enemy that sowed them is
the devil: and the harvest is the consummation of the age;[3] and
the reapers are angels. As therefore the tares are gathered up and
burned with fire; so shall it be in the consummation of the age.
The son of man shall send forth his angels, and they shall gather
out of his kingdom all things that cause stumbling, and them that
do lawlessness, and shall cast them into the furnace of fire: there
shall be weeping and the gnashing of teeth. Then shall the righteous shine forth as the sun in the kingdom of their Father. He
that hath ears, let him hear. The kingdom of heaven is like unto
a treasure hidden in the field; which a man found, and hid; and
for joy thereof he goeth and selleth all that he hath, and buyeth
that field. Again, the kingdom of heaven is like unto a man that
is a merchant seeking goodly pearls: and having found one pearl

3. Or *end of the world.*

of great price, he went and sold all that he had, and bought it.
Again, the kingdom of heaven is like unto a drag-net, that was
cast into the sea, and gathered of every kind: which, when it was
filled, they drew up on the beach; and they sat down, and gathered the good into vessels, but the bad they cast away. So shall it
be in the consummation of the age: the angels shall come forth,
and sever the wicked from among the righteous, and shall cast
them into the furnace of fire: there shall be the weeping and the
gnashing of teeth. Have ye understood all these things? They
say unto him, Yea. And he said unto them, Therefore every
scribe who hath been made a disciple to the kingdom of heaven
is like unto a man that is a householder, who bringeth forth out
of his treasure things new and old. And it came to pass, when
Jesus had finished these parables, he departed thence.

Matt. 13:54; Mark 6:1b. And he cometh into his own country.
And when the sabbath was come, he taught them in their synagogue: and many hearing him were astonished, saying, Whence
hath this man these things? and, What is the wisdom that is given
unto this man, and such mighty works wrought by his hands?
Is not this the carpenter's son? is not his mother called Mary?
and his brethren, James, and Joseph, and Simon, and Judas? And
his sisters, are they not all with us? And they were offended
in him. And Jesus said unto them, A prophet is not without
honor, save in his own country, and in his own house. And he
could there do no mighty work, save that he laid his hands on a
few sick fold, and healed them. And he marvelled because of
their unbelief.

Matt. 14:1; Mark 6:14. And Herod the tetrarch heard of him;
for his name had become known: and he said, John the Baptist
is risen from the dead, and therefore do these powers work in
him. But others said, It is Elijah. And others, A prophet, even
as one of the prophets. But Herod, when he heard of him, said,
John, whom I beheaded, he is risen. For Herod himself had sent
forth and laid hold upon John, and bound him in prison for the
sake of Herodias, his brother Philip's wife; for he had married
her. For John said unto Herod, It is not lawful for thee to have
thy brother's wife. And Herodias set herself against him, and
desired to kill him; and she could not; for Herod feared John,

knowing that he was a righteous and holy man, and kept him safe. And when he heard him, he was much perplexed; and he heard him gladly. And when a convenient day was come, that Herod on his birthday made a supper to his lords, and the chiliarchs, and the chief men of Galilee; and when the daughter of Herodias herself came in and danced, she pleased Herod and them that sat at meat with him; and he said unto the damsel, Ask of me whatsoever thou wilt, and I will give it thee. And he sware unto her, Whatsoever thou shalt ask of me, I will give it thee, unto the half of my kingdom. And she went out, and said unto her mother, What shall I ask? And she said, The head of John the Baptist. And she came in straightway with haste and asked, saying, I will that thou forthwith give me on a platter the head of John the Baptist. And the king was exceeding sorry; but for the sake of his oaths, and of them that sat at meat, he would not reject her. And straightway he sent forth a soldier of his guard, and commanded to bring his head: and he went and beheaded him in the prison, and brought his head on a platter, and gave it to the damsel; and the damsel gave it to her mother. And when his disciples heard thereof, they came and took up his corpse, and laid it in a tomb. And they went and told Jesus.

· *Matt. 14:13; Mark 6:32.* Now when Jesus heard it, he withdrew from thence in a boat, to a desert place apart: and when the multitudes heard thereof, they followed him on foot from the cities. And he came forth and saw a great multitude, and he had compassion on them, because they were as sheep not having a shepherd: and he taught them. And when even was come, the disciples came unto him, saying, The place is desert, and the time is already past; send them away, that they may go into the country and villages round about, and buy themselves somewhat to eat. But he answered and said unto them, They have no need to go away; give ye them to eat. And they say unto him, We have here but five loaves, and two fishes. And he said, Bring them hither to me. And he commanded them that all should sit down by companies upon the green grass. And they sat down in ranks, by hundreds, and by fifties. And he took the five loaves, and the two fishes, and looking up to heaven, he blessed, and brake, and gave the loaves to the disciples, and the disciples to the multitudes. And they did all eat, and were filled: and they took up that which remained over of the broken pieces, twelve baskets full. And they that ate the loaves were five thousand men. And straightway he constrained the disciples to enter into the boat, and to go before him unto the other side, till he should send the multitudes away. And after he had sent the multitudes away, he went up into the mountain apart to pray.

Matt. 14:23b; Mark 6:47. And when even was come, the boat was in the midst of the sea, and he alone on the land. And seeing them distressed in rowing, for the wind was contrary unto them, in the fourth watch of the night he cometh unto them, walking on the sea. And when the disciples saw him walking on the sea, they were troubled, saying, It is an apparition; and they cried out. For they all saw him, and were troubled. But he straightway spake with them, and saith unto them, Be of good cheer: it is I; be not afraid. And Peter answered him and said, Lord, if it be thou, bid me come unto thee upon the waters. And he said, Come. And Peter went down from the boat, and walked upon the waters, to come to Jesus. But when he saw the wind, he was afraid; and beginning to sink, he cried out, Lord, save me. And immediately Jesus stretched forth his hand, and took hold of him, and saith unto him, O thou of little faith, wherefore didst thou doubt? And when they were gone up into the boat, the wind ceased. And they that were in the boat worshipped him, saying, Of a truth thou art the Son of God.

Matt. 14:34; Mark 6:53. And when they had crossed over, they came to the land unto Gennesaret, and moored to the shore. And when they were come out of the boat, straightway the people knew him, and ran round about that whole region, and began to carry about on their beds those that were sick, where they heard he was. [And wheresoever he entered, into villages, or into cities, or into the country, they laid the sick in the marketplaces.] And they besought him that they might touch if it were but the border of his garment: and as many as touched were made whole.

Matt. 15:1; Mark 7:1. And there are gathered together unto him Pharisees, and certain of the scribes, who had come from

Jerusalem, and had seen that some of his disciples ate their bread with defiled hands. And they ask him, Why walk not thy disciples according to the tradition of the elders, but eat their bread with defiled hands? And he answered and said unto them, Why do ye also transgress the commandment of God because of your tradition? For God said, Honor thy father and thy mother: and, He that speaketh evil of father or mother, let him die the death. But ye say, Whosoever shall say to his father or his mother, That wherewith thou mightest have been profited by me is [Corban, that is to say,] given to God; he shall not honor his father. And ye have made void the word of God because of your tradition. Ye hypocrites, well did Isaiah prophesy of you, saying,

> This people honoreth me with their lips,
> But their heart is far from me.
> But in vain do they worship me,
> Teaching as their doctrines the precepts of men.

And he called to him the multitude again, and said unto them, Hear and understand: Not that which entereth into the mouth defileth the man; but that which proceedeth out of the mouth, this defileth the man. Then came the disciples, and said unto him, Knowest thou that the Pharisees were offended, when they heard this saying? But he answered and said, Every planting which my heavenly Father planted not, shall be rooted up. Let them alone: they are blind guides. And Peter answered and said unto him, Declare unto us the parable. And he said, Are ye also even yet without understanding? Perceive ye not, that whatsoever goeth into the mouth passeth into the belly, and is cast out into the draught? But the things which proceed out of the mouth come forth out of the heart; and they defile the man. For out of the heart come forth evil thoughts, murders, adulteries, fornications, thefts, false witness, blasphemies: these are the things which defile the man; but to eat with unwashen hands defileth not the man.

Matt. 15:21; Mark 7:24. And Jesus went out thence, and withdrew into the parts of Tyre and Sidon. And behold, a Canaanitish woman came out from those borders, and cried, saying,

Have mercy on me, O Lord, thou son of David; my daughter
is grievously vexed with a demon. But he answered her not a
word. And his disciples came and besought him, saying, Send
her away; for she crieth after us. But he answered and said,
I was not sent but unto the lost sheep of the house of Israel. But
she came and worshipped him, saying, Lord, help me. And he
answered and said, It is not meet to take the children's bread
and cast it to the dogs. But she said, Yea, Lord: for even the dogs
eat of the crumbs which fall from their masters' table. Then
Jesus answered and said unto her, O woman, great is thy faith:
be it done unto thee even as thou wilt. And her daughter was
healed from that hour.

Matt. 15:29; Mark 7:31. And Jesus departed thence, and came
nigh unto the sea of Galilee. And they bring unto him one that
was deaf, and had an impediment in his speech; and they beseech
him to lay his hand upon him. And he took him aside from the
multitude privately, and put his fingers into his ears, and he spat,
and touched his tongue; and looking up to heaven, he sighed,
and said unto him, [Ephphatha, that is,] Be opened. And his ears
were opened, and the bond of his tongue was loosed, and he
spake plain. And they were beyond measure astonished, saying,
He hath done all things well: he maketh even the deaf to hear
and the dumb to speak. And they glorified the God of Israel.

Matt. 15:32; Mark 8:1b. And he called unto him his disciples,
and saith unto them, I have compassion on the multitude, because they continue with me now three days, and have nothing
to eat: and I would not send them away fasting, lest haply they
faint in the way. And the disciples say unto him, whence shall
we be able to fill these men with bread here in a desert place?
And he saith unto them, How many loaves have ye? And they
said, Seven. And he commandeth the multitude to sit down on
the ground: and he took the seven loaves, and he gave thanks
and brake, and gave to the disciples, to set before them; and they
set them before the multitude. And they had a few small fishes:
and having blessed them, he commanded to set these also before
them. And they did eat, and were filled: and they took up that
which remained over of the broken pieces, seven baskets. And
they were about four thousand: and he sent them away. And

straightway he entered into the boat, and came into the borders of Magdalutha.

Matt. 16:1; Mark 8:11. And the Pharisees and Sadducees came, and tempting him asked him to show them a sign from heaven. But he answered and said unto them, An evil and adulterous generation seeketh after a sign; and there shall no sign be given unto it, but the sign of Jonah. [For as Jonah was three days and three nights in the belly of the sea-monster; so shall the son of man be three days and three nights in the heart of the earth.] And he left them, and again entering into the boat departed to the other side.

Matt. 16:5; Mark 8:14. And they forgot to take bread. [And they had not in the boat with them more than one loaf.] And he charged them, saying, Take heed and beware of the leaven of the Pharisees and Sadducees. And they reasoned among themselves, saying, We took no bread. And Jesus perceiving it saith unto them, O ye of little faith, why reason ye among yourselves, because ye have no bread? Do ye not perceive, neither remember the five loaves of the five thousand, and how many baskets ye took up? Neither the seven loaves of the four thousand, and how many baskets ye took up? How is it that ye do not perceive that I spake not to you concerning bread? Then understood they how that he bade them not beware of the leaven of bread, but of the teaching of the Pharisees and Sadducees.

Matt. 16:13; Mark 8:27. And Jesus went forth, and his disciples, into the parts of Caesarea Philippi: and in the way he asked his disciples, saying unto them, Who do men say that the son of man is? And they told him, saying, John the Baptist: and others, Elijah: and others, Jeremiah, or one of the prophets. He saith unto them, But who say ye that I am? And Simon Peter answereth and saith unto him, Thou art the Messiah, [the Son of the living God]. And Jesus answered and said unto him, Blessed art thou, Simon Bar-Jonah: for flesh and blood hath not revealed it unto thee, but my Father who is in heaven. And I also say unto thee, that thou art Peter;[4] and upon this rock[4] I will build my church; [and the gates of Hades shall not prevail against it.] I will give unto thee the keys of the kingdom

4. Aramaic *Kepha*.

of heaven: and whatsoever thou shalt bind on earth shall be bound in heaven: and whatsoever thou shalt loose on earth shall be loosed in heaven. Then charged he the disciples that they should tell no man that he was the Messiah.

Matt. 16:21; Mark 8:31. From that time began Jesus the Messiah to show unto his disciples, that he must go unto Jerusalem, and suffer many things of the elders and chief priests and scribes, and be killed, and after three days rise again. And Peter took him, and charging him saith, Be it far from thee, Lord: this shall never be unto thee. But he turned, and said unto Peter, Get thee behind me, Satan: thou art a stumbling-block unto me: for thou mindest not the things of God, but the things of men. Then said Jesus unto his disciples, If any man would come after me, let him deny himself, and take up his cross, and follow me. For whosoever would save his life shall lose it: and whosoever shall lose his life for my sake shall find it. For what shall a man be profited, if he shall gain the whole world, and forfeit his life? or what shall a man give in exchange for his life? For whosoever shall be ashamed of me and of my words in this adulterous and sinful generation, the son of man also shall be ashamed of him when he cometh in the glory of his Father with the holy angels. Verily I say unto you, There be some of them that stand here, who shall in no wise taste of death, till they see the son of man coming in his kingdom.

Matt. 17:1; Mark 9:2. And after six days Jesus taketh with him Peter, and James, and John his brother, and bringeth them up into a high mountain apart by themselves: and he was transfigured before them: and his garments became glistering, exceeding white; so as no fuller on earth can whiten them. And there appeared unto them Elijah with Moses: and they were talking with Jesus. And Peter answered and said unto Jesus, Rabbi, it is good for us to be here: if thou wilt, I will make here three tabernacles; one for thee, and one for Moses, and one for Elijah. While he was yet speaking, behold, a bright cloud overshadowed them: and behold, a voice out of the cloud, saying, This is my beloved Son, in whom I am well pleased; hear ye him. And when the disciples heard it, they fell on their face, and were sore afraid. [And Jesus came and touched them and said, Arise, and be not afraid.] And suddenly looking round about, they saw no one any more, save Jesus only with themselves. And as they were coming down from the mountain, Jesus commanded them, saying, Tell the vision to no man, until the son of man be risen from the dead. And his disciples asked him, saying, Why then say the scribes that Elijah must first come? And he answered and said, Elijah indeed cometh, and shall restore all things: and how is it written of the son of man, that he should suffer many things and be set at nought? But I say unto you, that Elijah is come already, and they knew him not, but have also done unto him whatsoever they listed [even as it is written of him]. Then understood the disciples that he spake unto them of John the Baptist.

Matt. 17:14; Mark 9:14. And when they were come to the multitude, there came to him a man, kneeling to him, and saying, Lord, have mercy on my son: for he is epileptic, and suffereth grievously; for oft-times he falleth into the fire, and oft-times into the water. And I brought him to thy disciples, and they could not cure him. And Jesus answered and said, O faithless and perverse generation, how long shall I be with you? how long shall I bear with you? bring him hither to me. And Jesus rebuked him, saying, Thou dumb and deaf spirit, I command thee, come out of him, and enter no more into him. And the demon went out of him: and the boy was cured from that hour. Then came the disciples to Jesus apart, and said, Why could not we cast it out? And he saith unto them, Because of your little faith: for verily I say unto you, If ye have faith as a grain of mustard seed, ye shall say unto this mountain, Remove hence to yonder place; and it shall remove; and nothing shall be impossible unto you. And he said unto them, This kind can come out by nothing, save by prayer [and fasting].

Matt. 17:22; Mark 9:30. And while they abode in Galilee, he would not that any man should know it. For he taught his disciples, and said unto them, The son of man is delivered up into the hands of men, and they shall kill him; and when he is killed, after three days he shall rise again. And they were exceeding sorry.

Matt. 17:24. And when they were come to Capernaum, they

that received the half-shekel came to Peter, and said, Doth not your master pay the half-shekel? He saith, Yea. And when he came into the house, Jesus spake first to him, saying, What thinkest thou, Simon? the kings of the earth, from whom do they receive toll or tribute? from their sons, or from strangers? And when he said, From strangers, Jesus said unto him, Therefore the sons are free. [Simon said, Yea. Jesus saith, Therefore give thou also unto them as a stranger.]

Matt. 18:1; Mark 9:33. In that hour came the disciples unto Jesus, saying, Who then is greatest in the kingdom of heaven? And he called to him a little child, and set him in the midst of them, and said, Verily I say unto you, Except ye turn, and become as little children, ye shall in no wise enter into the kingdom of heaven. Whosoever therefore shall humble himself as this little child, the same is the greatest in the kingdom of heaven. And whoso shall receive one such little child in my name receiveth me: [and whosoever receiveth me, receiveth not me, but him that sent me;] but whoso shall cause one of these little ones that believe on me to stumble, it is profitable for him that a millstone such as is turned by an ass should be hanged about his neck, and he should be sunk in the depth of the sea. And if thy hand cause thee to stumble, cut it off: it is good for thee to enter into life maimed, rather than having thy two hands to go into Gehenna, [into the unquenchable fire;] and if thy foot cause thee to stumble, cut it off: it is good for thee to enter into life halt, rather than having thy two feet to be cast into Gehenna. And if thine eye causeth thee to stumble, pluck it out, and cast it from thee: it is good for thee to enter into life with one eye, rather than having two eyes to be cast into Gehenna. See that ye despise not one of these little ones; for I say unto you, that in heaven their angels do always behold the face of my Father who is in heaven.

Matt. 18:15. And if thy brother sin against thee, go, show him his fault between thee and him alone: if he hear thee, thou hast gained thy brother. But if he hear not, take with thee one or two more, that at the mouth of two witnesses or three every word may be established. And if he refuse to hear them, tell it unto the congregation: and if he refuse to hear the congregation also,

let him be unto thee as the Gentile and the publican. Verily
I say unto you, What things soever ye shall bind on earth shall
be bound in heaven; and what things soever ye shall loose on
earth shall be loosed in heaven. Again I say unto you, that if two
of you shall agree on earth as touching anything that they shall
ask, it shall be done for them of my Father who is in heaven.
For where two or three are gathered together in my name, there
am I in the midst of them.

Matt. 18:21. Then came Peter and said to him, Lord, how oft
shall my brother sin against me, and I forgive him? until seven
times? Jesus saith unto him, I say not unto thee, Until seven
times; but, Until seventy times [and] seven. Therefore is the
kingdom of heaven likened unto a certain king, who would
make a reckoning with his slaves. And when he had begun to
reckon, one was brought unto him, that owed him ten thousand
talents. But forasmuch as he had not wherewith to pay, his lord
commanded him to be sold, and his wife, and children, and all
that he had, and payment to be made. The slave therefore fell
down and worshipped him, saying, Lord, have patience with me,
and I will pay thee all. And the lord of that slave, being moved
with compassion, released him, and forgave him the loan. But
that slave went out, and found one of his fellow-slaves, who
owed him a hundred denarii: and he laid hold on him, and took
him by the throat, saying, Pay what thou owest. So his fellow-
slave fell down and besought him, saying, Have patience with
me, and I will pay thee. And he would not: but went and cast
him into prison, till he should pay that which was due. So when
his fellow-slaves saw what was done, they were exceeding sorry,
and came and told unto their lord all that was done. Then his
lord called him unto him, and saith to him, Thou wicked slave,
I forgave thee all that debt, because thou besoughtest me: shouldest not thou also have had mercy on thy fellow-slave, even as I
had mercy on thee? And his lord was wroth, and delivered him
to the tormentors, till he should pay all that was due. So shall
also my heavenly Father do unto you, if ye forgive not every
one his brother from your hearts.

Matt. 19:1; Mark 10:1. And it came to pass when Jesus had
finished these words, he departed from Galilee, and came into

the borders of Judaea beyond Jordan; and great multitudes followed him; and he taught them again. And there came unto him
Pharisees, tempting him, and saying, Is it lawful for a man to
put away his wife for every cause? And he answered and said
unto them, Have ye not read that he which made them from
the beginning made them male and female, and said, For this
cause shall a man leave his father and mother, and shall cleave
to his wife; and the two shall become one flesh? So that they
are no more two, but one flesh. What therefore God hath joined
together, let not man put asunder. They say unto him, Why
then did Moses command to give a bill of divorcement, and to
put her away? He saith unto them, Moses for your hardness of
heart suffered you to put away your wives: but from the beginning it hath not been so. And he said to them, Whosoever shall
put away his wife, [except for fornication,] and shall marry
another, committeth adultery: and he that marrieth her when she
is put away committeth adultery. The disciples say unto him, If
the case of the man is so with his wife, it is not expedient to marry.
But he said unto them, All men cannot receive this saying, but
they to whom it is given. For there are eunuchs, who were so
born from their mother's womb: and there are eunuchs, who
were made eunuchs by men: and there are eunuchs, who made
themselves eunuchs for the kingdom of heaven's sake. He that
is able to receive it, let him receive it.

Matt. 19:13; Mark 10:13. Then were there brought unto him
little children, that he should lay his hands on them, and pray:
and the disciples rebuked them. But Jesus said, Suffer the little
children, and forbid them not, to come unto me: for of such
is the kingdom of heaven. And he took them in his arms, and
blessed them, laying his hands upon them.

Matt. 19:16; Mark 10:17. And as he was going forth into the
way, there ran one to him, and kneeled to him, and asked him,
Good Master, what shall I do that I may inherit eternal life?
And Jesus said unto him, Why callest thou me good? none is
good save one, even God. But if thou wouldest enter into life,
keep the commandments. He saith unto him, Which? And Jesus
said, Thou shalt not kill, Thou shalt not commit adultery, Thou
shalt not steal, Thou shalt not bear false witness, Honor thy

father and thy mother: and, Thou shalt love thy neighbor as thyself. And he said unto him, Master, all these things have I observed from my youth: what lack I yet? And Jesus looking upon him loved him, and said unto him, One thing thou lackest: go, sell whatsoever thou hast, and give to the poor, and thou shalt have treasure in heaven: and come, follow me. But his countenance fell at the saying, and he went away sorrowful: for he was one that had great possessions. And Jesus looked round about, and saith unto his disciples, How hardly shall they that have riches enter into the kingdom of heaven! And he saith unto them, It is easier for a camel to go through a needle's eye, than for a rich man to enter into the kingdom of God. And when the disciples heard it, they were astonished exceedingly, saying, Who then can be saved? And Jesus looking upon them saith, With men this is impossible, but not with God: for all things are possible with God. Then answered Peter and said unto him, Lo, we have left all, and followed thee; what then shall we have? Jesus said, Verily I say unto you, There is no man that hath left house, or brethren, or sisters, or mother, or father, or children, or lands, for my sake, and for the gospel's sake, but he shall receive a hundredfold now in this time, houses, and brethren, and sisters, and mothers, and children, and lands, [with persecutions,] and in the age to come eternal life. But many that are first shall be last; and the last first.

Matt. 20:1. For the kingdom of heaven is like unto a man that was a householder, who went out early in the morning to hire laborers into his vineyard. And when he had agreed with the laborers for a denarius a day, he sent them into his vineyard. And he went out about the third hour, and saw others standing in the marketplace idle; and to them he said, Go ye also into the vineyard, and whatsoever is right I will give you. And they went their way. Again he went out about the sixth and the ninth hour, and did likewise. And about the eleventh hour he went out, and found others standing; and he saith unto them, Why stand ye here all the day idle? They say unto him, Because no man hath hired us. He saith unto them, Go ye also into the vineyard. And when even was come, the lord of the vineyard saith unto his steward, Call the laborers, and pay them their hire, beginning from the last unto the first. [So the last shall be first, and the first last.]

Matt. 20:17; Mark 10:32. And they were in the way, going up to Jerusalem; and Jesus was going before them. And he took the twelve disciples apart, and said unto them, Behold, we go up to Jerusalem; and the son of man shall be delivered unto the chief priests and scribes; and they shall condemn him to death, and shall deliver him unto the Gentiles to mock, and to scourge, and to crucify: and after three days he shall rise again.

Matt. 20:20; Mark 10:35. Then came the mother of the sons of Zebedee with her sons, worshipping him, and asking a certain thing of him. And he said unto her, What wouldest thou? She saith unto him, Command that these my two sons may sit, one on thy right hand, and one on thy left hand, in thy kingdom. But Jesus answered and said, Ye know not what ye ask. Are ye able to drink the cup that I drink? [or to be baptized with the baptism that I am baptized with?] And they say unto him, We are able. And he saith unto them, The cup that I drink ye shall drink [and with the baptism that I am baptized withal shall ye be baptized]: but to sit on my right hand or on my left hand is not mine to give: but it is for them for whom it hath been prepared [of my Father]. And when the ten heard it, they were moved with indignation concerning the two brethren. And Jesus called them unto him, and saith unto them, Ye know that the rulers of the Gentiles lord it over them, and their great ones exercise authority over them. Not so shall it be among you: but whosoever would become great among you shall be your servant; and whosoever would be first among you shall be your slave. For verily the son of man came not to be ministered unto, but to minister, and to give his life a ransom for many.

Matt. 20:29; Mark 10:46. And they come to Jericho: and as he went out from Jericho, with his disciples and a great multitude, [the son of Timaeus,] Bartimaeus, a blind beggar, was sitting by the way side. And when he heard that it was Jesus the Nazorean, he cried out, saying, Jesus, thou son of David, have mercy on me. And many rebuked him, that he should hold his peace: but he cried out the more a great deal, Thou son of David, have mercy on me. And Jesus stood still, and said, Call ye him. And they call the blind man, saying unto him, Be of good cheer: rise, he calleth thee. And he, casting away his garment, sprang up, and came to Jesus. And Jesus answered him, and said, What wilt thou that I should do unto thee? And the blind man said unto him, Rabboni, that I may receive my sight. And Jesus said unto him, Go thy way; thy faith hath made thee whole. And straightway he received his sight, and followed him in the way.

Matt. 21:1; Mark 11:1. And when they drew nigh unto Jerusalem, and came unto Bethphage, unto the mount of Olives, then Jesus sent two disciples, saying unto them, Go your way into the village that is over against you: and straightway as ye enter into it, ye shall find a colt tied, whereon no man ever yet sat; loose him, and bring him. And if any one say unto you, Why do ye this? say ye, The Lord hath need of him; and straightway he will send him back hither. Now this is come to pass, that it might be fulfilled which was spoken through the prophet, saying,

> Tell ye the daughter of Zion,
> Behold, thy King cometh unto thee,
> Meek, and riding upon an ass,
> And upon a colt the foal of an ass.

And the disciples went away, and found a colt tied at the door without in the open street; and they loosed him. And certain of them that stood there said unto them, What do ye, loosing the colt? And they said unto them even as Jesus had said: and they let them go. And they bring the colt unto Jesus, and cast on him their garments; and he sat upon him. And many spread their garments upon the way; and others cut branches from the trees, and spread them in the way. And they that went before, and they that followed, cried, saying, Hosanna to the son of David: Blessed is he that cometh in the name of the Lord: Blessed is the kingdom that cometh, of our father David: Hosanna in the highest. And when he was come into Jerusalem, all the city was stirred, saying, Who is this? And the multitudes said, This is the prophet, Jesus, the Nazorean of Galilee.

Matt. 21:12; Mark 11:15. And he entered into the temple, and cast out all them that sold and bought in the temple, and overthrew the tables of the money-changers, and the seats of them that sold the doves. [And he would not suffer that any man should carry a vessel through the temple.] And he saith unto them, It is written,

> My house shall be called a house of prayer:

but ye make it a den of robbers. And the blind and the lame came to him in the temple: and he healed them. But when the chief priests and the scribes saw the wonderful things that he did, and the children that were crying in the temple and saying, Hosanna to the son of David; they were moved with indignation, and said unto him, Hearest thou what these are saying? And Jesus saith unto them, Yea: did ye never read,

> Out of the mouth of babes and sucklings thou
>   hast perfected praise?

And he left them, and went forth out of the city to Bethany and lodged there.

Matt. 21:18; Mark 11:12, 20. Now in the morning as he returned to the city, he hungered. And seeing a fig tree afar off having leaves, he came, if haply he might find anything thereon: and when he came to it, he found nothing but leaves [for it was not the season of figs].[5] And he answered and said unto it, No man eat fruit from thee henceforward for ever. And immediately the fig tree withered away. And when the disciples saw it, they marvelled, saying, Rabbi, behold, the fig tree which thou cursedst is withered away. And Jesus answering saith unto them, Verily I say unto you, If ye have faith, and doubt not, ye shall not only do what is done to the fig tree, but even if ye shall say unto this mountain, Be thou taken up and cast into the sea, it shall be done. Therefore I say unto you, All things whatsoever ye pray and ask for, believe that ye have received them, and ye shall have them.

Matt. 21:23; Mark 11:27. And when he was come into the temple, the chief priests and the elders of the people came unto him as he was teaching, and said, By what authority doest thou

---

5. It is hard to say whether the bracketed words stood in K or are a characteristic explanation by Mark for readers unfamiliar with Palestine. In the former case, the compiler of Matthew might have omitted them because of the psychological problem they raise.

these things? and who gave thee this authority? And Jesus answered and said unto them, I also will ask you one question, which if ye tell me, I likewise will tell you by what authority I do these things. The baptism of John, whence was it? from heaven or from men? And they reasoned with themselves, saying, If we shall say, From heaven; he will say unto us, Why then did ye not believe him? But if we shall say, From men; we fear the multitude; for all hold John as a prophet. And they answered Jesus, and said, We know not. He also said unto them, Neither tell I you by what authority I do these things. But what think ye? A man had two sons; and he came to the first, and said, Son, go work to-day in the vineyard. And he answered and said, I will not: but afterward he repented himself, and went. And he came to the second, and said likewise. And he answered and said, I go, sir: and went not. Which of the two did the will of his father? They say, The first. Jesus saith unto them, Verily I say unto you, that the publicans and the harlots go into the kingdom of God before you. For John came unto you in the way of righteousness, and ye believed him not; but the publicans and the harlots believed him: and ye, when ye saw it, did not even repent yourselves afterward, that ye might believe him.

Matt. 21:33; Mark 12:1. Hear another parable: There was a man that was a householder, who planted a vineyard, and set a hedge about it, and digged a winepress in it, and built a tower, and let it out to husbandmen, and went into another country. And when the season of the fruits drew near, he sent his slaves to the husbandmen, to receive his fruits. And the husbandmen took his slaves, and beat one, and killed another, and stoned another. And again he sent unto them another slave; and him they wounded in the head, and handled shamefully. And he sent another; and him they killed: and many others; beating some, and killing some. But afterward he sent unto them his son, saying, They will reverence my son. But the husbandmen, when they saw the son, said among themselves, This is the heir; come, let us kill him, and take his inheritance. And they took him, and cast him forth out of the vineyard, and killed him. When therefore the lord of the vineyard shall come, what will he do unto those husbandmen? They say unto him, He will miserably destroy those miserable men, and will let out the vineyard unto other husbandmen, who shall render him the fruits in their seasons. Jesus saith unto them, Did ye never read in the scriptures,

> The stone which the builders rejected,
> The same was made the head of the corner;
> This was from the Lord,
> And it is marvellous in our eyes?

And when the chief priests and the Pharisees heard his parables, they perceived that he spake of them. And when they sought to lay hold on him, they feared the multitudes, because they took him for a prophet. And Jesus answered and spake again unto them, saying, The kingdom of heaven is likened unto a certain king, who made a marriage feast for his son, and sent forth his slaves to call them that were called to the marriage feast. But they made light of it, and went their ways, one to his own farm, another to his merchandise: and the rest laid hold on his slaves, and entreated them shamefully, and killed them. But the king was wroth; and he sent his armies, and destroyed those murderers, and burned their city. For many are called, but few are chosen.

Matt. 22:15; Mark 12:13. Then went the Pharisees, and took counsel how they might ensnare him in his talk. And they send to him their disciples, with the Herodians. And when they were come, they say unto him, Master, we know that thou art true, and teachest the way of God in truth, and carest not for any one: for thou regardest not the person of men. Tell us therefore, What thinkest thou? Is it lawful to give tribute unto Caesar, or not? Shall we give, or shall we not give? But Jesus perceived their wickedness, and said, Why make ye trial of me, ye hypocrites? Show me the tribute money. And they brought unto him a denarius. And he saith unto them, Whose is this image and superscription? They say unto him, Caesar's. Then saith he unto them, Render therefore unto Caesar the things that are Caesar's; and unto God the things that are God's. And when they heard it, they marvelled, and left him, and went away. On that day there came to him Sadducees, they that say that there is no resurrection: and they asked him, saying, Master, Moses said, If a man die, having no children, his brother shall perform the duty of a husband's brother to his wife, and raise up seed unto his brother. Now there were with us seven brethren: and the first married and deceased, and having no seed left his wife unto his brother; in like manner the second also, and the third, unto the seventh. And after them all, the woman died. In the resurrection therefore whose wife shall she be of the seven? for they all had her. But Jesus answered and said unto them, Ye do err, not knowing the scriptures, nor the power of God. For in the resurrection they neither marry, nor are given in marriage, but are as the angels in heaven. But as touching the resurrection of the dead, have ye not read that which was spoken unto you by God, saying, I am the God of Abraham, and the God of Isaac, and the God of Jacob? God is not the God of the dead, but of the living. And when the multitudes heard it, they were astonished at his teaching.

Matt. 22:34; Mark 12:28. But the Pharisees, when they heard that he had put the Sadducees to silence, gathered themselves together. And one of them, a lawyer, asked him a question, trying him: Master, which is the great commandment in the Law? And he said unto him, The first is, Hear, O Israel; The Lord our God, the Lord is one: and thou shalt love the Lord thy God with all thy heart, and with all thy soul, and with all thy mind. This is the great and first commandment. And a second like unto it is this, Thou shalt love thy neighbor as thy self. On these two commandments the whole Law hangeth, and the Prophets.

Matt. 22:41; Mark 12:35. Now while the Pharisees were gathered together, Jesus asked them a question, saying, What think ye of the Messiah? whose son is he? They say unto him, Of David. He saith unto them, How then doth David in the Spirit call him Lord, saying,

> The Lord said unto my Lord,
> Sit thou on my right hand,
> Till I put thine enemies underneath thy feet?

If David then calleth him Lord, how is he his son? And no one was able to answer him a word, neither durst any man from that day forth ask him any more questions.

Matt. 23:1; Mark 12:38. Then spake Jesus to the multitudes and to his disciples, saying,[6] The scribes and the Pharisees sit on Moses' seat: all things therefore whatsoever they bid you, these do and observe: but do not ye after their works; for they say, and do not. But all their works they do for to be seen of men: for they make broad their phylacteries, and enlarge the borders of their garments, and love the salutations in the marketplaces, and chief seats in the synagogues, and chief places at feasts, and to be called of men, Rabbi. But be not ye called Rabbi: for one is your teacher, and all ye are brethren. And call no man your father on the earth: for one is your Father, he who is in heaven. Neither be ye called masters: for one is your master, the Messiah. But he that is greatest among you shall be your servant. [Woe unto you, scribes and Pharisees, hypocrites! for ye devour widows' houses, even while for a pretence ye make long prayers: therefore ye shall receive greater condemnation.] Woe unto you, scribes and Pharisees, hypocrites! for ye compass sea and land to make one proselyte; and when he is become so, ye make him twofold more a son of Gehenna than yourselves. Woe unto you, ye blind guides, who say, Whosoever shall swear by the sanctuary, it is nothing; but whosoever shall swear by the gold of the sanctuary, he is bound. Ye fools and blind: for which is greater, the gold, or the sanctuary that hath sanctified the gold? And, Whosoever shall swear by the altar, it is nothing; but whosoever shall swear by the gift that is upon it, he is bound. Ye blind: for which is greater, the gift, or the altar that sanctifieth the gift? He therefore that sweareth by the altar, sweareth by it, and by all things thereon. And he that sweareth by the sanctuary, sweareth by it, and by him that dwelleth therein. And he that sweareth by the heaven, sweareth by the throne of God, and by him that sitteth thereon. Ye blind guides, that strain out the gnat, and swallow the camel! Ye outwardly appear righteous unto men, but inwardly ye are full of hypocrisy and lawlessness. Ye serpents, ye offspring of vipers, how shall ye escape the judgment of Gehenna?

Mark 12:41. And he sat down over against the treasury, and beheld how the multitude cast money into the treasury: and

6. Note that the following discourse, like the Sermon on the Mount, follows immediately after incidents involving interpretation of the Torah.

many that were rich cast in much. And there came one poor widow, and she cast in two mites. And he called unto him his disciples, and said unto them, Verily I say unto you, This poor widow cast in more than all they that are casting into the treasury: for they all did cast in of their superfluity; but she of her want did cast in all that she had, even all her living.

Matt. 24:1; Mark 13:1. And he went out from the temple, and was going on his way; and his disciples came to him to show him the buildings of the temple. And he answered and said unto them, See ye not all these things? verily I say unto you, There shall not be left here one stone upon another, that shall not be thrown down. And as he sat on the mount of Olives, the disciples came unto him privately, saying, Tell us, when shall these things be? and what is the sign when these things are all about to be accomplished? And Jesus answered and said unto them, Take heed that no man lead you astray. For many shall come in my name, saying, I am the Messiah; and shall lead many astray. And ye shall hear of wars and rumors of wars: see that ye be not troubled: for these things must needs come to pass; but the end is not yet. For nation shall rise against nation, and kingdom against kingdom: and there shall be famines and earthquakes in divers places. But all these things are the beginning of travail. Then shall they deliver you up unto tribulation, and shall kill you: and ye shall be hated of all the Gentiles for my name's sake. And then shall many stumble, and shall deliver up one another, and shall hate one another. And many false prophets shall arise, and shall lead many astray. And because lawlessness shall be multiplied, the love of the many shall wax cold. But he that endureth to the end, the same shall be saved. And this gospel of the kingdom shall be preached in the whole inhabited earth for a testimony unto all the Gentiles; and then shall the end come. When therefore ye see the abomination of desolation, which was spoken of through Daniel the prophet, standing in a holy place (let him that readeth understand), then let them that are in Judaea flee unto the mountains: and let him that is on the housetop not go down [nor enter in] to take out the things that are in his house: and let him that is in the field not return back to take his cloak. But woe unto them that are with child and to

them that give suck in those days! And pray ye that your flight
be not in the winter, neither on a sabbath. For then shall be
tribulation, such as there hath not been the like from the beginning of the creation which God created until now, and never
shall be. And except the Lord had shortened the days, no flesh
would have been saved: but for the elect's sake, whom he chose,
he shortened the days.

Matt. 24:23; Mark 13:21. Then if any man shall say unto you,
Lo, here is the Messiah, or, Lo, here; believe him not. For there
shall arise false Messiahs, and false prophets, and shall show great
signs and wonders; that they may lead astray, if possible, even
the elect. But take ye heed: behold, I have told you beforehand.
But in those days, after that tribulation, the sun shall be dark-
ened, and the moon shall not give her light, and the stars shall be
falling from heaven, and the powers that are in the heavens shall
be shaken: and then shall appear the sign of the son of man in
heaven: and then [shall all the tribes of the earth mourn, and]
they shall see the son of man coming on the clouds of heaven
with power and great glory. And he shall send forth his angels
[with a great sound of a trumpet], and they shall gather together
his elect from the four winds, from one end of heaven to the
other. Now from the fig tree learn her parable: when her branch
is now become tender, and putteth forth its leaves, ye know
that the summer is nigh; even so ye also, when ye see these
things coming to pass, know ye that he is nigh, even at the doors.
Verily I say unto you, This generation shall not pass away, until
all these things be accomplished. Heaven and earth shall pass
away: but my words shall not pass away. But of that day or that
hour knoweth no one, not even the angels in heaven, neither the
Son, but the Father.

Matt. 25:1; Mark 13:33. Then shall the kingdom of heaven be
likened unto ten virgins, who took their lamps, and went forth
to meet the bridegroom. And five of them were foolish, and five
were wise. For the foolish, when they took their lamps, took no
oil with them: but the wise took oil in their vessels with their
lamps. Now while the bridegroom tarried, they all slumbered
and slept. But at midnight there is a cry, Behold, the bridegroom! Come ye forth to meet him. Then all those virgins arose,

and trimmed their lamps. And the foolish said unto the wise, Give us of your oil; for our lamps are going out. But the wise answered, saying, Peradventure there will not be enough for us and you: go ye rather to them that sell, and buy for yourselves. And while they went away to buy, the bridegroom came; and they that were ready went in with him to the marriage feast: and the door was shut. Afterward came also the other virgins, saying, Lord, Lord, open to us. But he answered and said, Verily I say unto you, I know you not. Watch therefore, for ye know not the day nor the hour. For it is as when a man, sojourning in another country, having left his house, and given authority to his slaves, to each one his work, commanded also the porter to watch. Now after a long time the lord of those slaves cometh, and maketh a reckoning with them. Watch therefore: for ye know not when the lord of the house cometh.

Matt. 25:31. But when the son of man shall come in his glory, and all the angels with him, then shall he sit on the throne of his glory: and before him shall be gathered all the nations: and he shall separate them one from another, as the shepherd separateth the sheep from the goats: and he shall set the sheep on his right hand, but the goats on the left. Then shall the King say unto them on his right hand, Come, ye blessed of my Father, inherit the kingdom prepared for you from the foundation of the world. Then shall he say also unto them on the left hand, Depart from me, ye cursed, into the eternal fire which is prepared for the devil and his angels. And these shall go away into eternal punishment: but the righteous into eternal life.

Matt. 26:1; Mark 14:1. And it came to pass, when Jesus had finished all these words, he said unto his disciples, Ye know that after two days the passover cometh, and the son of man is delivered up to be crucified. Then were gathered together the chief priests, and the elders of the people, unto the court of the high priest, who was called Caiaphas; and they took counsel together that they might take Jesus by subtlety, and kill him. But they said, Not during the feast, lest a tumult arise among the people. And while he was in Bethany in the house of Simon the leper,[7]

7. As C. C. Torrey points out (*The Four Gospels* [2d ed.; 1947], p. 296), in an Aramaic original the words for "leper" and "jar-merchant" would have had the same consonants.

as he sat at meat, there came a woman having an alabaster jar of ointment of pistic nard very costly; and she brake the jar, and poured it over his head. But there were some[8] that had indignation among themselves, saying, To what purpose hath this waste of the ointment been made? For this ointment might have been sold for above three hundred denarii, and given to the poor. And they murmured against her. But Jesus said, Let her alone; why trouble ye her? she hath wrought a good work on me. For ye have the poor always with you, and whensoever ye will ye can do them good: but me ye have not always. She hath done what she could; she hath anointed my body beforehand for the burying. Verily I say unto you, Wheresoever this gospel shall be preached in the whole world, that also which this woman hath done shall be spoken of for a memorial of her. Then one of the twelve, who was called Judas Iscariot, went unto the chief priests, and said, What are ye willing to give me, and I will deliver him unto you? And they, when they heard it, were glad. And they weighed unto him thirty pieces of silver. And from that time he sought how he might conveniently deliver him unto them.

Matt. 26:17; Mark 14:12. And on the first day of unleavened bread the disciples came to Jesus, saying, Where wilt thou that we go and make ready that thou mayest eat the passover? And he said, Go into the city, and there shall meet you a man bearing a pitcher of water: follow him; and wheresoever he shall enter in, say to the goodman of the house, The Master saith, Where is my guest-chamber, where I shall eat the passover with my disciples? And he will himself show you a large upper room furnished and ready: and there make ready for us. And the disciples went forth, and came into the city, and found as he had said unto them: and they made ready the passover. And when even was come, he was sitting at meat with the twelve disciples; and as they were eating, he said, Verily I say unto you, that one of you shall betray me. And they were exceeding sorrowful, and began to say unto him every one, Is it I? And he answered and said, He that dipped his hand with me in the dish, the same shall betray me. The son of man goeth, even as it is written of him:

8. Matt. 26:8 says it was the disciples.

but woe unto that man through whom the son of man is betrayed! good were it for him if that man had not been born. And Judas, who betrayed him, answered and said, Is it I, Rabbi? He saith unto him, Thou hast said. And as they were eating, he took bread, and when he had blessed, he brake it, and gave to them, and said, Take ye: this is my body. And he took the cup, and gave thanks, and gave to them, saying, Drink ye all of it; for this is my blood of the [new] covenant, which is poured out for many unto remission of sins. But I say unto you, I shall not drink henceforth of this fruit of the vine, until that day when I drink it new with you in my Father's kingdom.

Matt. 26:30; Mark 14:26. And when they had sung a hymn, they went out into the mount of Olives. Then saith Jesus unto them, All ye shall be offended in me this night: for it is written,

I will smite the shepherd,
And the sheep of the flock shall be scattered abroad.

But after I am raised up, I will go before you into Galilee. But Peter answered and said unto him, If all shall be offended in thee, I will never be offended. Jesus said unto him, Verily I say unto thee, that this night, before the cock crow, thou shalt deny me thrice. Peter saith unto him, Even if I must die with thee, I will not deny thee. Likewise also said all the disciples.

Matt. 26:36; Mark 14:32. Then cometh Jesus with them unto an enclosed piece of ground called Gethsemane, and saith unto his disciples, Sit ye here, while I go yonder and pray. And he took with him Peter and the two sons of Zebedee, and began to be sorrowful and sore troubled. Then saith he unto them, My soul is exceeding sorrowful, even unto death: abide ye here, and watch with me. And he went forward a little, and fell on his face, and prayed, saying, [Abba,] Father, all things are possible unto thee; remove this cup from me: howbeit not what I will, but what thou wilt. And he cometh unto the disciples, and findeth them sleeping, and saith unto Peter, What, could ye not watch with me one hour? Watch and pray, that ye enter not into temptation: the spirit indeed is willing, but the flesh is weak. Again a second time he went away, and prayed, saying, My Father, if this cannot pass away, except I drink it, thy will be done. And he came again and found them sleeping, for their eyes were heavy. And he left them again, and went away, and prayed a third time, saying again the same words. Then cometh he to the disciples, and saith unto them, Sleep on now, and take your rest: behold, the hour is at hand, and the son of man is betrayed into the hands of sinners. Arise, let us be going: behold, he is at hand that betrayeth me.

Matt. 26:47; Mark 14:43. And straightway, while he yet spake, cometh Judas, one of the twelve, and with him a multitude with swords and staves, from the chief priests and elders of the people. Now he that betrayed him gave them a sign, saying, Whomsoever I shall kiss, that is he: take him, and lead him away safely. And when he was come, straightway he came to him, and saith, Rabbi; and kissed him. Then they came and laid hands on Jesus, and took him. And behold, one of them that were with Jesus stretched out his hand, and drew his sword, and smote the slave of the high priest, and struck off his ear. Then saith Jesus unto him, Put up again thy sword into its place: for all they that take the sword shall perish with the sword. Or thinkest thou that I cannot beseech my Father, and he shall even now send me more than twelve legions of angels? How then should the scriptures be fulfilled, that thus it must be? In that hour Jesus answered and said unto them, Are ye come out, as against a robber, with swords and staves to seize me? I was daily with you in the temple teaching, and ye took me not. But all this is come to pass, that the scriptures of the prophets might be fulfilled. Then the disciples left him, and fled.

Matt. 26:57; Mark 14:53. And they that had taken Jesus led him away to the house of Caiaphas the high priest, where the scribes and the elders were gathered together. But Peter followed him afar off, unto the court of the high priest, and entered in, and sat with the officers, to see the end. Now the chief priests and the whole Sanhedrin sought witness against Jesus, that they might put him to death; and they found it not. For many bare false witness against him, and their witness agreed not together. And there stood up certain, and bare false witness against him, saying, We heard him say, I will destroy this sanctuary that is made with hands, and in three days I will build another made without hands. And not even so did their witness agree together. And the high priest stood up in the midst, and asked Jesus, saying, Answerest thou nothing? what is it which these witness against thee? But he held his peace, and answered nothing. And the high priest said unto him, I adjure thee by the living God, that thou tell us whether thou art the Messiah, the Son of the Blessed. Jesus saith unto him, Thou hast said: nevertheless I say unto you, Henceforth ye shall see the son of man sitting at the right hand of Power, and coming on the clouds of heaven. Then the high priest rent his garments, saying, He hath spoken blasphemy: what further need have we of witnesses? behold, now ye have heard the blasphemy: what think ye? They answered and said, He is liable to death. Then did they spit in his face and buffet him: and some smote him with the palms of their hands, saying, Prophesy unto us, thou Messiah: who is he that struck thee?

Matt. 26:69; Mark 14:66. And Peter was sitting without in the court: and a maid came unto him, saying, Thou also wast with Jesus the Nazorean. But he denied before them all, saying, I know not what thou sayest. And when he was gone out into the porch, another maid saw him, and saith unto them that were there, This man also was with Jesus the Nazorean. And again he denied with an oath, I know not the man. And after a little while they that stood by came and said to Peter, Of a truth thou also art one of them; for thy speech maketh thee known. Then began he to curse and to swear, I know not the man. And straightway the cock crew. And Peter remembered the word which Jesus had said, Before the cock crow, thou shalt deny me thrice. And he went out, and wept bitterly.

Matt. 27:1; Mark 15:1. And straightway in the morning, all the chief priests and the elders of the people took counsel against Jesus to put him to death: and they bound him, and led him away, and delivered him up to Pilate the governor. Then Judas, who betrayed him, when he saw that he was condemned, repented himself, and brought back the thirty pieces of silver to the chief priests and elders, saying, I have sinned in that I betrayed innocent blood. But they said, What is that to us? see thou to it. And he cast down the pieces of silver into the sanctuary, and departed; and he went away and hanged himself. And the chief priests took the pieces of silver, and said, It is not lawful to put them into the sacred treasury,[9] since it is the price of blood. And they took counsel, and bought with them the potter's field, to bury strangers in. Wherefore that field was called, The field of blood, unto this day. Then was fulfilled that which was spoken through Jeremiah the prophet, saying,

> And I took the thirty pieces of silver,
>   the price of him that was priced,
> Whom they priced on the part of the sons of Israel;
> And I gave them for the potter's field,
>   as the Lord appointed me.

Now Jesus stood before the governor: and the governor asked him, saying, Art thou the King of the Jews? And Jesus said unto him, Thou sayest. And when he was accused by the chief priests and elders, he answered nothing. Then saith Pilate unto him, Hearest thou not how many things they witness against thee? And he gave him no answer, not even to one word: insomuch that the governor marvelled greatly.

Matt. 27:15; Mark 15:6. Now at the feast the governor was wont to release unto the multitude one prisoner, whom they would. And they had then a notable prisoner, called [Jesus] Barabbas.[10] When therefore they were gathered together, Pilate said unto them, Whom will ye that I release unto you? [Jesus] Barabbas, or Jesus who is called Messiah? For he perceived that for envy they had delivered him up. Now while he was sitting on the judgment-seat, his wife sent unto him, saying, Have thou nothing to do with that righteous man; for I have suffered many things this day in a dream because of him. But the chief priests and the elders stirred up the multitude, that he should rather release Barabbas unto them. And the governor answered and said unto them, Which of the two will ye that I release unto

9. Gr., *eis ton Korbanan;* cf. Matt. 15:5 = Mark 7:11.

10. The reading *Jesus Barabbas* occurs in Koridethi and a few other manuscripts. It is hard to see how such a name could have been preserved at all unless there were some primitive tradition behind it. In the Gospel according to the Hebrews the criminal's name was apparently Bar-Rabban (Jerome, *Comm. in Matth.*).

you? And they said, Barabbas. Pilate saith unto them, What then shall I do unto Jesus who is called Messiah? They all say, Let him be crucified. And he said, Why, what evil hath he done? But they cried out exceedingly, saying, Let him be crucified. So when Pilate saw that he prevailed nothing, but rather that a tumult was arising, he took water, and washed his hands before the multitude, saying, I am innocent of the blood of this righteous man; see ye to it. And all the people answered and said, His blood be on us, and on our children.[11] Then he released unto them Barabbas: and delivered Jesus, when he had scourged him, to be crucified. Then the soldiers of the governor took Jesus into the palace, and gathered unto him the whole band. And they stripped him, and put on him a scarlet robe. And they platted a crown of thorns and put it upon his head, and a reed in his right hand; and they kneeled down before him, and mocked him, saying, Hail, King of the Jews! And they spat upon him, and took the reed and smote him on the head. And when they had mocked him, they took off from him the robe, and put on him his garments, and led him away to crucify him.

Matt. 27:32; Mark 15:21. And as they came out they found a man of Cyrene coming from the country,[12] Simon by name: him they impressed to go with them, that he might bear his cross. And they bring him unto [the place Golgotha, which is, being interpreted,] The place of a skull. And they offered him wine to drink mingled with gall: and when he had tasted it, he would not drink. And they crucify him, and part his garments among them, what each should take. And it was the third hour, and they crucified him. And the superscription of his accusation was written over, The King of the Jews. Then are there crucified with him two robbers, one on the right hand, and one on the left. And they that passed by railed on him, wagging their heads, and saying, Ha! thou that destroyest the sanctuary, and buildest it in three days, save thyself: [if thou art the Son of God,] come

11. These terrible words might be thought to be a gentile addition. However, they do not condemn Jewish *Christians*, but only those who rejected Messiah. The cry itself is thoroughly Jewish.

12. For "Cyrenean" an Aramaic original may have read "farm laborer." It would have been easy to mistake an Aramaic letter *waw* for a *nun* in the primitive translation.

down from the cross. In like manner also the chief priests mocking him, with the scribes and elders, said, He saved others; can he not save himself? He is the King of Israel; let him now come down from the cross, and we will believe on him. He trusteth in God; let him deliver him now, if he desireth him. [For he said, I am the Son of God.] And the robbers also that were crucified with him cast upon him the same reproach.

Matt. 27:45; Mark 15:33. And when the sixth hour was come, there was darkness over the whole land until the ninth hour. And at the ninth hour Jesus cried with a loud voice, Eloi, Eloi, lama sabachthani? which is, being interpreted, My God, my God, why hast thou forsaken me? And some of them that stood there, when they heard it, said, This man calleth Elijah. And straightway one of them ran, and took a sponge, and filled it with vinegar, and put it on a reed, and gave him to drink. And the rest said, Let be; let us see whether Elijah cometh to take him down. And Jesus cried again with a loud voice, and yielded up his spirit. And the veil of the sanctuary was rent in two from the top to the bottom. And when the centurion, who stood by over against him, saw that he so [cried out and] gave up the ghost, he said, Truly this man was a son of God. And there were also women beholding from afar: among whom was Mary Magdalene, and Mary the mother of James and Joses, and the mother of the sons of Zebedee; who, when he was in Galilee, followed him, and ministered unto him; and many other women who came up with him unto Jerusalem.

Matt. 27:57; Mark 15:42. And when even was come, there came Joseph of Arimathea, a councillor of honorable estate, who also himself was looking for the kingdom of God; and he boldly went in unto Pilate, and asked for the body of Jesus. And Pilate marvelled if he were already dead: and calling unto him the centurion, he asked him whether he were already dead. And when he learned it of the centurion, he granted the corpse to Joseph. And Joseph took the body, and wrapped it in a clean linen cloth, and laid it in his own new tomb, which he had hewn out in the rock: and he rolled a great stone to the door of the tomb, and departed. And Mary Magdalene was there, and the other Mary, sitting over against the sepulchre.

Matt. 27:62. Now on the morrow, which is the day after the Preparation, the chief priests and the Pharisees were gathered together unto Pilate, saying, Sir, we remember that that deceiver said while he was yet alive, After three days I rise again. Command therefore that the sepulchre be made sure until the third day, lest haply his disciples come and steal him away, and say unto the people, He is risen from the dead: and the last error will be worse than the first. Pilate said unto them, Ye have a guard: go, make it as sure as ye can. So they went, and made the sepulchre sure, sealing the stone, the guard being with them.

Matt. 28:1; Mark 16:1. And in the evening of the sabbath, Mary Magdalene and the other Mary bought spices, that they might come and anoint him. And very early on the first day of the week, they come to the tomb when the sun was risen. And they were saying among themselves, Who shall roll us away the stone from the door of the tomb? and looking up, they see that the stone is rolled back: for it was exceeding great. And entering into the tomb, they saw a young man sitting on the right side, arrayed in a white robe; and they were amazed. And he saith unto them, Be not amazed: ye seek Jesus the Nazorean, who hath been crucified: he is risen; he is not here: behold, the place where they laid him! But go quickly, and tell his disciples, He is risen from the dead; and lo, he goeth before you into Galilee; there shall ye see him, as he said unto you. And they went out, and fled from the tomb; for trembling and astonishment had come upon them: and they said nothing to any one; for they were afraid. And behold, Jesus met them, saying, All hail. And they came and took hold of his feet, and worshipped him. Then saith Jesus unto them, Fear not: go tell my brethren that they depart into Galilee, and there shall they see me.

Matt. 28:11. Now while they were going, behold, some of the guard came into the city, and told unto the chief priests all the things that were come to pass. And when they were assembled with the elders, and had taken counsel, they gave much money unto the soldiers, saying, Say ye, His disciples came by night, and stole him away while we slept. And if this come to the governor's ears, we will persuade him, and rid you of care. So they took the money, and did as they were taught: and this saying was spread abroad among the Jews, and continueth until this day.

Matt. 28:16. But the eleven disciples went into Galilee, unto the mountain where Jesus had appointed them. And when they saw him, they worshipped him: but some doubted. [And Jesus spake unto them, saying, Go ye and make disciples,] teaching them to observe all things whatsoever I commanded you: and lo, I am with you always, even unto the end of the world.

Appendix

APPENDIX

TABLE I

MATTHEAN EXPRESSIONS WHICH IN M OCCUR ONLY
IN TEACHINGS OF JESUS

	TOTAL MATTHEW	M	Genealogy, Infancy	Q Dubious	TOTAL Q	Parallels to Mark
ἄλλος with article	4	1	......	1	1	3
ἀνομία	4	3	......	1	1	......
ἀποδίδωμι	18	13	......	......	1	4
ἄρτι	7	2	......	......	2	4
βασιλεία τῶν οὐρανῶν	32	15	......	1	9	8
βρυγμὸς τῶν ὀδόντων	6	3	......	2	3	......
γενηθήτω	5	1	......	2	2	2
γεννάω	44	1	42	......	......	1
δεῦτε	6	2	......	1	1	3
δικαιοσύνη	7	4	......	1	3	......
διψάω	5	4	......	......	1	......
διώκω	7	3	......	......	4	......
δῶρον	8	5	1	......	......	2
εἷς = τις	5	1	......	......	1	3
ἔνοχος	5	4	......	......	......	1
ἐργάζομαι	4	1	......	2	2	1
ἐρρέθη	6	6	......	......	......	......
εὐώνυμος	5	2	......	......	......	3
ἡμέρα κρίσεως	4	1	......	......	3	......
θυσιαστήριον	6	5	......	......	1	......
κλαυθμός	7	3	1	2	3	......
κρυπτός	7	6	......	......	1	......
λυπέω	6	1	......	......	......	5
μισθός	10	7	......	......	2	1
μωρός	7	6	......	......	1	......

TABLE I—*Continued*

	Total Matthew	M	Genealogy, Infancy	Q Dubious	Total Q	Parallels to Mark
ὀλιγόπιστος, ὀλιγοπιστία	5	1	......	1	2	2
ὀμνύω	13	12	......	......	......	1
ὁμοιόω	8	3	......	1	4	1
ὅρκος	4	1	......	......	......	3
ὅσος ἄν, ἐάν	6	3	......	1	2	1
παρθένος	4	3	1	......	......	......
Πατὴρ ἡμῶν, ὑμῶν, σου, αὐτῶν	20	11	......	2	8	1
Πατὴρ ὁ ἐν (τοῖς) οὐρανοῖς	13	5	......	2	7	1
Πατὴρ ὁ οὐράνιος	7	3	......	......	3	1
περί with accus. of time	5	4	......	......	......	1
πονηρός, ὁ· πονηρόν, τό	5	2	......	2	2	1
πρόβατον	11	6	......	1	3	2
πρὸς τό with infinitive	5	4	......	......	......	1
πυρὸς γέεννα, κάμινος	4	3	......	......	......	1
σαπρός	5	1	......	4	4	......
σκάνδαλον	5	1	......	......	3	1
συλλέγω	7	6	......	1	1	......
σύνδουλος	5	4	......	......	1	......
συντέλεια	5	4	......	......	......	1
σφόδρα	7	1	1	......	......	5
τάλαντον	14	1	.....	13	13	......
τί σοι, ὑμῖν δοκεῖ;	6	2	......	......	1	3
τυφλός metaph.	7	4	......	......	3	......
ὑποκριτής	15	5	......	1	8	2
ὕστερον	7	1	......	1	1	5
φονεύω	5	2	......	......	2	1
φρόνιμος	7	5	......	......	2	......
χρυσός	4	2	1	1	1	......
ὥσπερ	14	7	......	2	6	1
54 expressions	449	207	47	46	119	77

TABLE II

Matthean Expressions Which in M Occur Both in Teachings of Jesus and in Narrative or Editorial

	Total Matthew	M, Discourse	M, Narr. or Edit.	Total M	Genealogy, Infancy	Q Dubious	Total Q	Parallels to Mark
ἔνδυμα	7	3	1	4	. . . . .	. . . . .	2	1
κατοικέω	4	1	1	2	1	. . . . .	1	. . . . .
κελεύω	8	1	2	3	. . . . .	. . . . .	. . . . .	5
κρίσις	8	3	2	5	. . . . .	. . . . .	3	. . . . .
κρύπτω	7	3	1	4	. . . . .	2	3	. . . . .
ξένος	5	4	1	5	. . . . .	. . . . .	. . . . .	. . . . .
ὅπως	18	7	2	9	2	1	3	4
πληρόω used of Scripture	12	1	6	7	4	. . . . .	. . . . .	1
προσέρχομαι	52	3	11	14	. . . . .	5	9	29
προσκυνέω	13	1	2	3	3	. . . . .	2	5
προσφέρω	15	3	2	5	1	1	2	7
συμφέρει	4	2	1	3	. . . . .	. . . . .	. . . . .	1
συνάγω	24	7	3	10	1	3	7	6
τηρέω	6	1	3	4	. . . . .	. . . . .	. . . . .	2
τότε	91	17	13	30	3	4	13	45
φαίνομαι	13	6	1	7	4	. . . . .	2	. . . . .
16 expressions	287	63	52	115	19	16	47	106

TABLE III

Matthean Expressions Which in M Occur Only in Narrative or Editorial

	Total Matthew	M	Genealogy, Infancy	Q Dubious	Total Q	Parallels to Mark
ἀναχωρέω	10	1	4	. . . . . .	. . . . . .	5
ἀργύρια plural	8	7	. . . . . .	1	1	. . . . . .
ἀρχιερεῖς καὶ πρεσβύτεροι	8	2	. . . . . .			6
διὰ προφήτου, προφητῶν	13	6	5	. . . . . .	. . . . . .	2
ἐκεῖθεν in narrative	11	2	. . . . . .			9
εὐθέως	12	1	. . . . . .	1	1	10
ἡγεμών	11	1	1	. . . . . .	. . . . . .	9
ἰδού after genitive absolute	11	2	4	. . . . . .	. . . . . .	5
κλέπτω	5	2	. . . . . .	1	2	1
ὄναρ	6	1	5	. . . . . .	. . . . . .	. . . . . .
ῥηθέν, ῥηθείς	13	6	4	. . . . . .	. . . . . .	3
Σαδδουκαῖοι	7	1	. . . . . .	1	2	4
σεισμός	4	1	. . . . . .			3
συμβούλιον λαμβάνω	5	2	. . . . . .			3
τάφος	6	2	. . . . . .		2	2
15 expressions	130	37	23	4	8	62

TABLE IV

Matthean Expressions That Do Not Appear in M

	Total Matthew	Genealogy, Infancy	Q Dubious	Total Q	Parallels to Mark
ἀνατολή	5	3	....	2	....
ἄνεμοι	5	....	....	2	3
ἀστήρ	5	4	....	....	1
γάμος	9	....	9	9	....
ἐγερθείς	9	5	....	....	4
Ἰησοῦς Χριστός	6	3	....	....	3
κερδαίνω	6	....	5	5	1
λεγόμενος with names	13	2	....	....	11
μετάβαινω	5	....	1	1	4
μόνον, adverb	7	....	....	2	5
ὅθεν	4	....	2	3	1
ὁμολογέω	4	....	1	3	1
παρουσία	4	....	....	3	1
σκανδαλίζομαι ἐν	4	....	....	1	3
τροφή	4	....	....	3	1
ψυχή contrasted with σῶμα	4	....	....	4	....
ὥρα ἐκείνη	8	....	1	1	7
17 expressions	102	17	19	39	46

TABLE V

Expressions Characteristic of the Q Document

	Total Matthew	M	Genealogy, Infancy	Parallels to Mark	Matthew's Q Dubious	Total Matthew's Q	Luke's Q	Luke, other	Mark
ἀγαθός	14	1	....	3	6	10	6	10	3
ἄξιος	9	....	....	....	2	9	3	5	....
ἀποκαλύπτω	4	1	....	....	....	3	4	1	....
ἄρα	7	1	....	3	....	3	3	3	....
Βεεζεβούλ	3	....	....	....	1	3	3	....	1
γενεά, singular	9	....	....	3	....	6	7	5	5
δένδρον	12	....	....	1	8	11	6	1	1
δοκός	3	....	....	....	....	3	3	....	....
δοῦλος	30	7	....	5	11	18	15	11	5
ἐκβάλλω ἐν	5	1	....	....	1	4	5	1	2
ἐξέρχομαι with purpose clause	5	1	....	1	....	3	4	2	2
ἐρῶ, future indicative	10	4	....	3	1	3	3	13	2
ἐσθίω .... πίνω	4	....	....	....	....	4	7	7	1
ἔσομαι, future	50	14	....	17	14	19	18	32	17
ἕτερος	9	2	....	1	....	6	12	23	....
ἥξω, future	4	....	....	1	....	3	3	1	....
θερίζω	3	....	....	....	2	3	3	....	....
θησαυρός	9	1	1	2	1	5	3	1	1
ἰδού	61	8	6	35	3	12	12	44	8
καρπὸν ποιεῖν	10	2	....	....	5	8	4	2	....
καρφός	3	....	....	....	....	3	3	....	....
μακάριος	13	5	....	....	....	8	7	8	....
μεριμνάω	7	....	....	1	2	6	4	1	....
ὅς in attrac. constr. followed by noun	5	....	....	....	....	5	5	7	2
οὐαί	10	3	....	2	....	5	7	7	2
οὐρανὸς καὶ γῆ	6	2	....	1	1	3	4	1	2
πετεινόν	4	....	....	1	1	3	3	1	2
πλεῖον	5	2	....	....	....	3	3	4	1
πλήν	5	....	....	1	1	3	7	8	1
πονηρός, adjective	19	3	....	3	5	13	7	3	2
σῶμα	14	3	....	3	....	7	7	6	4
ὑπό with accusative	5	....	....	....	1	5	6	....	3
32 expressions	357	61	7	89	66	200	187	208	67

TABLE VI

Expressions Characterizing Matthew's Parallels to Mark*

Luke	Mark		Total Matthew	Genealogy, Infancy	M	Parallels to Mark	Q
10	8	ἀγρός	16	.....	8	4	4
3	3	ἀδελφός, of Jesus	6	.....	1	5	.....
8	4	ἁμαρτίας ἀφίημι	4	......	......	4	.....
7	5	ἀμπελών	10	.....	6	4	.....
.....	1	ἀναχωρέω	10	4	1	5	.....
4	4	ἀπαρνέομαι	4	......	......	4	.....
13	11	ἅπτομαι	9	.....	2	7	.....
1	2	ἀρχιερεῖς καί πρεσβύτεροι	8	.....	2	6	.....
4	5	ἄρτον λαμβάνω	6	......	......	6	.....
31	28	ἄρχω	13	.....	4	7	2
.....	.....	βασιλεία τῶν οὐρανῶν	32	.....	15	8	9
14	23	γραμματεύς	23	1	5	7	10
1	4	δαιμονίζομαι	7	.....	2	4	1
3	3	Δαυείδ, υἱός/υἱέ	9	2	2	4	1
12	10	διδάσκαλε, voc.	6	......	......	4	2
14	15	ἐκβάλλω without ἐν	22	.....	5	8	9
3	5	ἐκεῖθεν	12	.....	1	10	1
3	3	ἐκτείνω	6	.....	1	5	.....
4	3	ἐλεέω	5	1	......	4	.....
8	9	Ἐλείας	9	......	......	8	1
5	3	ἐμπαίζω	5	1	......	4	.....
2	6	ἐν τῇ ὁδῷ	5	......	......	5	.....
17	25	ἐπερωτάω	8	......	......	8	.....
12	10	ἐπιτιμάω	7	......	......	7	.....
1	42	εὐθύς, adv.	7	......	......	7	.....
1	4	Ζεβεδαῖος	6	......	......	6	.....
2	1	ἡγεμών	11	1	1	9	.....
13	8	Ἡρώδης,	4	......	......	4	.....
3	5	θέλω with fin. vb.	5	.....	1	4	.....
14	5	θεραπεύω	16	.....	3	10	3
1	.....	ἰδού after gen. abs.	11	4	2	5	.....

* Occurring at least 4 times in Matthew's parallels to Mark, and oftener there than in John, Acts, the Epistles, and Revelation combined.

TABLE VI—*Continued*

Luke	Mark		Total Matthew	Genealogy, Infancy	M	Parallels to Mark	Q
2	4	Ἰορδάνης	6	.....	2	4	.....
2	8	καθεύδω	7	.....	2	5	.....
2	4	κακῶς	7	.....	1	6	.....
2	7	κατ' ἰδίαν·	6	.....	.....	6	.....
.....	5	κοινόω	5	.....	.....	5	.....
.....	5	ὅρια	6	1	1	4	.....
.....	5	ὀψία	7	.....	1	5	1
13	12	παιδίον	18	9	1	7	1
18	13	παραβολή	17	.....	3	12	2
1	7	πέραν	7	.....	2	5	.....
4	3	ποιέω . . . ἐν	5	.....	1	4	.....
3	6	πόσος other than πόσῳ					
		μᾶλλον	5	.....	1	4	.....
11	6	προσέρχομαι	52	.....	14	29	9
3	7	προσκαλεσάμενος	6	.....	1	5	.....
2	8	σκανδαλίζω	14	.....	3	10	1
3	4	σπλαγχνίζομαι	5	.....	1	4	.....
3	4	συκῆ	5	.....	.....	5	.....
1	1	σφόδρα	7	1	1	5	.....
1	.....	ὕστερον	8	.....	.....	7	1
1	1	ὥρα ἐκείνη	8	.....	.....	7	1
286	365	51 expressions	503	25	97	322	59

TABLE VII

MATTHEW-MARK EXPRESSIONS*

Luke	John	Acts		TOTAL MARK	TOTAL MATTHEW	M	Genealogy, Infancy	Q Dubious	TOTAL Q	Parallels to Mark, Same Form in Mark	Parallels to Mark, Partly Same in Mark	Parallels to Mark, No Such Form in Mark	TOTAL PARALLELS TO MARK
1	.	.	ἀγανακτέω	3	3	1	.	.	.	.	2	.	2
2	.	.	ἀπολύω γυναῖκα	3	8	2	1	.	2	1	2	.	3
1	1	.	βλασφημία	4	4	.	.	.	.	.	1	3	4
1	.	.	γέεννα	3	7	3	.	.	2	.	2	.	2
2	.	1	γρηγορέω	6	6	1	.	1	2	3	.	.	3
1	1	.	δαιμονίζομαι	4	7	2	.	.	1	1	2	1	4
1	2	.	δεῦτε	3	6	2	.	1	1	2	1	.	3
1	.	.	ἐπιτιμάω . . . ἵνα	3	3	.	.	.	.	1	2	.	3
.	.	2	εὐαγγέλιον	8	4	1	.	.	.	1	1	1	3
1	1	.	Ζεβεδαῖος	4	6	.	.	.	.	3	.	3	6
3	.	.	θέλω + fin. vb.	5	5	1	.	.	.	2	1	1	4
2	.	.	καθεύδω	8	7	2	.	.	.	4	1	.	5
2	1	1	κακῶς	4	7	1	.	.	.	2	1	3	6
1	.	1	καλόν ἐστιν, ἦν	7	5	.	.	.	.	1	4	.	5
2	1	1	κατ' ἰδίαν	7	6	.	.	.	.	4	.	2	6
.	.	.	κηρύσσω (τὸ εὐαγγέλιον)	3	4	1	.	.	.	1	2	.	3
2	1	4	κρατέω	15	12	2	.	1	2	4	3	1	8
1	.	.	λίαν	4	4	.	1	.	1	.	.	2	2
.	1	.	νοέω	3	4	1	.	.	.	3	.	.	3
1	1	.	ξηραίνω	7	3	.	.	.	.	1	2	.	3
1	.	.	ὅπου ἄν, ἐάν	5	3	.	.	.	2	1	.	.	1
.	.	1	ὅρια	5	6	1	1	.	.	2	.	2	4
.	2	.	ὀψία	5	7	1	.	1	1	1	3	1	5
.	2	.	παράγω	3	3	1	.	.	.	1	.	1	2
1	.	.	παραλυτικός	5	5	1	.	.	1	3	.	.	3
1	1	.	πέραν, τό	6	4	.	.	.	.	3	.	1	4
.	1	.	περιτίθημι	3	3	.	.	.	.	2	1	.	3
1	2	.	πλανάω	4	8	1	.	.	3	3	1	.	4
1	1	.	ποτήριον, metaph.	3	4	.	.	.	.	3	.	1	4

* Occurring at least 3 times in Mark; and in Mark, and in Matthew's parallels to Mark, as often as in Luke-John-Acts combined.

TABLE VII—*Continued*

Luke	John	Acts		TOTAL MARK	TOTAL MATTHEW	M	Genealogy, Infancy	Q Dubious	TOTAL Q	Parallels to Mark, Same Form in Mark	Parallels to Mark, Partly Same in Mark	Parallels to Mark, No Such Form in Mark	TOTAL PARALLELS TO MARK
1	..	3	προάγω	5	6	..	1	1	1	4	....	....	4
..	..	..	πῦρ, metaph.	3	6	4	..	..	..	2	....	....	2
2	..	..	ῥίζα	3	3	..	..	..	1	2	....	....	2
1	1	..	σκανδαλίζω, ac.	4	6	2	..	..	..	1	2	1	4
..	..	..	σκανδαλίζομαι without ἐν	3	4	2	..	..	..	....	2	....	2
5	2	..	σπείρω	10	17	4	..	2	3	2	6	2	10
3	..	..	σπλαγχνίζομαι	4	5	1	..	..	..	3	....	1	4
2	..	..	ὑπάγετε	4	6	4	..	..	..	1	....	1	2
44	22	14	37 expressions	179	207	42	4	7	23	66	44	28	138

TABLE VIII

Additional Matthew-Mark Expressions*

Luke	John	Acts		Total Mark	Total Matthew	M	Genealogy, Infancy	Q Dubious	Total Q	Parallels to Mark, Same Form in Mark	Parallels to Mark, Partly Same in Mark	Parallels to Mark, No Such Form in Mark	Total Parallels to Mark
1	1	2	ἀκοή	3	4	2	..	..	..	1	....	1	2
3	1	3	ἄνεμος, sing.	6	4	1	..	..	1	2.	..	..	2
15	1	4	γραμματεύς	22	24	7	1	1	8	5	3	....	8
2	4	13	δέω (to bind)	8	8	4	..	..	..	4	..	..	4
4	..	4	ἐκ δεξιῶν	5	7	2	..	..	..	5	..	..	5
3	..	1	ἐκπλήσσομαι	5	4	1	..	..	1	1	1	..	2
3	2	3	ἐκπορεύομαι	11	6	..	..	1	1	1	3	1	5
3	..	1	ἐνδύω, ἐνδύνω	4	4	1	..	..	1	1	1	..	2
6	..	8	ἑπτά	9	9	..	..	1	2	5	2	..	7
2	..	2	ἔρημος, adj.	5	3	..	..	..	1	2	..	..	2
8	7	10	εὐθέως, εὐθύς	42	18	1	..	1	1	6	8	2	16
3	..	4	ἥλιος	4	5	1	..	1	1	1	1	1	3
3	9	10	θάλασσα	19	17	4	..	..	..	8	4	1	13
..	2	5	θλίψις	3	4	..	..	..	..	3	....	1	4
..	1	5	κακεῖ	3	3	2	..	1	1	....	....	....	....
2	..	4	κλάω	3	3	..	..	..	..	2	1	..	3
4	6	11	κράζω	12	12	4	..	..	..	2	4	2	8
4	..	3	νηστεύω	6	8	5	..	..	..	2	1	..	3
7	2	3	ὁ, ἡ, τό with gen.	11	12	..	1	1	1	5	2	3	10
7	..	22	παρακαλέω	9	9	3	1	..	2	1	2	....	3
3	2	4	πειράζω	4	6	..	..	..	1	3	..	2	5
5	1	8	περί with accus.	9	8	4	..	..	..	2	..	2	4
5	1	18	πρεσβύτερος	7	13	3	..	..	..	4	2	4	10
4	..	10	προσκαλέομαι	9	6	1	..	..	..	3	1	1	5
..	4	1	πρωί, πρωία	5	4	1	..	1	1	....	1	1	2
4	..	..	σάββασιν, τοῖς	5	5	2	..	..	1	2	..	..	2
2	3	4	σπέρμα	5	7	3	..	1	1	2	1	....	3
2	2	9	συνάγομαι	5	11	5	..	..	1	..	1	4	5
1	1	14	συνέδριον	3	3	2	..	..	..	1	....	..	1
4	..	4	συνίημι	5	9	4	..	..	..	..	2	3	5
1	1	2	τελευτάω	4	4	..	1	..	..	1	..	2	3
1	4	..	ὕπαγε, sing.	7	11	4	..	2	3	4	....	....	4
5	1	8	ὥστε	13	15	1	..	1	3	4	....	7	11
117	56	200	33 expressions	271	266	68	4	12	32	83	41	38	162

* Occurring 3 times in Matthew, 3 in Mark, and as often in each of these as in Luke and John combined.

Indexes

GENERAL INDEX

INDEX OF SCRIPTURE REFERENCES

rs in